RUSSIAN PULP

RUSSIAN PULP
The *Detektiv* and the Russian Way of Crime

Anthony Olcott

ROWMAN & LITTLEFIELD PUBLISHERS, INC.
Lanham • Boulder • New York • Oxford

ROWMAN & LITTLEFIELD PUBLISHERS, INC.

Published in the United States of America
by Rowman & Littlefield Publishers, Inc.
4720 Boston Way, Lanham, Maryland 20706
www.rowmanlittlefield.com

12 Hid's Copse Road
Cumnor Hill, Oxford OX2 9JJ, England

British Library Cataloguing in Publication Information Available

Library of Congress Cataloging-in-Publication Data

Olcott, Anthony, 1950–
    Russian pulp : the *detektiv* and the Russian way of crime / Anthony Olcott.
      p. cm.
    Includes bibliographical references and index.
    ISBN 0-7425-1139-1 (cloth : alk. paper)—ISBN 0-7425-1140-5 (paper : alk. paper)
     1. Detective and mystery stories, Russian—History and criticism. 2. Russian
fiction—20th century—History and criticism. I. Title.

    PG3098.D46 O43 2001
    891.73'08720904—dc21
                                   2001018060

♾™ The paper used in this publication meets the minimum requirements of
American National Standard for Information Sciences—Permanence of Paper for
Printed Library Materials, ANSI/NISO Z39.48–1992.

Посвящается моим детям

Алисон, Андрью, и Хиллари

и, особенно, моей любимой жене

Марте

Двадцать пять лет супружеской жизни не шутка, конечно,

но за то

смеемся почти каждый день!

This book is dedicated to my children,

Alison, Andrew, and Hillary,

and, especially, to my beloved wife,

Martha

twenty five years of married life is no joke, of course,

but we do laugh almost every day!

Contents

Acknowledgments   ix

A Note on Transliteration   xi

Introduction   1

1   Defining the Genre   15

2   The Peculiarities of Russian Crime   49

3   Good Guys and Bad Guys   85

4   Punishment and Rehabilitation   117

5   Confirmation from Afar   153

Bibliography of Works Consulted   189

Index   201

About the Author   207

Acknowledgments

I have consulted with a number of people during the preparation of this manuscript. I owe the original idea to Nina King, whom I misunderstood when she asked me to write about "detective fiction in Russia." What she wanted is reflected in this book's final chapter, but her question got me thinking about what became the rest of this book. Much of what I know of the mystery genre, and of the literary life, I learned from Tim Steele, to whom I have remained as close in spirit as I have been removed by geography. Andrey Kivinov, Nikita Filatov, and Andrey Izmaylov offered valuable insights in the early stages of my research, while Nina Katerli and Shamil Umerov helped me considerably at later stages. Catherine Nepomnyashchy was kind enough to share her work and to invite me to participate in a panel on this subject, during which my thinking was challenged and changed. In the book's final stages I was the grateful beneficiary of thoughtful comments by Pavel Palazchenko and—especially—William DeSmedt. I met Wayne Allensworth when the book was almost finished, but he helped me to see some valuable points, which I was able to incorporate into the text. In the agonizing final prepublication stage, Erik Scott helped me untangle the mess I had made of transliteration. I would also like to thank Lynn Gemmell and Jamie O'Hara, whose ability to solve manuscript problems fortunately exceeded my ability to create them. Throughout this project I have received financial support from Colgate University, for which I am grateful. As it is traditional to note, any errors in the book that follows are mine, not theirs.

A Note on Transliteration

The system used in this book renders the Russian vowels Ё, Ю, Ы, and Я as, respectively, *Yo, Yu, Y,* and *Ya.* The letter Й is also written Y. When Russian E is in initial position or follows a vowel, it is rendered *Ye,* but after consonants is written *E.* Hard signs are ignored entirely, as are soft signs save in the combination ьE, which is rendered in English as *Ye.* А, И, О, У and Э are rendered as *A, I, O, U,* and *E.* Russian consonants Ж, Х, Ц, Ч, Щ, and Щ are, respectively, *Zh, Kh, Ts, Ch, Sh,* and *Shch,* while the rest of the Russian consonants are rendered by their Latin analogues. Words and names that have become anglicized, such as "perestroika," remain in their familiar form. Russian names and words quoted from English-language originals are left as in the source.

Introduction

Lord, this Russian soul of ours! We even commit our crimes like Russians, and not just to make money!

—A militia inspector in Aleksandra Marinina's *The Ghost of Music* (175)

RUSSIA HAS CHANGED SO MUCH since the end of the Soviet Union that some of the country's less obvious transformations, important though they unquestionably are, have yet to be fully cataloged, examined, and taken into account. Among these less remarked but significant changes is the utter transformation of the Russian reading public that has taken place since the early 1990s.

While no one expects anymore that Russia should be "the most reading nation on earth," as Soviet propagandists once claimed it to be, the dimensions of this collective turn away from literature are nevertheless striking. Although the number of individual titles published per year has remained relatively steady since 1990 (41,234 in 1990, which was already well down from its highest point in the 1970s, versus 36,244 in 1996), the drop in the total number of copies of books printed has been breathtaking, from 1,553 million copies in 1990 down to 422 million in 1996.[1] An obvious companion to this trend is that the number of Russians who buy no books at all is growing, reaching nearly a quarter of the population by 1996.

This drop in book production has several causes. Some are economic. Even though the price of the average Russian book in 1997 was the ruble equivalent of less than two dollars, this still represents a sizable slice of the average family budget. The new Russia also offers a great many more ways in which discretionary money may be spent, with these new temptations proffered by the full arsenal of western advertising blandishments. From the publishers' point of view, there is also an economic justification for this drop in book production: Costs of production have skyrocketed as the market demand has dropped, making it ever less profitable to put money into publishing, particularly given the relatively greater return possible from other kinds of investments. Publishing has also been affected by the fact that much of the actual printing has been moved out of Russia, which means that production cost has now been effectively tripled by the foreign currency crisis and the ruble's nose dive.

While impossible to separate from the strictly economic reasons for this precipitious decline in book publishing in Russia, the cultural reasons for it are even more important. The Soviet Union is remembered as a place that tormented its writers, painters, and musicians with incessant ideological demands, but it should equally be recalled that the justification for that steady interference in the life and work of the country's artists lay in the central role that the USSR assigned to "high culture." The Soviet system created enormous numbers of mechanisms to support and sustain "serious" writers, painters, and musicians that, among other things, protected these artists from the rigors of the marketplace. The Soviet people bought those serious books and went to those serious concerts in part because they had it drummed into them incessantly that such activities were a sign of the respectablity, the *kulturnost*, toward which most of them aspired, and in part, too, because art, save perhaps for the most ideologized of its Soviet expressions, could give its consumers a sense of belonging to some higher allegiance outside the value system of the USSR. In retrospect, however, probably the single largest reason why people devoted so much time and energy to high culture in the Soviet period was that they really had no other choice—pop culture, or mass culture, as we know it in the west, barely existed.

The new Russia boasts a vigorous pop culture. Vulgar music, trashy movies, pulp magazines, and junk fiction abound, offered by vendors on nearly every street corner. Flashy paperback books are particularly in evidence in the streets and in the surviving book stores (the number of book stores in Moscow has been more than halved since the end of communism[2]), where mysteries, romances, and science fiction have pushed out weightier fare. A recent survey of book buyers found that nearly two-thirds of all readers preferred either romances (27 percent) or *ostrosyuzhetnaya literatura* (32 percent), a catch-all phrase that covers mysteries, thrillers, and adventure stories. As happens in market economies, this enthusiasm for the genres both feeds the publishing industry and is conditioned by it. The number of copies printed of serious fiction or scholarly tomes is often as small as a few hundred, with the printing and distribution often coming from some sort of corporate or institutional sponsor; by contrast, the print runs in the mystery and romance genres can be in the hundreds of thousands, since the more popular authors can sell a print run of ten thousand copies in as little as three weeks.[3] The publishers have also learned the market trick of continuing to print as long as there is reader demand, permitting the most popular authors to rack up phenomenal sales figures. Andrey Kivinov, a lesser-known St. Petersburg mystery writer, claims to have more than two million copies of his books in print, while Aleksandra Marinina, who in November 1997 placed six of her novels on the top-ten list of fiction bestsellers in Moscow, was said the same year to have more than nine million copies of her eighteen novels in print.[4]

Coming from Nowhere?

In the case of the romance, it is relatively easy to argue that this conquest of the market is entirely a product of the new commercial age in Russia, since the overwhelming majority of published novels are translations of American, English, and German originals, most of them marketed—and with great sophistication—by the international corporations who published these genre romances in the first place. Although there have been a few attempts at "domestic" romances, Russia's consumers of this genre— who, statistics say, are women of middling years and middling education, living in Russia's smaller cities and towns—seem to prefer translations of foreign books.[5]

Exactly the opposite situation obtains in the case of the mystery, which is usually known by the generic name of *detektiv* or *boyevik*, depending upon whether the story is more about crime solving (the first type) or Rambo-like action (the second). When censorship was first loosened, then removed, in 1989–90, publishers rushed out translations of western writers like Ian Fleming, John le Carré, Tom Clancy, and Martin Cruz Smith, whom Russian readers had seen denounced but had never been able to read. Simultaneously, however, domestic *detektivy* began to appear as well, and quickly conquered the field. With the exception of Clancy, Ed McBain, and the English writer James Hedley Chase, whose books are relatively widely available, the mystery selection at most kiosks and bookstores is almost entirely Russian.

This extraordinary flourishing of the mystery genre in Russia is all the more striking for the fact that, as recently as a few years ago, many people were not even sure whether Russia had the genre. As writer-publisher Stanislav Gagarin remarked in a 1992 interview, "As a Russian, I am offended that, until we published our six-volume *Russkiy detektiv* there were [collections of] English detective stories published, and French, German, Swedish, Polish, Bulgarian, and Latvian [too], but no Russian *detektivy*."[6]

Actually, Gagarin's statement is more self-serving than accurate. Although Russian and Soviet intellectuals have nursed a fulminating dislike of detective fiction, Russia has seen several flowerings of the genre. Fyodor Dostoyevsky's novels *Crime and Punishment* and *The Brothers Karamazov* are frequently put forward by mystery fans, in Russia and elsewhere, as examples of "serious" crime fiction; whether or not his novels may properly be considered whodunits, there is no question that both these novels grew in part from Dostoyevsky's fascination with the vigorous "vulgar press" of the 1860s and 1870s, which supported a mixture of what today would be considered "true crime" and crime fiction.

Jeffrey Brooks, in his book *When Russia Learned to Read*, provides an exhaustive account of the pulp fiction explosion that catered to the growing numbers of Russia's newly literate in the 1890s and early 1900s. Most of these books consisted of translations or imitations of Sherlock Holmes, Nick Carter, and Nat Pinkerton; indeed, *pinkertony* became a generic shorthand term for the pulpy products of this boom. The surge in pulp fiction abated for a time, and then got new life in the early 1920s, when the Russian publishing industry began to revive before the Soviets imposed strict ideological constraints upon it.

There are a number of reasons why Joseph Stalin's ideologists not only put a complete stop to the publication of mystery-like stories but even went so far as to remove books already published from libraries (including such classics as the works of Arthur Conan Doyle).[7] Some have to do with the Soviets' general impulse to harness society to higher purposes, thus making *any* activity undertaken for mere pleasure a definitional waste of time, and others more specifically concern the nature of the western mystery genre, which depends upon a number of features that are deeply antithetical to the Socialist, totalitarian world that Stalin wished to construct. Those differences between the western genre and the Socialist worldview are considered in detail in the following chapters. In brief, though, detective fiction depends upon an individual actor who is pursuing a private form of retribution for what often was another individual's loss of private property—all concepts to which the Bolsheviks were deeply hostile.

It is probably a testament to the enduring human appetite for a good tale of danger and adventure, though, that some vestige of the mystery survived even the Stalin years, in the form of children's stories, by the likes of Anatoliy Rybakov and Arkadiy Gaydar.[8] When Stalin died, censorship was relaxed, permitting the return of recognizable mystery fiction for adult readers in the works of authors like Ivan Lazutin, Lev Sheynin, and Lev Shapovalov (who used the pseudonym Ovalov).[9] There was also a surprising amount of translation, albeit of relatively nonpolitical writers like Agatha Christie (some fifteen of whose works appeared between 1966 and 1970).[10]

In the late 1960s and early 1970s, there appeared a whole slew of "Red mystery writers"—Arkadiy Adamov, Leonid Slovin, the fraternal writing team of Georgiy and Arkadiy Vayner, and, above them all, Yulian Semyonov who, by his death, was said to have published more than 35 million copies of his many books.[11] This publishing popularity was further buttressed by the transformation of a number of these works into movie and television versions. Russia's President Vladimir Putin credits the 1968 film made from Vadim Kozhevnikov's massive *Shield and Sword* with inspiring him to join the KGB, while the televised serial version of Semyonov's *Seventeen Moments of Spring* was so popular that it was rumored Leonid Brezhnev changed the meeting times for the Politburo, so as not to miss an episode. (It seems more logical that the all-powerful head of the USSR might have changed the program's air time instead, but such at least is the rumor.)

For all the popularity that the mystery genre enjoyed earlier, however, its real apotheosis might be dated to 1986, when three pillars of the Soviet literary establishment suddenly turned to the *detektiv* genre to address pressing social concerns. This was the first public evidence of the policy of glasnost, which Mikhail Gorbachev, at the time the brand-new general secretary of the Communist Party, was introducing in the hopes of revitalizing Soviet society.

Valentin Rasputin's *The Fire* described a Siberian logging town filled with drunken louts who were indifferently destroying the Russian forests on the orders of party officials, who were using the proceeds to pay for what the fire of the title reveals, at the end of this short novel, to be a warehouse stuffed to bursting with jeans, Japanese tape recorders, and the other unobtainable and (to Rasputin) unnecessary consumer trash of western life.

Chingiz Aitmatov's *The Executioner's Block* (published in English as *The Place of the Skull*) comprised two unrelated plots threaded together by a subplot of a peripatetic family of wolves; the first of these plots concerned the efforts of a young Russian journalist to trace the illegal hashish industry of Central Asia.

The most caustic of the three was Viktor Astafyev's novel *Sad Detective*, which detailed the degraded horrors of provincial Russian life, where drunken mothers might abandon their infants in bus station coin lockers, or ignore their toddlers so fully that the youngsters taught themselves to live on the cockroaches they could catch; where drunken farm workers let their animals die of cold and hunger in their stalls; and where those Russians who survive and prosper do so, not through their labor, but through guile, deceit, and flattery.

Although none of these was a *detektiv*, as narrowly defined, each of them used the general structure of the genre. Astafyev's novel, closest of the three to the genre, even had as its hero a militiaman. These three high-culture authors turned simultaneously to the once-spurned low-culture genre of the *detektiv* for several reasons. By the mid-1980s most Soviet readers had grown deeply indifferent to the "serious" literature that the official publishing houses were churning out, producing a flood of what came to be called *seryatina*—"literary grayness." The government must also have have been aware of the readers' indifference; one of the rationales for glasnost was that the Soviet people had grown deaf to the usual appeals for political mobilization, making it necessary to try reaching them with sensationalism. The *detektiv* genre was a perfect vehicle for airing social concerns because mysteries were so rare that readers avidly snapped them up whenever they found them. This meant that the government could be more certain of getting its message across.

The *detektiv* was more than simply popular, however. The genre proved to be well suited to the era of glasnost and perestroika because it combines the fresh immediacy of journalism (which quickly outstripped fiction in popularity in the late Soviet era) with the ability to ask the traditional "Big

Question" of Russian fiction—*kto vinovat* (Who is guilty?). On a more mundane level, the pent-up demand for *detektiv* fiction also proved to be a godsend for Soviet publishers, who were being forced by Gorbachev's economic reforms toward greater fiscal accountability. Readers would actually purchase *detektivy* if the publishers printed them, thereby permitting the publishers to survive the rigors of the early versions of Gorbachev's market reforms.

Once the restraints of ideology were removed, the *detektiv* enjoyed what can only be described as an explosion of popularity, which continues to the present, when, as noted above, it has all but pushed most other forms of literature from the Russian book market, making a number of authors and publishers extremely wealthy in the process.

Some Other Sources of the *Detektiv* Boom

Some of those who have turned their attention to the *detektiv* genre have noted that the genre's ebb and flow corresponds to the larger ebb and flow of the attempt to control Russian society. When censorship is tight, the Russian version of the genre tends to be among the first victims of repression; conversely, the reappearance of mystery novels and stories has tended to be a reliable indicator that the intellectual atmosphere, as a whole, is lightening. As noted, this was particularly vividly illustrated in 1986, when Aitmatov's *The Executioner's Block* and Astafyev's *Sad Detective* suddenly signaled that the flat gray waters of official Soviet publishing were about to be replaced by the tidal wave of glasnost that followed.

What does not seem so much to have been remarked upon, however, is that these periods of greater freedom have also been times when the social compass of Russian society has swung its needle toward its westernizing pole. In fact, one of the most important measures westerners have used to *define* "loosening up" is to look for ways in which Russian society has begun to admit into itself institutions, practices, and artifacts from the western way of life. Thus, the appearance of "junk fiction" is taken as a sign that Russia is becoming more "normal"—by which is meant, invariably, more like the west.

From the Russian perspective, however, the causality has often run the other way; that is, these practices have not been "admitted" into society, but rather have been consciously and deliberately adopted. Westerners like to assume that the adoption of portions of their culture signifies approval of "westernism," and the desire to become as much like the west as possible. To a certain extent this is true. One reason why Russians have adopted western artifacts and institutions is what might be called metonymic wish-fulfillment, as if, by possessing physical and institutional accoutrements like those of New York or London, the country will, in some indefinable way, *become* those places, or, at least, will come to resemble the west in more ineffable ways.

However, Russians also adopt portions of western culture for antagonistic reasons as well. This may be demonstrated particularly well by the period of forced industrialization, when Stalin and his lieutenants not only adopted western designs and products, but even imported them wholesale from the west, often also bringing along westerners to set them up and get them running. As the newspapers of the time made absolutely explicit, though, the purpose of this imitation was to "overtake and surpass" the west and, in so doing, to improve upon and correct what the west had already done. Thus, the factories of forced industrialization would not be the dank quasi-prisons of capitalism, but rather the bright labor temples of socialism; the workers would live, not in the squalor of capitalist cities, but in the efficient, well-planned splendor of socialist cities; and the standard of living would not only become the material equal of that in the west, or even better, but would also be morally superior, by being based upon socialism rather than capitalism.

This second impulse of transformation is manifestly ideological, which makes it easy to explain the differences between Russia and the west as deriving from differing philosophies. This also made it possible, when Russian socialism collapsed, to see the process as the objective triumph of one philosophy over another. Russia's apparent "conversion" to the western way of life, however, has left a great many westerners deeply puzzled as to why the west's institutions and artifacts function so poorly once transposed to Russia. Particularly as Russia's economy has collapsed and its politics have slumped back toward the Byzantine opacity of the Communist era (or the tsarist one, for that matter), there has been a growing temptation to ascribe these failures of things western to flourish in Russia to some innate Russian incompetence.

Such explanations fail to see that *both* sorts of the impulse to transform share the common conviction that anything brought in from the outside must be modified so as to fit Russian society, and thus preserve the country's distinctive character. As Tim McDaniel puts it in his book, *The Agony of the Russian Idea*, "Russianness was always defined *in opposition* to something else" (28). In other words, there is a quality of Russian thought that is innately and instinctively ideological, attempting always to resolve the unresolvable paradox that Russia is exactly like the rest of the world—or at least its rich, powerful, and civilized part—and yet is at the same time unique, specially favored, and *superior to* the rest of the world.

That this spirit of simultaneous possession and opposition extends even to the humble reaches of junk fiction may be seen in the curiously large number of publishers' series which contain the adjective *russkiy*— *Russkaya voyna*, by the AST publishing house; *Russkiy proyekt*, by Olma-Press; *Russkiy bestseller* by Eksmo-Press; and the *Russkiy syshchik* of Stanislav Gagarin, already mentioned. All of these series share the odd quality to which McDaniel is referring, of being related to the western models on which they are based, and yet of also being transformed in some way which makes them perceptibly "Russian." The mysteries of that transformation are deepened by the fact that "Russian" is the only nationality for which the Russian language has only an adjective, and not also a proper noun. Thus, linguistically at least, an *anglichanin* (Englishman) or *nemets* (German) is an object, a palpable thing, while the *russkiy* is an attribute, a description of qualities, the presence of which is as surely sensed as its nature is ill-defined.

Most of the examples in McDaniel's book are what might be called consciously ideologized artifacts—institutions and objects that have been deliberately "Russified" in order to correct what to Russians seem inadequacies or evils. As McDaniel points out, this permits observers to see what Russia is *not*, but it does not easily coalesce into an ideology of Russianness that can be articulated. To get at the essence of that "Russianness" is a problem that has vexed scholars, largely because the coherent whole of Russianness is a deeply ingrained and largely reflexive entity, of which most of its exemplars are not even aware. That is, they are not conscious of their Russianness, any more than most Americans are of their Americanness, because their attitudes, reactions, and opinions seem *natural.* In McDaniel's words, "the Russian idea . . . is an interweaving of social practices, ideological interpretations of these social practices, and transformative activity with respect to these practices based partly on the ideas that they helped generate" (31).

The unarticulated quality of this "interweaving" has always presented a certain problem to outsiders interested in the anatomy of Russianness because of the conundrum of what legitimately might serve as evidence. Many have done as McDaniel does, using the pronouncements of the many philosophers of Russianness, such as Pyotr Chaadayev and Nikolay Berdayev; others have done as Daniel Rancour-Laferriere does in his *The Slave Soul of Russia*, using the classics of Russian literature to explore the Russian soul; still others do as both McDaniel and Rancour-Laferriere do, drawing upon personal experiences, anecdotes, and observations to delineate the typically Russian. Nor should it be assumed that this approach is typical only for "russophobes" (perhaps too strong a term for the kind of exasperated impatience that both McDaniel and Rancour-Laferriere demonstrate in their respective books); the books of "russophiles" such as Suzanne Massie and James Billington also tend to draw upon similar bodies of evidence.

As valuable as the insights that such approaches have generated unquestionably are, they also are, or ought to be, a little discomfiting, since the western observers themselves tend to be ideologized, making it difficult to be confident that the evidence presented is typical, and thus significant. Whether written by russophobe or russophile, many books about Russianness have a circular quality, in that the author begins with a certain attitude toward the polemic between Russianness and non-Russianness, and then finds the evidence to support his or her contention, most often drawing it from other sources that themselves either are equally ideologized (in the case of such sources as Chaadayev, Berdayev, or Dostoyevsky) or are unique, and thus possibly contingent (for example, arguments based upon the classics of Russian literature, or the anecdotes of Russian friends).

It is in this regard that the genre of the *detektiv* proves such a rewarding source of insights into the specifics of Russianness. For one thing, the *detektiv*, like its western cousins, is genre literature, which means that its readers come to it with far greater expectations of familiarity than do readers of more serious fare; as with any genre literature, there is a relatively tightly defined set of options among which the authors of *detektivy* may move as they construct their plots. Indeed, as will be shown at much greater length below, the *detektiv* is even more tightly confined by unwritten genre rules than is the murder mystery, which serves to highlight the genre's essential features of Russianness even more clearly.

By definition, genre literature also has a large social dimension; part of what makes a kind of fiction into genre literature is that subsequent authors imitate their predecessors in the hope of easily gaining a wide readership. One of the reasons that critics condescend to genre literature is that the desire of an author to express himself or herself is subordinated to the need to supply the readership what it wants, or at least what the author supposes the reader to want. This may reduce the quality of the prose, but it also makes much more valid any conclusions that such literature may prompt about the nature of the readers. That is so because, in the process of selection, or, more succinctly, in what they do and do not buy, readers reveal their own needs and desires, providing the market tool that shapes the genre's further evolution.

Speculation about why people read mysteries is a popular but inexact activity, as can be demonstrated by the variety of explanations that people have offered for it. Nicolas Freeling, himself a genre practitioner, suggests that "Materialist philosophy, and a refusal to believe in an afterlife, has [given us] a great and paralyzing fear of death, because all the goodies are here and now, and death will take them away. . . . Fictional death then becomes rather popular,"[12] presumably because contemplation of the fictional thing keeps the real thing at bay in the reader's mind. Michael Holquist argues rather that it is the "supremely rational quality which accounts for the popularity of [mystery fiction]—the magic of mind in a world that all too often seems impervious to reason. Popular—but with whom? . . . it is largely intellectuals. . . . Not only do intellectuals read detective stories, they write them."[13] As for the Russian reader, Gagarin speculates "that a man reads detective stories in order to forget his confining, dead-end and tedious life, in order at least in his thoughts, and maybe in his emotions, to participate in very tense situations, to experience incredible adventures, and all without the slightest risk to his own life. In the second place, in detective stories, and this is normal in Russian detective stories, justice sooner or later wins" (362).

That such explanations are not exhaustive is suggested by the fact that, in the west at least, exactly the same benefits as those that Gagarin names are also provided by another kind of genre literature—the western. Although not as popular as the murder mystery, science fiction, or the romance, the western nevertheless has an undeniable vigor in the American marketplace. However, in spite of many similarities between America's westward expansion and that of Russia eastward into Siberia, nothing like this genre has appeared in Russia. As Gagarin laments in the interview just quoted, "When I was just starting as a publisher, I announced a contest to create a Russian western, or more precisely, an 'eastern.' So far, though, no one has responded" (365). Given that the only censorship that now exists in Russia is the thoroughly dispassionate and objective "censorship" of market forces, the only possible conclusion is that there is nothing about the genre that Russia's readers "need"—even at a time when Russia's readers are turning increasingly to works about their nation's past.[14]

By contrast, the millions of *detektivy* that appear and are snapped up every year clearly meet a need, the outlines of which can be deduced by the shape of the dynamic tension between readers' expectations that they will find something familiar and predictable in a new book and their desire, nevertheless, for novelty and surprise. Although it would be suspect to take any single *detektiv* as representative or typical, the cumulative similarities among large numbers of these books unquestionably begin to create a kind of "rules of the genre" that, in their aggregate, may fairly be taken as a reflection of how Russians—or at least that part of them who buy *detektivy*—look at the world.

It is the constituency of the *detektiv*'s readership which makes analysis of those rules of the genre particularly useful for the attempt to define modern Russianness. Surveys indicate that most of the people who read *detektivy* are educated, urban, and between 25 and 40 years of age.[15] To be sure, there are important regional dimensions to Russia's book business that must be taken into account. Russian publishing is overwhelmingly concentrated in Moscow, which, in 1996, produced 55 percent of the titles and 80 percent of the total books printed in the country; St. Petersburg, the closest runner-up, in the same year, produced about 10 percent of the titles, and 7 percent of the total volume. For all the insignificance of its impact on the country's overall figures, however, regional publishing is strong; publishing firms are listed in more than 200 Russian cities and towns, 32 of which boast 20 publishers or more.[16] The nearly total collapse of the Soviet book distribution network, followed now by the apparent collapse of the Russian mail system, however, has meant that it is all but impossible for books from one city to reach another. As might be expected, the Moscow publishers have had better luck getting their products into other parts of Russia than provincial publishers have had placing their products in the capital; even the most popular of the St. Petersburg writers, for example, are all but unknown in Moscow, because their books are unobtainable. Although there is evidence of a vigorous *detektiv* industry in places as far-flung as Rostov-na-Donu, Kharkov, and even Magadan, not enough of their products are available to be certain that developments in each of these smaller cities are entirely like those in Moscow.

Still, just as Moscow so frequently seems a metonymy for Russia, so too would the *detektiv*'s readership seem to be broadly typical of the Russian population. What makes the tastes of this segment of Russian society particularly valuable to analyze is the raw stuff from which the *detektiv* is concocted: the innumerable tales of crimes, their perpetrators, and those who seek to bring them to justice. To a degree not true of any other genre, crime fiction—in any society—describes what the people of a given place fear most, and describes, too, how they would defend against it. By definition, crime fiction must establish the values that a society views as most dear, just as it must delineate, or at least imply, the consequences of transgression of those values. Equally important, however, it must also explain what leads individuals to such a transgression; otherwise, it has no way of justifying why it is that some people are able to defend those values as assiduously, and as imaginatively, as others are driven to violate them. Even more valuably, because this is literature people read for entertainment rather than for uplift or enlightenment, there is a homey and uncomplicated quality in the assumptions that the genre makes about the world. Whether or not Russia is truly as the *detektiv* describes it is a question that would be exceedingly difficult to answer. The enormous popularity of the genre, however, makes it seem entirely safe to suppose that the *detektiv* describes Russia as the readers *understand* the country to be—which makes the portrait of Russia and Russians that emerges from the *detektiv* as valuable as it is vivid.

Notes

1. *Itogi*, 18 November 1997, 36.
2. *Itogi*, 18 November 1997, 39.
3. *Itogi*, 18 November 1997, 39.
4. Interview, *Kapital*, no. 39, 22–28 October 1997, 5.
5. *Itogi*, 6 October 1998, 54.
6. Anatoliy Gagarin, "Detektiv—literatura plyus igra," in *Russkiy syshchik* (Moscow: Otechestvo, 1994), 361.
7. C. Nepomnyashchy, "Markets, Mirrors, and Mayhem: Aleksandra Marinina and the Rise of the New Russian *Detektiv*," in *Consuming Russia: Popular Culture, Sex, and Society Since Gorbachev*, ed. Adele Barker (Durham: Duke University Press, 1999).
8. Nepomnyashchy, 2.
9. Gagarin, 361.

10. Nepomnyashchy, 4.

11. Richard Stites, *Soviet Popular Culture* (Cambridge, U.K.: Cambridge University Press, 1992), 152.

12. Nicolas Freeling, *Criminal Convictions* (Boston: Godine, 1994), xxi.

13. Michael Holquist, "Whodunit and Other Questions," in *The Poetics of Murder*, ed. Glenn Most and William Stowe (New York: Harcourt Brace Jovanovich, 1983), 159.

14. *Itogi*, 6 October 1998, 55.

15. *Itogi*, 6 October 1998, 54.

16. *Itogi*, 6 October 1998, 54.

CHAPTER ONE

Defining the Genre

Perhaps the best way to introduce the Russian *detektiv* is to explain why the most tempting translations for the Russian name of this genre are misleading and inaccurate.

Why the *Detektiv* Is Not a Murder Mystery

Although the English and American crime fiction genres have shown an extraordinary vigor in their evolution and transformation, encompassing an ever larger number of locales, detective types, motivations, and even settings in time, in virtually all of the books that might be ascribed to the genre, the focus of the story is on murder. It is of course for that reason that a common name for the genre is "murder mystery."

The two elements of this metonymy essentially contain the full plot concern of the western genre, in its thousands and thousands of expressions; in order to "work" as a murder mystery, a story must have one or more people who have been, in the legal phrase, "unjustly deprived of life," and another person or people who have done the depriving. This is the murder. The bulk of the book is then the author's revelation, through one or more agents, of who did the depriving, how, and—very important—why, so supplying the mystery.

In the case of the *detektiv*, however, this description is inadequate, if only for the reason that very few books in this genre are centered on murders.

There are a number of reasons for this. Some are straightforward, but others are less expected, and thus tell a great deal about the differences between Russian and western thought.

Particularly for those *detektivy* that were subject to Soviet censorship, the publishers had no interest in depicting murder as anything but an extraordinary event in the context of Soviet Russia. As Stanislav Gagarin has said, there was in the Soviet period an unwritten but universally known rule that the censors would not permit *detektivy* to feature more than one death (Gagarin, 363). In fact, as Adamov's *Evil Wind* demonstrated, it was not even necessary that there be a death at all for a plot to become the Soviet version of a murder story. In that novel a burglar who specializes in rifling hotel rooms while the guests are out is surprised by a hotel maid; the burglar knocks the unlucky woman unconscious, then stuffs her under a bed. Even though the maid survives, and indeed has suffered no significant injury, the novel's hero, Investigator Losev, decides to treat his search for the burglar as if this were *already* a murder case, because, as he explains, "Internally, psychologically, [the burglar] had gone as far as murder, so he was a murderer" (36).

Only marginally closer to the western canons was a work like Arkadiy and Georgiy Vayner's *Telegram from the Other World*, which was considered to be among the best of the Soviet *detektivy*. The "murder" in that book comes when an elderly man suffers a fatal heart attack after receiving a telegram (that later proves to have been a hoax) informing him that his daughter, son-in-law, and grandsons had been killed in a car wreck. Inspector Tikhonov, the novel's hero, investigates the case as a murder, even though there had been no intention of causing death when the telegram was sent, nor provable causal responsibility for that death when it was received.

It was not just the delicacy of Soviet censorship, however, that made western-style murder such a rarity in the Russian *detektiv*. It was also in part a reflection of the actual conditions of life in the USSR, where murder was something of a rarity. This is not to suggest that there was no violent crime in the Soviet Union, but rather to stress that, statistically, murder of the sort that figured in British and American mysteries was so rare as to be nonexistent. Figures compiled in 1966, for example, indicated that 77.4 percent of all victims of crimes resulting in death were either relatives or acquaintances of the killer; moreover, two-thirds of the victims were between the ages of 18 and 40, and 71.4 percent of them were male.[1] Thus, for most of the Soviet period, approximately 70 percent of all real-life Russian crimes of death were little more than one drunk bashing another on the head for reasons that no one was likely to remember once sobriety returned.[2] This supposition is further buttressed by other statistics, suggesting that, for most of the Soviet period, the instrument most often used to cause death was a knife, axe, or other sharp instrument; firearms, the most common weapon in the United States, were almost never used,[3] to say nothing of the arcane poisons and other fiendish inventions that turn up with predictable regularity in the murder mysteries of the west.

To be sure, most of the ingenious literary murders of the western genres also had no hard analogue in reality. What the literary murders in the west did have in common with their real counterparts, however, was a social and physical environment that Soviet Russia completely lacked. For one thing, Soviet society did not have the sort of secondary positions that traditionally allowed western literary villains to get close to their victims—to put it schematically, there were no butlers in Soviet Russia, so the butler *couldn't* have "done it." More substantively, the nationalization of all land and most personal property, at least of anything that had an intrinsic value, meant that few Soviet citizens had the kind of inheritance that might make it worth killing them to secure it. Nor could one business partner set out to murder another in order to gain greater control of a business; everything in Soviet Russia belonged to the state, so there was little direct point in killing for it.

Perhaps the most important difference between Soviet Russia and the west, however, was that the laws of the two places were based upon entirely different kinds of assumptions. In part, this difference is a formal one; both American law and British law are based on English Common Law, while Russian law is based upon a French model. There are profound differences in the fundamentals that underlie these two systems; in criminal cases, these differences are expressed in the way that investigations, arrests, and trials are handled. Whereas in the English system, the burden to prove guilt lies upon the state and is decided at trial, in the French model, although a formal presumption of innocence is usually maintained, in fact, most of the determination of whether or not an individual is guilty has been made in the pretrial process. And so, at the actual trial the burden lies on the accused, essentially to *disprove* that he or she is guilty. This presumption of guilt was even greater in Russia for most of this century, since Soviet jurisprudence specifically, and vehemently, rejected the concept of presumptive innocence

in criminal cases. Indeed, in 1968, when one of the primary textbooks of Soviet criminology dared to suggest in a new edition that such a presumption
should be included in Soviet jurisprudence, the entire print run was seized
at the printing press, and the book not released until the page bearing that
suggestion was ripped out of all 13,200 copies and replaced with an inof-
fensive substitute.[4]

In addition to the formal systemic differences between Russian law and
its western counterparts, however, there are a number of differences between Russians and westerners in how they understand many basic notions
of jurisprudence. Several of these differences are sufficiently important to
warrant fuller examination below. For the moment, the different emphasis
that Russian law has put on various crimes for much of this century may
be adequately suggested by the plot of *His Master's Voice*, a murder mystery
written by Ivy Litvinov, an Englishwoman who married Maksim Litvinov,
one of the most prominent of Stalin's foreign emissaries. This novel says a
great deal about the differing sensibilities of Russians and westerners, because, although Litvinov set out very consciously to create an English-style
mystery with a Russian setting and a Russian detective, the intimate knowledge she had gained from living in Russia led her to violate the genre's English canons in telling ways.

Written in the 1930s but set during NEP, the period of the early 1920s
when Lenin and the Bolsheviks permitted capitalism to make a temporary
return to Russia for purposes of national economic recovery, *His Master's
Voice* shows District Procurator Nikulin attempting to learn why "Arkady
Petrovich Pavlov, Moscow representative of the Obless timber firm, had
been found dead," slumped over a recording of Chalyapin, "with a Caucasian dagger in his neck" (29). The prime suspect, who proves to be a red
herring, is Tamara Dolidzey, a tempestuous Georgian ballerina, and the
threads of Litvinov's plot wind through black marketeers speculating in
platinum, underground anti-Bolshevik conspiracies, and a skein of false
identities. Like his fictional English counterparts of the day, Nikulin pa-
tiently collects testimonies and sorts through physical evidence, trying to
establish the sequence of various stages of the murder, in order to demonstrate, in the best traditions of the genre, that the unlikely will prove true,
once the impossible has been eliminated.

A note of Soviet reality asserts itself, however, when Nikulin is forced to
go to the OGPU, one of the earlier incarnations of the KGB, to act upon his
evidence. Although praised for his work in uncovering the speculators,

Nikulin protests that he would much rather have found Pavlov's murderer, at which the OGPU officer scolds Nikulin sharply.

It's an open question . . . who is more dangerous to society, a man who deprives it of a not particularly valuable life, or one who continues for years systematically undermining trade and the development of industry, thus affecting the lives of countless hundreds. If I could rid society of the speculators, I would leave it to deal with the murderers itself. (157)

The same point about the relative seriousness of murder and economic crimes against the state is also made by the fact that, in Stalin's later years, as one gulag survivor recalls, "Steal two truckloads of potatoes or two million rubles—[they'll give you] twenty-five years. The guy who's murdered three people, though, just walked around laughing—him they gave ten years."[5]

It would be logical to assume that the vast changes that have ensued in Russia since the collapse of communism would have altered what seems, to westerners anyway, a nonchalant attitude toward murder. After all, most of the conditions that were true of Soviet Russia, as described above, are no longer to be seen in modern Russia. Certainly, there is no longer a limit on the number of corpses that a book might feature; indeed, the corpses pile up so quickly in most of the new *detektivy* that one could begin to suspect authors are paid by the body. Serial killers are a popular genre topic, as, for example, in Aleksandra Marinina's *Stylist*, which begins with an investigation into the serial deaths of seventeen young males of similar appearance. Even bloodier are the *boyeviki*, or action-thrillers in which the heroes can dispatch bad guys in enormous numbers; Lev Puchkov's *Blood Matter*, for example, ends with the obliteration of an entire Chechen village.

Social conditions have changed too. Russian life, or at least Russian fiction, may not yet have come as far as to offer actual butlers, but the live-in assistant to a very rich paraplegic translator proves a handy suspect in Marinina's *Stylist*. The need to "bump off" somebody before a will is altered and an inheritance is lost figures as a possible motivation in novels like Dmitriy Petrov's *Setup for a Sucker* (mother and daughter want rich but stingy papa's money) and Irina Zarubina's *Mrs. Inspector* (son-in-law without legal permission to live in Moscow wants mother-in-law out of the picture so wife can inherit apartment and, thus, the right to register him there). As for motivations for murder arising from business, virtually every one of the post-Soviet *detektivy* offers one variation or another upon this theme. In some works, such as Andrey Kivinov's "Track of the Boomerang," the logic of business is shown to be such that two partners, once the closest of friends, both end up taking out murder contracts on each other. Other books show murder itself to be a business. A particularly clever example is Marinina's *Small Fry Die First*, in which a would-be gun-for-hire ends up receiving orders to eliminate herself. Igor Vinnichenko's *Honeymoon* has a slightly different take on the morality of business. In that novel, enterprising businessmen use the cover of a Satanic cult in a provincial Russian city to lure children, whom they then butcher in order to "harvest" their organs. Nikita Filatov's story "Static" suggests precisely the same crime, but for the even simpler purpose of turning kidnapped children into sausages and meat patties.

Despite all the gore in the post-Soviet *detektivy*, however, almost none of them have as a primary focus the investigation of how and why one or more humans have "unjustly deprived" one or more of their fellows of life, making it as difficult to use the term "murder mysteries" for the post-Soviet *detektivy* as it was for the Soviet-era ones. There are a number of reasons for this continued similarity, but the simplest of them may surprise westerners: Russia's notions of criminal behavior were governed by the same Criminal Code from 1960 until 1997. To be sure, before the code was replaced in its entirety on January 1, 1997, the old code was modified more than seven hundred times, with some specific statutes rewritten as many as seven times.[6] However, those changes were introduced in an incoherent and generally hasty way, not only leaving a number of laws on the books that contradicted one another, but also leaving others in nominal force, even though they were no longer applied. This confusion of Soviet and post-Soviet laws and practices is what allows the heroine of Zarubina's *Mrs. Inspector*, published in 1998, to chide a prosperous businessman whom she had arrested in Soviet days for black marketeering, "Just remember! Nobody has changed the laws on illegal hard-currency transactions yet!" (180).

Perhaps even more influential, however, was the fact that, as one commentary to the new Russian Criminal Code rather blandly puts it, "Criminal legislation [in the 1960–1997 code] did not formulate sharp categories of distinction between criminal and non-criminal violations of rights."[7] To put matters more bluntly, the 1960 Criminal Code permitted similar actions to incur greater or lesser consequences, depending upon the jurisdiction to which a particular act was consigned. Under the 1960

Criminal Code the perpetrators of essentially similar acts might variously be tried by

- the ordinary criminal courts, which could impose prison sentences;
- the so-called comrades' courts, which were under the control of the trade unions and the party, and which could not impose prison sentences, but instead could levy "educational" penalties, such as fines, reduction of job status, censure, and others;
- the party's own internal discipline procedures, which imposed penalties solely in terms of further advancement within the party.

Once the Communist Party was outlawed, these last two administrative options disappeared, but it remains a feature of Russian law that what constitutes a crime is only partially defined by the act itself. The context in which the act takes place, and the actor's intentions at the time of commission, play a much larger role in Russian criminal law than either factor does in the west. One consequence of this is that confession—the acknowledgment by the actor that his or her act was criminal—is much more essential to a successful prosecution than is true in the west. Indeed, as Robert Cullen wrote in *The Killer Department*, his account of the real-life serial killer Andrey Chikatylo, "Russians are accustomed to the idea that a guilty man must confess; some Russians, even now, hold the mistaken belief that a defendant who does not confess cannot be convicted" (40).

One consequence of the centrality of confession to the Russian system of justice with particular impact on the crime fiction genre is that physical evidence has much less importance than it does in the west. A post-Soviet handbook for procedural investigators warns explicitly that "facts received by investigative means [*operativno-rozyskim putyom*] cannot be used as the basis for a formal accusation."[8] The same point is put more vividly in a textbook on the criminal process in Russia. Quoting Dostoyevsky, the author of that text says, "Just as a hundred rabbits don't make an elephant, so might a hundred clues fail to make a single proof."[9]

There is even a certain circularity in the Russian view of evidence, since it is illegal for an investigator to begin to collect physical evidence until a formal *ugolovnoye delo*, or criminal case, has been opened by one of the small number of government organs permitted to do so.[10] The decision whether or not a crime has occurred—which is what the opening of a criminal case formally registers—depends upon the competent officials' evaluation of the evidence for it, but the elements on which that decision is based do not become "evidence" until that decision is taken. That necessity to formally open a case before evidence is collected would thus make almost impossible Russian versions of the American and British mysteries in which a hero painstakingly accumulates anomalies that turn out to be evidence for a murder. This conundrum is spelled out explicitly at the end of Marinina's *The Ghost of Music.* After the heroine, Nastya Kamenskaya, has discovered, by processes of classical deduction, who is responsible for the novel's three murders, and then has proven that her deduction is correct by a piece of elegantly staged "police theater" (provoking her suspect to reveal himself by sending him an artfully constructed letter of blackmail, supposed to be from someone in the "murder-for-hire" firm he had employed for his first killing), her supervisor asks her, "But where are the facts? Where is the proof?" To this Kamenskaya is forced to respond:

> Nowhere. I have no proof. But you aren't a *sledovatel* [the procurator's investigator, explained below], so what do you need proof for? You need truth. Let Gmyra [the head *syshchik*—the police investigator, explained below] have the headache. He doesn't have the right to open a case against Yermilov [the killer], he has to pass that to the procurator, but he can only pass it to the procurator when proof of Yermilov's guilt turns up or there is at least some weighty reason to suspect him. We have to find at least one serious proof for Gmyra, and then we can consider that we have earned our keep. Otherwise [Gmyra] is going to send me and all my clever constructions to that address we all know so well [i.e., send me and my crazy ideas to hell]. (302)

It might also be said that, in a technical sense, the *detektiv* cannot be a murder mystery because the Russian language does not recognize "murder" as such; unlike English, which distinguishes linguistically between manslaughter (criminal but unintended death) and murder (desired, anticipated, and planned death), Russian uses the same word, *ubiystvo*, for both. To a certain extent, of course, this point is disingenuous, because Russian can, and in the criminal code does, distinguish between *umyshlennoye ubiystvo* [intentional killing] and, for example, *ubiystvo sovershennoye v sostoyanii affekta* [killing while under the influence of a heightened emotional condition]. At least in the world of the *detektivy*, however, this lack of linguistic distinction tends to result in a reduced *moral* distinction between kinds of victimization, so that what is important in many plots is not that death itself is the crime, as in a murder mystery, but rather that *any* crime can lead to death. In the Soviet-era novels, that supposition was obviously a powerful argument in the genre's overall attack on criminal behavior of any sort. Perhaps paradoxically, though, in the post-Soviet novels, very much the same logic seems to have led to nearly complete indifference to violent death, which in many novels seems little more than a cost of doing business. The implications of both attitudes are explored at greater length below.

This relative devaluation of physical evidence, as compared to its place in western law, or at least in western crime literature, should not be understood to mean that it has no place at all in the Russian tradition. Russian *detektivy*, just like their western counterparts, feature such staples of the murder mystery as fingerprints, bullet marks, footprints, and the like, because while evidence is not of great value in court cases, it is important in the investigative stage. This is in part because one of the key features of the Russian criminal system is that before a case can proceed, the procurator and judge, who stand at the apex of the system, must be convinced both that a crime has occurred and that the accused is likely to be guilty of having committed it. In part because of that systemic requirement, but even more because of the cultural assumptions that gave rise to it, both the Soviet legal system and its Russian successor place a much higher value on confession than do the western legal systems. One consequence of this Russian insistence upon confession is that, in the *detektivy* at least, physical evidence most often serves as a kind of lever, or bludgeon, that investigators use to convince suspected criminals to "come clean."

Finally, although arguments from absence are perhaps less compelling than arguments from presence, it is nevertheless striking how completely Russia has failed to develop one particularly evidence-dependent crime fiction subgenre, in spite of the subgenre's enormous popularity—and profitability—in the west. As one Russian observer of the *detektiv* phenomenon put it, "It is characteristic [of Russia] that the literary and film genre that is most popular in Europe and, especially, America—the courtroom drama—can find absolutely no space beneath our heavens."[11]

Why the *Detektiv* Is Not a Detective Story

One literary consequence of this rather different attitude toward physical evidence is that the *detektiv* is very rarely a logical puzzle of the sort that many western mystery readers enjoy. As is explained below, the structure of the *detektiv* genre is such that there is seldom any doubt about who the villain is; indeed, not only is it quite rare for a book to offer more than two or three possible suspects, but often there is only one, whose identity is known almost immediately. In several *detektivy*, in fact, the authorial point of view will suddenly shift in order to let the reader find out who is the villain even before the nominal detective does.

The few exceptions to this pattern are so rare, and so like their western counterparts, that it is tempting to presume they were written as self-conscious imitations of western genres. A good example of this is *A Night at Elk Farm*, written in the late 1980s by Viktors Lagzdins, who, very importantly, is Latvian rather than Russian. Since the novel was written at a time when Latvians were increasingly at pains to distance themselves from Russia and the Soviet Union in which they felt themselves trapped, it seems very likely that the plot of the novel is intentionally "western." A classic "locked-room" mystery, *A Night at Elk Farm* features a group of fortyish intellectuals from Riga who have gathered in a remote cabin to celebrate a birthday, only to have the birthday boy himself turn up dead. The plot of the book turns upon precisely the kinds of clues that might drive such a novel in the west, as the investigator, who happens also to be one of the guests, sorts through the conflicting testimonies and emotions of the various guests—all of them showing various signs of very European *weltschmerz* and *angst*—until at last he determines the unexpected villain.

For all that *A Night at Elk Farm* seems a conscious imitation of western murder mysteries, and thus a departure from the usual *detektiv* form, Lagzdins's novel remains absolutely typical of the genre in another, and very significant, regard: by having as the investigator a member of the state procurator's office. Although there are a great number of western mysteries that also feature detectives who are sheriffs or policemen, the word itself, and the wider notion of the detective story generally, evokes a figure like Lord Peter Wimsey, Miss Marple, Hercule Poirot, or, of course, Sherlock Holmes—an individual who takes upon himself or herself the investigation of crime. However, as one description of the present-day Russian genre points out, "There is no *detektiv* in which the main hero is an amateur private investigator; apparently there is no eccentric or stranger (aristocrat, foreigner, or well-intentioned old lady) in modern Russia who is suitable for this role" (56).

To a certain extent, as T. J. Binyon has demonstrated in his exhaustive but odd book, *Murder Will Out*, the problem of finding suitable detective heroes is a universal one, particularly if an author wishes to keep his or her options open for creating a series should a book prove popular. Even in the west, there are surprisingly few professions that can plausibly provide a character with sufficient income to stay alive between jobs. The central character also needs a motivation to pursue criminals and sufficient intelligence to be successful in that pursuit.

In Russia, though, the choice of possible detective is even more restricted, for reasons that are both cultural and legal. As may perhaps be expected, the choice was most limited in the Soviet period, when the hero of a *detektiv* was really limited to one of only four professions: *uchastkovyy* (simple policeman), *syshchik* (detective), *sledovatel'* (investigator), or agent of the KGB.

This last figure is probably the easiest to understand, for it is most like the secret agent of the western genres. However, some important differences should be noted. For one thing, the KGB was also investigating large-scale internal economic crimes, so that novels featuring these agents might also be about black-marketeering; for another, the KGB had a cult of "facelessness" for its agents, which meant that novels featuring them—of which there are surprisingly few, at least in comparison with the huge body of spy literature in the west—usually depicted teams of agents, rather than individuals. Even more debilitating for the dictates of the genre was that KGB sensibilities prevented the slightest whisper of possibility that its agents might fail to understand a clue or catch a criminal; thus, plots that used the KGB (or its earlier avatars) tended to be formulaic and predictable in the extreme. To be sure, there were some notable exceptions, such as Semyonov's *Seventeen Moments of Spring*, discussed above. Featuring the double agent Otto Shtirlits, this novel became one of the Soviet Union's best-known and best-loved pieces of junk fiction. Used in more detective-like roles, however, the KGB agents depicted in books such as Igor' Aryasov's *Three Hours to Clarify the Truth* or instances such as Yuzef Printsev's "Wedding Postponed" tend to be reliable, nearly perfect, and thoroughly dull.

The other three professions from which Soviet authors might choose their detectives, while similar to some types of detectives in the western crime literature, were much more specifically Russian, with particular consequences for the genre of the *detektiv*. The *uchastkovyy* and *syshchik* are both members of the *militsiya* (militia), as the Russian police were renamed shortly after the Revolution. The *uchastkovyy* is basically a patrol cop, who has responsibility for a particular territory, or *uchastok*. Especially in the

Soviet era, but also in the new Russia, the *uchastkovyy* combines elements
of the western policeman with those of a social worker, and even a bit of an
uncle. One of the most famous figures of Soviet children's books is Samuil
Marshak's Uncle Styopa, a kind-hearted and extremely tall *uchastkovyy*
who does things like reach up to change the bulbs in burned-out traffic
lights and help small children to get home. The *uchastkovyye* of adult crime
fiction tend to be of more normal height, but otherwise they resemble
Uncle Styopa; the figure usually is depicted as elderly, avuncular, and intimately knowledgeable about the citizens of his particular territory. (In literature at least, there don't seem to have been any female *uchastkovyye*.)
Such figures know when citizens have suddenly come into unexpected
money or are living beyond their means; they know who abuses alcohol
and who beats his wife. In any number of books, they also know who is
most likely to be the prime suspect, if a crime of a certain sort has been
committed on their turf. A typical example is the following scene in Kivinov's "Doomed Cop": An apartment has been burgled, apparently by
someone who has squeezed in through a small ventilation window. The
novel's hero, Andrey from the criminal investigation office, is taken to the
scene by the *uchastkovyy*, who is described as a bit plump, and who is called
"Palych," a form of address that suggests that he is both older than Andrey,
and also a bit rural, avuncular, and simple. Noting that this is Palych's turf,
Andrey asks:

> "So, and what about elements? This is the third job in your territory."

> "Elements?" Palych blew smoke in the direction of the mail boxes. "This isn't
> a region, it's nothing *but* 'elements'. . . . Of course, though, we *could* drop
> around to one particular little address. Three years ago or so we shut down
> Vitka Kopylov doing these kinds of B&E [breaking and entering], through
> ventilation windows . . . the method in this one here sure looks like his." (308)

As the relationship between Andrey and Palych might suggest, however,
the *uchastkovyy* also has a number of definitional deficiencies that make his
appearance as a literary hero relatively rare. Normally, this seems to have
been a dead-end kind of job for militiamen who were too limited to have
risen higher. One of the characters who nearly ruins the heroine's investigation, and who ultimately manages to get himself killed, in Marinina's
Stolen Dream is an *uchastkovyy* who sets out on his own to solve a murder
that has turned up on his pitch because he feels this is the last opportunity
he has to pull himself up the career ladder before retirement. Marinina's

story makes clear, however, that this is a bad decision on the *uchastkovyy's* part, in large part because the beat cop does not have the resources to deal with all that he has stirred up.

This reflects the fact that the territory for which the *uchastkovyy* has responsibility is generally very small; this means that the figure's sphere of movement, and thus his available resources of "detection," are highly restricted. The nature of the job is such that most *uchastkovyye* would have no reason, or, more importantly, no jurisdictional right, to extend an inquiry beyond their small plot of land. The only exception to this seems to be in Siberia, where even *uchastkovyye* are responsible for hundreds or even thousands of square miles of mostly empty territory. Most mysteries set in Siberia thus feature *uchastkovyye*. Probably the most famous of these were the many stories in the 1970s that featured Vil Lipatov's *uchastkovyy* Aniskin, who also was the hero of a popular television serial.

Probably because the figure has much greater latitude, and also perhaps for reasons of status, the more common police-type figure in *detektivy* is the *syshchik*, an appellation that may literally be translated as "the searcher." This figure is probably the closest analog to the British and American police inspector, or detective, because it is his or her job to establish, first, that a crime has taken place, and then to gather the physical evidence that might lead to the arrest of a suspect. The comparison is limited, however, by certain constraints that the western counterparts do not share.

These are best suggested by a description of the stages of a Russian criminal case. Because the same Criminal Code was in force until 1997, as well as because of the continuation of many important structural practices since then, this description is valid for the full period from 1960 until today.

> The criminal process begins with the opening of a case, *after which* [emphasis added] the organs of investigation and preliminary examination, working under the supervision of the procurator, investigate the crime of which they have been made aware. If in the course of their investigation there are assembled proofs attesting to the guilt of a particular person in having committed the crime, the case then moves to the next stage of the process, the stage of submitting the case for hearing. After this point the case is investigated in the stage of judicial consideration, at which the judge, on the basis of an examination of all the materials together, will establish a verdict. (Larin et al., 22)

As this description suggests, one significant way in which the *syshchik* differs from the usual western notion of a detective is that the *syshchik* is deeply imbedded in an administrative structure, or process, that sharply limits the degree of autonomy he might demonstrate. Indeed, for most of the Soviet period, the narrative emphasis was put not on individuals, but on investigative teams. For example, in Semyonov's *Petrovka, 38* (the street address of the headquarters of Moscow's criminal investigation unit), another of the classics of the Soviet genre, the various *syshchiki* are all but indistinguishable from one another, even though one of them, Kostyenko, was later to emerge as Semyonov's serial hero when social conditions changed enough to permit this closer similarity to western practice. Also typical of the genre was Semyonov's use of the senior *syshchik* who, like Nero Wolfe, seems never to go outside the office, but who is indispensable to coordinating the efforts of the investigators, making sure that they are observing Soviet laws in the course of their investigation, and, most important of all, that they are moving properly toward the solution, one that he seems almost to know in advance.

By the late Soviet period, Kostenko's kind of transformation, from team member to main hero, had become more common, as authors increasingly depicted their heroes as disaffected from the normal police practices of their fellows, at odds with their lazy, dishonest colleagues, and deliberately hiding their work from their corrupt superiors. Adamov's Inspector Losev, Leonid Slovin's Inspector Denisov, and Lyubov Arestova's hero all were examples of *syshchiki* who in the late 1980s emerged from the group identity of their investigative teams, and so became more similar to the detective heroes of the western genre.

Unlike in the west, however, even the most independent of the *syshchiki* still remains bound within the Russian legal process, unable to function except insofar as he, or she, is able eventually to move a given criminal case further up the staircase of jurisprudence. One of the more curious consequences of that fact is that the senior official remains a fixture of the *detektiv*, not only through the end of the Soviet period, but also into the present day. In the late Soviet period, this figure sometimes becomes an enemy to the hero, as in Slovin's 1989 novel *Bulletproof Vests*, where what "[*syshchik*] Igumnov and his men mostly had to watch out for wasn't armed criminals, but their own bosses," but in a surprising number of instances, this senior official figure remains positive. Perhaps even more surprising, at least against what the conventions of the western genre might lead us to expect, is that this avuncular senior official remains a fixture even of the post-Soviet *detektivy*. Sometimes, as in the stories of Andrey Kivinov (who is himself a working *syshchik* and thus may have fewer romantic notions about the nature of senior militia administrators), this senior official is negative, but even today it is far more common to find, as in the many novels of Marinina, that this senior official remains a crucial part of the *syshchik*-hero's ability to function.

The many cultural reasons why this is so will be explored at greater length below, but there is also a strictly functional explanation for the continued importance of the senior militia official. As the jurisprudential "flow chart" sketched above suggests, the militia's responsibility only extends as far as the demonstration that a crime has indeed taken place and that a given person or persons is very likely to have been responsible for that crime. Once that condition has been satisfied, the militia has fulfilled its duty and passes the case on to the procurator. It is the senior *syshchik* who maintains the prestige and honor of his office by making certain that the procurator will not send the case back as incomplete.

It is the responsibility of the procurator, at the next step on the ladder, to make certain that a given case has been assembled so thoroughly that there is no chance that a judge will not find the accused guilty, that the rights of the accused have not been violated in any way, and that the militia have not exceeded their powers in drawing up their case. These latter points may seem unrealistic to westerners who are accustomed to thinking of the Soviet Union as a lawless society, but there is in fact a strong thread running through novels of the late Soviet period, and even of the post-Soviet period, that suggests that the procurators not only can, but frequently do, release suspects when, for example, they have been kept in custody longer than the seventy-two hours that the law permits, or because a search has taken place without proper sanction. A particularly striking instance of the ways in which a judge might derail a case on procedural grounds is mentioned in the memoirs of A. N. Yegorov, who was head of Moscow's Criminal Investigation Division from 1989 to 1991. Yegorov describes a case in which two murderers had actually confessed to their crimes, but the presiding judge refused to accept their confession without the corroborating evidence of the murder weapons that the militia were unable to find. The confessed killers kept changing their stories about where they had disposed of the weapons until they nearly succeeded in having the case dismissed, prompting Yegorov to remark laconically that "Even then [the late 1980s] our courts were humanitarian not to the victims but, to put it mildly, to the lawbreakers."[12]

Since the procurator is a person of some importance, the actual investigation of cases is usually performed by a subordinate known as the *sledovatel*. The name might be translated as "the follower" or "the follower-up," which suggests the way in which this job nearly duplicates that of the *syshchik*. The difference is that the *sledovatel* does most of his (or her) work in offices, jail cells, and courtrooms, rather than in the field. In part because he or she must have legal as well as criminology training, the *sledovatel* tends to be more cerebral than the *syshchik*. This is most often reflected in the attempt to get a given criminal to confess. In Russian law, a criminal case may be opened either against a particular individual or, based upon the factual evidence that a crime has been committed, by person or persons unknown. However, this second method is used sparingly and generally only for situations, such as a murder, about which there can be no arguing that a crime has occurred. This is because the *syshchiki*, just like the procurators who are their bosses, must show a high rate of successful prosecutions. I. G. Fedosev, who followed Yegorov as head of Moscow's CID from 1991 to 1994, has argued that the Russian insistence upon statistical demonstrations of judicial efficiency, as measured by a very high rate of crimes to convictions, is probably the single most harmful element in the way that Russia currently deals with crime.[13] Because of this insistence upon an unrealistically high conviction rate, *syshchiki* see no advantage in opening criminal cases that they are unlikely to be able to conclude. One consequence is that, in the *detektivy* at least, *syshchiki* tend to seem less concerned with the physical facts of a case than with the psychological aspects, presumably because of the perceived necessity to force the accused to confess.

Curiously enough, the relaxation of censorship that marked the late Soviet era had only a minimal effect on this restricted choice of fictional detectives. The changing of the legal environment did offer some new professional affiliations, such as investigators who worked for the Division for the Struggle Against Theft of Socialist Property (OBKhSS), but such investigators were little more than variations on the three varieties of "detective" who had existed throughout the Soviet period. There were also some experiments with new possibilities. Nikolay Aleksandrov, for example, made an investigative journalist the hero of at least the first part of his novel, *Two Leaps Across a Chasm;* Danil Koretskiy and Andrey Izmaylov introduced heroes who were versed in oriental martial arts; and Anatoliy Stepanov, even more innovatively, made a soccer coach the detective of his "Soccer Star."

The difficulties that each of these attempted innovations presented, however, tell a great deal about the wider structure of the Russian *detektiv*. Aleksandrov's novel, which begins as a depiction of high-level corruption and economic malfeasance, is able to use the journalist-hero, Orlov, as a narrative device only to the point where the crimes he is investigating become public knowledge. It is precisely at that point that the plot suffers a technical breakdown, because Orlov, like any Russian journalist, can only expose actions that have taken place; what transforms these actions into crimes is the decision of the militia or other competent government organ to actually open a criminal case. "If there is no case, there is no criminal process," says one of the textbooks on the subject.[14] This automatically transfers further action to either the *syshchik* or the *sledovatel*. In fact, in Aleksandrov's book, Orlov disappears completely from the second half of the novel, his place taken by *syshchik* Vashko.

The novels by Koretskiy and Izmaylov avoided this difficulty of jurisdiction, but only because the crimes they pictured were assaults directly on the person of the martial arts expert whom each created for a main character. Thus, the hero has a motivation to solve the crime (since otherwise the bad guys would kill him), and also has the means to bring the malefactors to "justice" (by killing them first). This type of hero may be said to have been a successful addition to the genre, since this basic model has subsequently been imitated hundreds of times. At the same time, though, this success has come at the price of a marked narrowing of the possible crimes this kind of *detektiv* might explore, since, if these plots are to be logical, the crimes must continue to be personal ones, so that the hero may then personally avenge them.

It will, of course, be immediately obvious that one consequence of featuring personal crimes is that heroes such as martial arts experts must inevitably have an individual motivation, rather than being able to take up broader or less personal types of crimes. What will be less obvious, to western readers at least, is that this logical requirement of a personal motivation for the crime against the hero that is necessary to set the plot in motion runs rather quickly into one of the most peculiar features of the *detektiv* and, it would seem, of Russian thought: a lingering suspicion that the victim of a crime is generally complicit, at least for having tempted the criminal into his attack in the first place. Thus, further experimentation with this kind of hero was quickly limited by the kinds of assaults that might logically be made upon an individual, without having the hero himself be so disproportionately wealthy, gifted, or situated as to have "justified" the initial attack in some way.

The limitation is perhaps best illustrated by Stepanov's innovation of having a soccer coach as the hero of "Soccer Star." The motivation for the hero, Oleg, to investigate is that bookmakers are paying young soccer players to throw games and thus, in Oleg's estimation, are ruining the purity of a game he loves. He is wealthy enough, and has enough free time, to be able to fly to the Caucasus to search out the bad guys, and he is fit enough to deal with them when he finds them. Moreover, justice is easy enough to establish, because what Oleg wants is not that anyone be punished for game fixing, but simply that it stop. Thus, what this particular *detektiv* celebrates, atypically for the genre, is Oleg's individual qualities of bravery, honesty, selflessness, and self-reliance, much like the stereotype of the detective in western mystery novels. The fact that Oleg is shown to be reading Mickey Spillane's *I, The Jury* (and in English at that) suggests, however, that this character was the product of conscious imitation of the western canonical norms. If that supposition is correct, it is thus even more indicative of the nature of the Russian genre that Oleg seems to have proved to be a one-time hero, for whom Stepanov apparently could not find any further cases to solve.

Perhaps the biggest surprise, however, is that the collapse of the Soviet Union, and the introduction of the market economy that came with it, has also done almost nothing to broaden the choice of possible detectives for Russian mystery fiction. To be sure, there have been some curious innovations, among the most striking of which are several novels that take criminals as their heroes. If for no other reason than that the "heroes" of these books are causing the crimes that the books depict, and, therefore, there is no mystery whatever about who has committed them and why, it is impossible to see these as detective stories. Obviously, though, they fit into the broader category of crime fiction and thus play a role in the post-Soviet boom in *detektivy*.

While there are several important nuances to this choice of lawbreakers as literary heroes, in terms of simple plot mechanics, this kind of main character is essentially identical to the heroes who have grown out of the Koretskiy and Izmaylov heroes we have discussed. Indeed, while Izmaylov has not much enlarged his reputation beyond that which he won for himself with *Russian Transit*, Koretskiy has become one of the most popular of the post-Soviet writers. Along with colleagues like Lev Dvoretskiy, Viktor

Dotsenko, and Fyodor Butyrskiy, Koretskiy has created the subgenre of the so-called *superboyevik*, or action-thriller. The plots and heroes of these novels are so similar as to be interchangeable, but all of them have in common that their heroes—most of whom seem invariably to be known only by nicknames, such as Dvoretskiy's Yaryy (Savage), Dotsenko's Beshenyy (Rabid—now joined by a female counterpart, known as Beshenaya), and Butyrskiy's Lyutyy (Fierce), are fighters of all-but-superhuman skill, hardened in battles in Afghanistan and Chechnya, with no close human attachments, no frailties, and no second thoughts. Indeed, at least in the case of Dotsenko's Beshenyy, the hero steps over the boundary from human to superhero. Beshenyy, in various novels, is able to heal wounds by glancing at them, read minds, and even manipulate a computer to disarm a "pocket-sized atom bomb," not only without turning the computer on, but without even opening the suitcase in which it is secured.[15]

Especially when taking account of the flights of fancy to which this kind of post-Soviet literary hero has soared, it is perhaps doubly surprising how few realistic additions there have been to the number of possible heroes. The creation of the tax police in 1993 made it possible for authors to add the operatives of this service to their repertoire, but, since the members of this force are simply another specialized kind of militia inspector, this did not widen the cast of possible heroes in any fundamental way. The specificity of this service branch's sphere of activity seems also to have had an inhibiting effect on the use of such policemen as main characters, no doubt because plots of financial chicanery are difficult to make seem as exciting as murders.

The explosion of corruption and, even more so, interethnic conflict and civil war has made it possible for authors to make much greater use of members of Russia's intelligence forces, particularly the GRU (the military intelligence unit), in plots concerning Chechen nationalists and mafia who traffic in nuclear secrets or nuclear scientists. Interestingly enough, the FSB, heir to the major security functions of the KGB, seems to maintain much of the same control over depiction of its agents as did the KGB, for there remain very few books with star fictional agents from this agency, at least by name (more shadowy "security forces" are reasonably common in post-Soviet *detektiv* plots).

Equally instructive about the assumptions and motivations of the *detektiv* genre, however, is the almost complete *failure* of the genre to elaborate the private detective as a genre hero. This failure may seem odd to westerners, since the collapse of the Soviet system has given Russia enormous private fortunes, corruption, and evil on mind-boggling scales, and no shortage of lubricious babes—all social elements upon which the tough-guy fictions of Raymond Chandler, Ross MacDonald, and Elmore Leonard depend. To be sure, Russian *detektiv* writers have experimented with something like the private eye, but again, the differences between western and Russian versions are instructive. Igor Vinnichenko comes close to the western private eye in the figure of his television writer/ producer, the hero of *Honeymoon*. Like a western private detective, this character accepts responsibility for solving what to him are clearly crimes, long before they have reached the attention of public officials. However, Vinnichenko, too, runs into the usual procedural problem, i.e., that there is nothing much that a private citizen can do to evoke an official response to a perceived crime, and thus, Vinnichenko is forced to provide his hero with friends in the police, who can take care of the necessary legal steps.

A common solution to the jurisdiction problem, even during the Soviet days, this "friend-in-the-militia" device has become more frequent in the post-Soviet period, as writers attempt to widen their choice of heroes. Vinnichenko's novel adds an additional wrinkle, though; his hero is also an Orthodox believer, so that the "court" to which Vinnichenko's hero is attempting to refer the crimes he discovers is much higher than is usually true for detective stories.

Nikita Filatov, a St. Petersburg writer, has a serial hero, Vinogradov, who begins as a militia inspector, but who, in later stories, is turned into a true private eye. At least as illustrated by Filatov's stories, however, the problems this character faces are enormous. In addition to all those mentioned above—that he has no means to investigate crimes, nor procedures for having them treated as crimes once he achieves some kind of solution or resolution—Filatov's hero also encounters the dilemma of the private eye inevitably taking on the moral coloration of his employer. To be sure, this is a problem that arises in certain of the western private eye novels as well. In postcommunist Russia, though, authors seem to have had difficulty imagining private clients who are not at least as reprehensible as the people whom those clients would hire the imagined private detectives to investigate. Thus the private eye, in his Russian variant, becomes nothing more than a hired gun, as Filatov's Vinogradov sadly realizes, as in this stake-out with another former cop, also turned private security.

"Come on, damn it, Vinogradov! Who are you and me working for right now? Honestly?"
Vladimir Aleksandrovich [Vinogradov] pictured the face of his employer. "Swindlers, I guess. All of them...." ("Static," 315)

This quandary is even more explicit in Yelena Yakovleva's *All Joking Aside*, a novel that features, in part, a former senior official of the militia named Rumyantsev who has now gone into private security. As part of his duties to his boss, Rumyantsev "cleans up" a murder scene by picking up a spent cartridge and digging the slug out of a wall, then leaves the apartment, with the corpse—a former colleague—still lying on the floor. As he shuts the door,

> something like a sense of guilt entered his soul. In the first place, guilt toward Mikhail, who would continue to lie on the floor for who knows how long. And in the second place because he understood perfectly well that for the first time in his life he had broken the law, and so had become in a way complicit in the crime. He reassured himself that [his boss] would pay him for the risk he was taking . . . but the loss of self-respect can not be bought with any amount of money. It's far too expensive a thing, and, by today's standards, an unacceptable luxury. (144)

Yakovleva also struggles with the jurisdictional problems that face a Russian private detective. Her solution is to make the major investigator in her novel a certain Remezov who, though still employed by the militia, has taken vacation time while trying to decide whether to leave the force entirely (for reasons both of disillusionment with the militia and because of the enticements of the much better paying private work). He thus is able to have the freedom of the private citizen while still retaining most of the legal powers of a militiaman.

The heroine of Anna Danilova's *I'm Coming to Find You* is one of the few true private detectives to emerge in the post-Soviet genre, but neither Danilova's solutions to the generic problems nor her plots are even remotely realistic. Yuliya Zemtsova, the private detective, works for a prosperous private investigation agency in "a southern city" that provides her with a snazzy Ford, a mobile telephone, and sufficient funds to spend most of the novel either driving to the beach or eating in one of this resort town's many restaurants. When she needs to do some actual detecting, Zemtsova and her entire agency seem to act as a kind of subcontractor of the militia, for, as Danilova writes, "Krymov [the agency head] paid not only hundreds of agents and employees of the city's criminal investigation bureau, including [the senior inspector] . . . but also the senior *sledovatel* of the oblast procuracy. . . . The higher authorities closed their eyes to this discrete cooperation, since it brought them obvious benefit" (14). It must also be said that, to judge from her plot, Danilova does not seem to know very much about Russian criminal law. Zemtsova, for example, not only is given the right to arrest suspects at the point of a gun but also to handcuff them and then search their apartments, with official permission. Thus, her book may more properly be assigned to the fantasy world of the action-oriented *boyeviki*. This is particularly well demonstrated by the novel's ending, in which Zemtsova, crazed with secret drugs and psychiatric manipulation, is featured in an all-female gladiatorial "fight to the death" that an underworld figure stages for the pleasure of the local bigwigs. However, despite the basically fantastic nature of Danilova's plot, even her heroine Zemtsova is aware of an ethical nuance pertaining to the private detective business that doesn't seem to surface in the genre's American counterparts:

> She no longer saw [her client] as a businessman, as a client; now there stood before her just a human being, who had appealed to her for help. And she was going to take money from him for that. Was that moral? (26)

Varvara Klyuyeva illustrates another dimension of the problem in her *Unicum*, a novel that features an eponymous heroine who, like Miss Marple, solves the puzzling murders of two of her acquaintances while she and a large group of her friends are camping in the Crimea. Part of a series titled "Cozy *detektiv*," the novel is clearly an attempt to create a Russian version of the "cozy" mystery, in which a civilian, usually female, solves a crime by dint of logic alone. Klyuyeva generally succeeds in this imitation, but the cultural constraints of the Russian genre produce telling deviations from what would have been expected in a western cozy. The heroine of this novel does succeed in puzzling out who has killed the two victims and nearly killed a third, but then she does nothing with her information, beyond explaining to the killer that she knows. She has no authority for arresting the killer herself—especially since the crime takes place in Ukraine—and she refuses to assist the authorities, since to turn in the killer would be informing. Rather, the heroine simply leaves the killer, because she is confident that "A person who has committed a murder . . . will not ever be happy again"(160).

These difficulties in creating a Russian version of Sam Spade or Miss Marple are entirely consistent with an observation made by Jeffrey Brooks in *When Russia Learned to Read*. After studying the masses of pulpy "Pinkerton" fiction that Russian publishers churned out to feed the appetites of the newly literate in the late tsarist period, Brooks noted that, in the west, "The private detective is a defender of civil society and not the state. He is stronger than the official representatives of order, and it is to him, rather than to the authorities, that society must look for security. The detective serves society, but he does so from the outside, on his own terms, and at society's insistence" (208). By contrast, in the early Russian crime genres, "The relationship between the individual and society is explored and society is shown inevitably to be the stronger of the two. The states of freedom and order are juxtaposed and the latter is shown inevitably to be the stronger of the two" (169). This elevation of the state above the individual continues to be the basic predisposition of the Russian *detektiv*, even when the state itself seems to be in serious decline. In discussing recent *detektivy*, one Russian critic has noted that

> The System itself—both the state and its law-enforcement arm—have disintegrated in a very serious fashion. In part it is precisely The System (especially the "Brezhnev system") which is guilty in these novelistic crimes. But there is no other system, these books say, and, bad as it is, duty must be done. In the name of what ideas, values, and symbols The System exists is also not terribly clear from the novels (the novels of today no longer provide such explanatory scenes).[16]

Thus, despite the fact that "The System" either has decayed beyond utility or itself has become the enemy, the heroes of nearly all of the thousands of new *detektivy* and *boyeviki* remain pretty much what their Soviet-era ancestors were—representatives of "The System." As the same critic put it in his article,

> Strictly speaking, there is no *detektiv* where the main hero is an amateur private investigator. . . . There is [only] the modern variation on the militia novel, where the "main role" is taken by a professional, a person from The System. . . . There is the revitalized counter-espionage novel, also about professionals, special agents on special assignments, . . . who also have The System standing behind them. . . . And there is the social novel about a private person who is living in today's criminalized society and who either becomes a victim . . . or a weapon.

Paradoxically enough, as the last clause in the quote above suggests, even the heroes of novels who are themselves actual lawbreakers nevertheless are depicted as defenders, proponents, and even representatives of this abstract, disembodied "state." In Vladimir Shitov's *Cathedral without Crosses*, for example, the hero is an extremely adept safecracker and senior criminal boss, who, in the course of the novel, steals large quantities of gold that he uses first to set up fraudulent businesses and then to swindle huge sums of money out of American and European businessmen. Near the novel's end, however, this hero confesses to his mistress (who herself has decided to enter an Orthodox convent) that the reason he has worked the wrong side of the law so energetically is to prove that, as he says, "Russians know how to think globally and know how to work" (234). Even more importantly, though, the hero, at novel's end, announces that all his wealth is going to be turned over to "the state," because, as he says,

> If we simple people, the backbone of our people, don't love our Motherland just as she is, and defend her interests everywhere and all the time, then who will defend her against insults and shame? . . . I won't let anyone put my Motherland down, and . . . I will give all my capital to defend her interests. (483)

Beshenyy, the hero of Dotsenko's series, goes Shitov's safecracker hero one better. In the novel *Beshenyy's Love*, after swindling Dzhokar Dudayev, the now-dead president of the breakaway republic of Chechnya, out of $3 million, Beshenyy personally takes this money directly to Viktor Chernomyrdin, who was prime minister of Russia when the novel was published.

Thus, despite several post-Soviet experiments with possible heroes, the basic shape of the *detektiv* genre remains just as it was in Soviet days. As a handbook on Russian criminal procedure points out, the typical criminal investigator, in life as in fiction, is "a state servant, and in this capacity is a part of the mechanism of the government machine, just like any civil servant."[17]

Why It Is Sometimes Difficult Even to Call the *Detektiv* a Mystery

There are so many thousands of examples that it is undoubtedly foolhardy to speak of a "typical" mystery. Still it seems fair to suggest that all but the most unusual of British and American mysteries will, at the very least, wait until almost the end of the novel before revealing who it is that has committed the crimes. Not always, but very frequently, the reader of British and American mysteries will be offered a variety of possible suspects for a given crime. This means that, generally, the reader gains knowledge about the crime and its perpetrators at approximately the same pace as does the novel's main investigator. This does not mean that the reader may not be given advance views of the criminal as he or she commits the crimes, but in the west it is a generally accepted rule of the genre that, if a work is to deserve the designation "mystery," the reader must be left in some suspense about who this perpetrator is, and why he (or she) is doing whatever is being done.

This is not the case in the Russian *detektiv*. Although plots can, and often do, begin with the discovery of a body or a missing item of value, the purpose of a given work seldom seems to be simply the discovery of who is responsible for that crime. Indeed, in the Soviet-era genre, that lack of interest in "whodunit" was sometimes explicit, as one critic remarked in his "afterword of appreciation" for Ivan Lazutin's classic of the 1950s, *Militia Sergeant:*

> [This novel's point] is not the suspensefulness of the search for the criminal trio . . . [rather] in *Militia Sergeant* we see our contemporary depicted life-size, a man who during the war, not sparing his own life, battled against fascism for the Fatherland, and who when he came back traded his soldier's greatcoat for that of the militia, to go out on a new front of battle. (475)

As such a comment suggests, the point of the Soviet-era *detektivy* was much less to explore the specific nature of specific crimes and their specific perpetrators than it was to illustrate the general principle that crime harmed the state as much as war once had. Indeed, as the more detailed discussion of what constitutes crime in the *detektiv* in the following chapter will show, this was entirely consistent with the nature of Soviet law, which was fundamentally different from that of the west. Maria Los, one of the leading scholars of Soviet legal thought, has pointed out that

> the existence of . . . fixed sets of laws suggests that society is basically static in nature. Such an assumption, however, is contrary to the Marxist view of society which gives much importance to the constant change and dialectic transformations of socioeconomic life. Given the dynamic nature of [Marxist] society, the law has to be able to respond quickly to change by assuming the form of the versatile elements of the evolving social reality. According to this view, defended strongly by many Soviet law professors in the 1950s, law must be "dialectically" applied as the circumstances require. (56)

To be sure, the "flexibility" that this view of law permitted the Stalin-era organs of law-enforcement was considerably stiffened by the introduction of the 1960 legal code, which replaced the infamous "crimes of analogy" and other flagrant uses of "dialectal" jurisprudence with a legal code that more closely resembled a western model. However, up until the adoption of Russia's new Criminal Code in January 1997, the fundamental assumption underlying the country's legal code was that crime did not consist in specific actions, but rather in their result; in the words of one critic, "The Soviet concept of law was that a crime was something that was harmful to society." Essentially the same point was made even more straightforwardly by Adamov's Lt. Losev in *Evil Wind*: "As we know, there are no abstract truths; truth is always concrete. What is good? What is evil? Can't the one become the other in certain concrete circumstances? The wound of the bandit's knife is evil, but the wound of the surgeon's knife is good" (175).

Although the 1997 Criminal Code was based on the more western notion that a crime is the commission of an act forbidden by the Criminal Code, the members of the committee given responsibility for drawing up the new criminal code are said to have been still committed to the broader, Soviet-era notion of crime. Thus it was necessary to strike a compromise in the drafting of the Criminal Code, as a result of which crime is now understood to be the commission of an act in violation of a law that causes harm to society.[18]

It was not surprising, given this rather generalized view of crime, that the battle against crime in Russia has tended to have a similarly abstract character, both in the Soviet period and since. This is captured particularly neatly in "Gone with the Wind," a story by Kivinov. In the story, the hero is looking for some help from his fellow *syshchiki* in trying to solve a murder, and so appeals to one who is spending his day in one of the city's new supermarkets, arresting shoplifters. Asked to help, the other detective refuses, pointing out that

> anyone [here in the supermarket] who takes so much as a box of matches, I can arrest him on a 144. And the statistics for "crimes solved" don't say anything about what sort of crimes get solved. So let's say there's a murder of some kind, but instead of solving it, let's say I solve a burglary instead, the statistics are the same, right? So why should I shackle myself to a murder, when I can stand here peacefully catching shoplifters? . . . As soon as [our squad] gets behind in the stats, I come right on over here. (128)

Such thinking might seem in part to explain why Russia has enjoyed so exponential a growth in crime since the breakup of the Soviet Union. While Russian statistics can be notoriously unreliable, it is nevertheless sobering to note that the number of registered crimes (of all types) grew from 751,000 in 1965 (for the entire USSR) to 2,786,600 in 1990 (again for the entire USSR), and, by 1995, had reached very nearly that same number, or 2.7 million, for just Russia alone.[19] As Los suggests, however, the purpose of law enforcement in Soviet Russia and even, it would seem, in post-Soviet Russia, is not so much to solve a particular crime, as much as it is to demonstrate that, in the words of the senior inspector in one of Marinina's novels puts it, "[the militia] are defending ourselves with our last ounce of strength, trying to cling to the pitiful remnants of what we used long ago to call professional pride and honor" (341).

Whatever effect such an attitude may have upon society, its significance for the way that authors lay out the plots of their *detektivy* is profound. Because the fact of crime itself is more important than the specifics of any particular crime, authors as a rule do not supply large numbers of suspects. Much more commonly, both in the Soviet-era novels where this might have been expected, and also very frequently in their post-Soviet descendants where it might not be, the *detektivy* reveal who the perpetrator is soon after the crime has been depicted. In the Soviet-era books, this revelation could come almost immediately. We learn who is the villain in Ivan Shevtsov's *Theft*, for example, on page seven. Leonid Medvedovskiy, in his *Interrupted Journey*, allows his Inspector Ageyev about thirty pages of first-person narrative before breaking away to a disembodied authorial third-person to let us see, at least, the lesser characters of the gang of bad guys at work. Leonid Zalata goes a step farther in his "Wolf Berries." Here, the mystery begins with the discovery of the body of a murdered young woman, who turns out to have accidentally learned of the existence of an illegal private turtleneck factory. Once the militia have found out about the factory, however, they lose interest in the murder entirely and set out instead to find the owner of the illegal factory.

The post-Soviet *detektivy* are not quite as quick to reveal their perpetrators as were their forebears. This is in part dictated by changes in the social atmosphere that make it considerably easier for authors to imply that crime is not so limited a phenomenon as, for reasons of censorship and propaganda, the Soviet-era *detektivy* had to maintain. Thus a novel like Marinina's *Stylist* can put forward two separate possible—but false—perpetrators of that novel's seventeen drugs-and-sex murders before offering up the final and correct solution. Much more commonly, however, the plots, even of the post-Soviet *detektivy*, tend to resemble those of the earlier period. Zarubina's *Mrs. Inspector*, for example, is not able to explain precisely how or why the novel's evildoers have committed their various crimes (murder, arson, dope peddling, and dognapping) until near the book's end, but there are no red herrings or false leads; most of the malefactors are firmly in sight throughout the greater part of the book, making the focus of the book's tension not who "dunit" but rather, when and how will they be caught. It can even happen, as it does in Yakovleva's *All Joking Aside*, that the "crime" that begins the mystery proves by novel's end not to have been a crime at all; in that book, the "kidnapping" that sets the plot in motion turns out to have been caused by a young woman's explanatory note of farewell to her mother disappearing when teenage vandals in search of kicks set fire to the mail boxes in her apartment building. It can also happen, as it does in Shitov's *Cathedral without Crosses* or, not quite so extravagantly, in Valeriy Maslov's *Made Mafia*, that the "heroes" themselves are committing the crimes that a given novel features. The peculiarities of Russian plot construction extend as well to the typical denouement of the *detektiv*, which, only in the rarest of novels, proves to be the arrest of that particular work's villain. Even in Soviet-era novels, which tended to be so constructed that readers were left in no doubt that the villain would soon fall into the hands of the militia, the moment of actual arrest is very seldom pictured. Adamov's *Evil Wind* builds for more than two hundred pages toward a confrontation between the villain and Inspector Losev only to skip over what would seem obligatory, the arrest of the villain, a black marketeer. Instead the novel ends with the words: "Yes, criminal investigation had done its job. The criminal has been arrested. Now it's the *sledovatel*'s job" (272).

The self-assurance of this ending, implying that the criminal, once arrested, will be convicted, is in part a product of the Russian legal process in which, as noted, a person cannot (or at least will not) be arrested until there is virtual certainty of conviction. It is also, of course, a reflection of a Soviet propaganda system that could not very well imply that Soviet militiamen might make a mistake in an investigation or an arrest. In the post-Soviet novels, by contrast, very nearly the opposite kind of ending is the rule. Rather than being arrested, it can sometimes happen, as in Dmitriy Petrov's *Setup for a Sucker*, that the villain is appointed procurator for the entire region, and thus would have, in effect, to punish himself—which obviously he will not do. More frequently, as in Marinina's *Stolen Dream* or Dashkova's *Flesh for Sale*, a *detektiv* will end, as it were, in a tie. As the husband of Marinina's heroine philosophizes on the novel's final page, "from a mathematical point of view, [the militia and the criminal world] will always exist parallel to one another, never intersecting. Never. They won't break you, but you won't crush them either" (444).

What the *Detektiv* Is

For all their apparent dissimilarities, these two kinds of endings share some common traits, which by and large define the social purpose of the *detektiv*, both in the Soviet era and since. Focusing upon the arrest of an evildoer, as the western genres tend to do, suggests that there is something essentially anomalous about the crime that has been committed. Showing the police, or its equivalent, depriving a malefactor of his or her freedom, including the freedom to do further harm, demonstrates that crime represents a disruption of the social pattern. This is put right by the apprehension of the disrupter—thus making further disruptions impossible.

By concentrating rather upon the process of *explaining* the crime, and the companion process of getting the perpetrator to understand and admit those explanations (for that is what a *sledovatel* is essentially doing, as he or she works a case up for presentation to the judge), the Soviet-era *detektivy* are attempting to deal with one of the most puzzling features of the Soviet environment—the continuing presence of crime. After all, Lenin had assured his followers, in *State and Revolution*, that

> we know that the fundamental social cause of excesses which violate the rules of social life is the exploitation of the masses, their want and poverty. With the removal of this chief cause, excesses will inevitably begin to "wither away." We do not know how quickly and in what stages, but we know that they will be withering away. (Connor, 221)

Since this "withering" seemed to take an ever longer time to get started, the Soviet *detektivy* were concerned less with the mechanics of specific crimes and much more with the broader causes of crime itself. Thus, the focus of a book had to be not so much the way in which a particular crime was accomplished, as much as the broader failings and shortcomings in a person that had caused him, or her, to wish to bring harm to society. The interest in a novel was less on the arrest of a person and more on the interrogation—and the sparring with the *sledovatel* that that interrogation permitted.

By the late Soviet period, and even more so by the post-Soviet period, the authors of the *detektivy* were growing ever more pessimistic that crime was a temporary or "withering" phenomenon. Increasingly, authors began instead to posit a kind of Manicheanism, suggesting that evil is probably eternal, and that the best for which humankind may hope is to maintain a kind of dynamic equilibrium between that evil and some kind of good. This thinking resulted in the more typical ending of the post-Soviet *detektivy*, which suggest that, in the words of one critic, "Both sides [militia and criminals] settle their accounts with one other practically identically, meaning, completely professionally and absolutely pitilessly."

In terms of the typical plot, however, the conviction that evil is ubiquitous and eternal has very nearly the same effect as does the Soviet-era conviction that a crime is a rare and inexplicable error. In neither event is the arrest upon which the western genres insist likely to do very much to reduce the future likelihood of further crime. What is far more important, regardless of the era from which the *detektiv* is drawn, is the demonstration of how evil comes about, and the effect that this has, not upon the individual, as it might be in the west, but upon society as a whole. Similarly, just as the effect of crime is social in the Russian *detektiv*, so too is the manner in which it must be battled. The hero of Kivinov's "Gone with the Wind" states this explicitly:

> What's [preventing crime] got to do with the militia? If the [country's] economy is down the hole why should the militia have to be the best in the world? ... Crime is the result of the collapse of society, so that the first to battle with it should be politicians and economists. (95)

Although the *detektiv* resembles its western counterparts in that the ultimate center about which the genre revolves is the question of what is good and what is evil, the fact that the question is being posed in terms of society as a whole, rather than of individuals, gives the *detektiv* a much wider canvas. The plots of *detektivy* are never intended to be specific, but, rather, are written to be representative, and, as such, to be instructive. The fact that criminals are caught, and so presumably punished, in western mystery novels may, of course, be understood to be a kind of didacticism, a lesson in good and evil. The far broader canvas of the *detektiv*, however, makes the Russian genre much more overtly didactic. To be sure, this is, to a certain extent, true of all Russian literature, which has always taken it as its duty the need to shape and educate its readers. What is particularly striking about the state of literature in Russia today, however, is the degree to which readers seem no longer to find that the concerns of more serious literature speak to them or give shape to their world. The astounding success of the *detektiv* may perhaps lie in a new national need for less ponderous, more entertaining fare. Given the continued and even enlarged dose of social morality that infuses every new *detektiv*, however, it seems safe to conclude that at least a part of that success is due to readers searching to give moral shape to a world they find otherwise inexplicable. In turn, the authors of the *detektiv* seem more than ready to oblige. As one writer and publisher, Stanislav Gagarin, pontificates,

> the Russian *detektiv* has always carried a large spiritual burden. . . . The primary difference [between Russian and western mysteries] is in the mentality of the readers themselves, in the national character, in the differences between the western individual character and our collective one. Where the western detective is interested primarily in the size of his reward, and in defending the law, for the Russian detective and his genre the most important thing is the moral side of crime. The tradition of morality has always been very important for our state. . . . The Russian *detektiv* is always a defender of the humiliated and insulted, a fighter for justice. (360)

It is this preoccupation with the moral issues, not of individual behavior but rather of the individual in relationship to society, that makes the Russian *detektiv* so revealing a source for understanding nuances of the national character. The *detektivy* are not intended to be puzzles of logic that their readers delight in solving; nor are they written to be celebrations of acts of individual heroism, initiative, or daring. The central subject in the *detektiv*, in the Soviet-era books and in those of the present-day alike, is the collective harm that is done to society when society itself is unable to control all of its members.

In his study of the pulp fiction that Russia's newly literate snapped up at the turn of the century, Jeffrey Brooks found that the

> tales of bandits and criminals illustrate two fundamental issues in Russian culture. The relationship between the individual and society is explored and society is shown inevitably to be the stronger of the two. The states of freedom and order are juxtaposed and the latter is shown inevitably to be the stronger of the two. Those who choose freedom must live outside the social

order, and they are doomed by their decision. . . . Russian outsiders differed from their American, French, and English counterparts in their means of reentry into respectable society [for those western rebels]. The judgement of the community legitimates their rebellion against an unjust authority in the name of another conception of justice or virtue. For the heroes of Russian popular culture there is no unofficial court of appeal. Only the state and Church had moral authority to pardon the rebellion of Russian fictional bandits, and they could earn a full pardon by patriotic feats, such as heroism during wartime, or, occasionally, through acts of religious penitence such as pilgrimages. (169, 171)

As the following chapters will demonstrate, very much the same thing continues to be true of Russian crime fiction today. The *detektiv* is a social morality play, the various plots of which all reinforce the notion that society is simultaneously strong—stronger than any individual desire or intention—and yet at the same time very weak, for it can be harmed by the actions of even one of its members. It is in the continuing affirmation of that necessity for the individual to subordinate himself or herself to the larger entity of the state that the genre provides its most illuminating lessons about the way in which Russians understand themselves and their place in the world about them. In a word, if it is true, as writer Igor Vinnichenko avers, that "even *detektivy* . . . may serve to better the soul," then it is worthwhile to examine precisely what lessons it is that the genre is teaching its readers.

Notes

1. L. V. Frank, *Nuzhna li sovetskaya viktimologiya? Voprosy ugolovnogo prava.* (Dushanbe, 1966), 153, as quoted in V. L. Vasilyev, *Yuridicheskaya psikhologiya* (St. Petersburg: Piter, 1998), 393.

2. N. F. Kuznetsova, *Kriminologiya* (Moscow: Izd. BEK, 1998), 103.

3. Maria Los, *Communist Ideology, Law, and Crime* (New York: St. Martin's Press, 1988), 265.

4. A. M. Larin, E. B. Melnikov, and V. M. Savitskiy, *Ugolovnyy protsess Rossii* (Moscow: Izd. BEK, 1997), 16.

5. Vladimir Yanitskiy, "Mugface Kingdom," in *Poyedinok #16* (Moscow: Moskovskiy rabochiy, 1986), 278–79.

6. *Kommentariy k ugolovnomu kodeksu Rossiyskoy Federatsii* (Moscow: Infra-Norma, 1997), v.

7. *Kommentariy,* v.

8. U. A. Usmanov, *Spravochnik sledovatelya* (Moscow: PRIOR, 1998), 19.

9. Larin, et al., 26.

10. Larin, et al., 24.

11. *Itogi*, 6 October 1998, 56.

12. *Moskovskiyy ugolovnyy rozysk: Istoriya v litsakh* (Moscow: Ob"ed. red. MVD Rossii, 1998), 508.

13. *Moskovskiy ugolovnyy rozysk*, 527.

14. Larin, et al., 24.

15. T. Morozova, "Slyshish', vremya gudit: Blyam!" *Literaturnaya gazeta*, 28 October 1998, 10.

16. *Itogi*, 6 October 1998, 56.

17. Pavel Yani, *Pod sledstviyem:* Besedy o prave (Moscow: Raduga, 1997), 73.

18. *Itogi*, 1 October 1996, 54.

19. N. F. Kuznetsova, *Kriminologiya* (Moscow: Izd BEK, 1998), 103, 111.

CHAPTER TWO

The Peculiarities of Russian Crime

A GREAT DEAL HAS BEEN WRITTEN about the wide variety of activities that westerners perceive as innocent, but that the Soviets defined as criminal. Peter Juviler, a western scholar of Soviet law, offers a typical catalog for the Stalin years:

> Ten or more years of labor camp, followed by exile (if one survived until then) usually awaited the following: anecdote tellers; a person turning off the radio when the announcer began reading letters to Stalin; Soviet commissars who had fought during the Spanish Civil War; the middle classes; intelligentsia; non-Communist politicians of the Baltic states and other occupied areas; targets of slanderers' and informers' grudges or opportunism; Esperantists and North Caucasus mountaineers; possibly, the first person to stop applauding Stalin's name at a meeting; Latvian sharpshooters and Chekists who spearheaded the Bolshevik struggle; suspected collaborators; returning POWs; persons who stayed with Stalin in Moscow instead of evacuating during the German attack in 1941; entire Soviet or party organizations; persons who described the horrors of the Leningrad siege or a retreat; returning troops who praised the living standards they saw in war-torn Germany and Europe to the West; émigrés encountered by Soviet forces; the million slave laborers taken by the Nazis, who had to be forcibly repatriated in 1946–47; whole suspect nationalities carted off into exile; Jewish intellectuals; the flower of Soviet culture, from director Meyerhold to poet Mandelstam. (62–63)

Precisely because these excesses of Soviet law are so familiar to western readers, it is instructive to examine areas of human activity that the west has criminalized, while the Soviet Union or Russia has not.

Crime, Sex, and Sex Crimes

Given the prominent place that the subject plays in most western detective fiction, it is particularly striking how infrequently the subject of sex, and especially of criminal sex, appears in the *detektivy*. In the Soviet-era novels, of course, this absence was to a large extent due to the prudishness of government censors; the degree to which they controlled the "decorum" of published fiction was confirmed after the fact by Leonid Slovin, who confessed in 1992 that he was throwing as much sex into his new plots as he could dream up, simply because he had been forbidden to put *any* sex into his plots before.[1]

Another reason why sex probably did not figure in the Soviet-era plots is that most of the Soviet populace was deeply ignorant about matters of human sexuality and particularly about the more extreme ways in which that sexuality might be expressed. As Robert Cullen explains in *The Killer Department*, his true-crime account of the mass murderer Andrey Chikatylo, found guilty in the sex-mutilation deaths of more than fifty children, one of the many things that made investigation of Chikatylo's horrendous crimes all but impossible was the nearly complete absence of public discussion of sex and the equally complete absence among law enforcement personnel and other public officials of the most rudimentary knowledge about human sexuality, deviant or otherwise.

This lack of knowledge, or perhaps of imagination, seems clearly to be reflected in the general paucity of sex scenes in the *detektivy*, even after the disappearance of censorship cleared the way for them. The following scene, from Ilya Derevyanko's *Thugs*, might serve to illustrate the most common kind of sex scene in the new *detektivy*. The commander of a special military prison decides to pass a slow afternoon in dalliance with his secretary, which Derevyanko renders in toto as

Ten minutes later he was clutching the smooth springy thighs of the well-built brunette, who, her chest on the table, was passionately moving in time to his rhythmic movements. (12)

Vladimir Shitov doesn't manage to get much racier in *Cathedral without Crosses*, even though he is trying to build his criminal-hero up to proportions just less than those of a superman. Although the hero and his other rich criminal friends repair frequently to Russian baths for frolics with flocks of naked girls, Shitov never tries to show us what might go on there. This enormous novel's closest approximation to a sex scene is the following.

> They had long ago outgrown the age of hurried and mindless fumbling. Like professional wine tasters, slowly and with good knowledge of what they were doing, they gave themselves up to erotic love. . . . (481)

What is even more curious, given the efforts Shitov has expended in depicting his hero as a fellow of extra-grand aspirations, the woman with whom this scene is played is the hero's wife.

About the best that most of the new *detektivy* seem to manage by way of sex scenes are ones similar to the following, which is taken from Nikolay Ivanov's *Tax Police*. In that novel, the bad guy, a Russian Jew who has earlier emigrated to America and who has now returned to profit from the misfortunes of his former motherland, maintains a pleasure island on which he keeps two well-tanned, totally naked

> young blonde girls without an ounce of extra fat, with precisely curved hips which, though not yet fully formed, were already shamefully bared and summoning, underlining their femaleness. They had sharp little breasts and pertly thrust, taut nipples, the kind of breasts which there was no need to bring to their most divine form by indolently placing their arms on their heads, as older photo-models were forced to do. (22)

The most graphic activity that Ivanov permits these two lovelies, however, is, when asked to do so by their boss, first, to "embrace and kiss one another," and then, on order, "to turn from nunnish Madonnas into whorish Magdalenes, who like female devils flung themselves upon their victims, demonstrating . . . that this was their work" (24).

To be sure, the freedoms of the post-Soviet world, especially in the heady days right after censorship vanished, let some authors exercise their most lurid imagination. Igor' Bunich depicts a horrific revenge in *Absolute License*, where rats gnaw a bound man's genitals as his tormentor urinates on him, while Leonid Slovin, in one of his novels, is said to depict a character using the severed head of a crime victim to fellate himself in Lenin's Tomb.[2]

Given that such scenes had been forbidden before, and that even more graphic scenes are possible—as some American mystery writers have proven—they nevertheless remain surprisingly infrequent in the post-Soviet *detektivy*.

There is another, and perhaps more surprising reason why sex figures so infrequently in the *detektivy*, particularly as a motivator for a crime, or as a crime itself. That is that most sexual activity was not considered criminal, either in the Soviet Union or in post-Soviet Russia.

The most striking omission of this kind, from the western point of view, is that neither Soviet nor Russian law has statutes forbidding prostitution. The subject seems to have been entirely overlooked by the Khrushchev criminal code, perhaps in part because it was always possible for procurators who wished to do so to charge those practicing prostitution under other clauses of the Criminal Code, such as the statutes forbidding "non-labor income." The fact that it was possible for the courts to deal with the *practice* of prostitution, however, does not obviate the fact that the act of exchanging money for sexual favors was not in and of itself considered to be criminal.

The Criminal Code of 1997 is perhaps even more striking, in that it specifically recognizes the *fact* of prostitution, but only regards activities subsidiary to it to be criminal, while prostitution itself appears to remain legal. Article 241 of the new Criminal Code forbids the establishment and maintenance of places devoted to the practice of prostitution, while Article 240 forbids the activity of procurement for prostitution, but specifically limits criminal culpability to acts that coerce or force people into prostitution. The right to become a prostitute appears to be a freedom that Russian law preserves, in contrast to most western countries, which have long ago revoked it.

This "freedom" finds a particularly vivid expression in Andrey Kivinov's story "Gone with the Wind." There, a businesslike and resourceful young woman appears at the front desk of her local militia station, complaining that she has had trouble breaking into her "chosen profession," and thus has decided to ask the assistance of the militia in setting herself up as a hard-currency prostitute in a nearby hotel, in return for which she will keep the militia informed about goings-on in the hotel. The desk officer to whom she makes this proposal, though startled, decides to accept the deal she offers because, as he says, "It's odd that a prostitute would come to the militia looking for work . . . but I suppose, with our life, it's nothing surprising" (90–91).

The new Criminal Code is equally silent on other forms of sexual activity that many western countries have criminalized. Article 116 of the Criminal Executive Code, adopted July 1, 1997 to regulate the function of Russia's prisons and other places of punishment, lists lesbianism and *muzhelovstvo* (a fusty, almost biblical, word for male homosexuality) as two activities that constitute a violation of the legal order inside labor colonies and prisons, along with use of narcotics, organizing or taking part in prisoners' strikes, or failing to treat prison authorities with due respect. Commentaries on the new criminal-executive law seem to regard lesbianism of any sort within prisons as definitionally illegal, but they appear to accept male homosexuality that is not coerced as not in and of itself illegal.[3] The Criminal Code also seems to permit consensual homosexual activities between adults: Article 132 of the code forbids only homosexual activities that are achieved with coercion or force; Article 133 forbids the same thing achieved by deception or threat; and Article 134 forbids both homosexual and heterosexual activity with partners who are "obviously" younger than 16.[4] Article 135, which forbids "perverse acts" (*razvratnyye deystviya*), explicitly applies only to sexual activities directed at very young children, such as fondling and flashing, and so does not permit application to a broader range of activities, no matter how elastic the statute's title might seem. It is conceivable that Article 121, which forbids the knowing transmission of venereal disease, and Article 122, which forbids the transmission of immunodeficiency diseases, might be used against homosexuals, but either application would be an extension of criminality that these laws themselves do not seem to intend. Thus homosexuality, like prostitution, appears in and of itself to be entirely legal in Russia.

Very much the same situation now appears to obtain with respect to pornography. Although the Soviet criminal code specifically forbade possession of pornographic materials in any form, the 1997 code seems concerned only to prevent the unregulated distribution of pornography, and the commentaries themselves appear exceedingly reluctant to grasp the nettle of deciding precisely what it is that constitutes pornography. After attempting to define this as "the coarsely naturalistic detailed depiction of anatomic and/or physiological details of sexual relations," commentaries on the Criminal Code then confess that recent judicial attempts to stop the sale both of the *Kama Sutra* and of a physiology text on the grounds that they were pornographic had equally ended in failure.[5]

The fact that the Criminal Code seems so accepting of sexual activity does not mean, however, that the *detektivy* share the law's broadmindedness. Especially in the Soviet-era works, but also to a surprising degree in the *detektivy* of the present, sexuality tends to appear as a negative trait far more often than it seems positive.

In the Soviet books, sexuality of any sort, but especially anything that might be termed "abnormal," was generally permitted only in order that authors might better illustrate the overall depravity of their fictional criminals. In Ivan Shevtsov's *Theft*, for example, one proof that, in Shevtsov's words, "all criminals are moral monsters" (230) is that the novel's bad guy, Prishelets, receives an unexpected visit from his daughter, whom he had abandoned in her infancy. Now grown up to be an attractive Aeroflot stewardess, the young woman has made the sentimental decision to seek out her father and has come to Prishelets, thinking him to be an acquaintance of her father who might help her to locate him. Taken both by her beauty and by the possibilities that her job might present for letting him smuggle money out of the USSR, Prishelets first woos this girl with gifts of cubic zirconia (which, villain that he is, he passes off as diamonds), then gets her drunk on champagne. Unaware that this apparently charming suitor is her father, the girl eventually falls into his bed, where her father happily, and knowingly, indulges in incest.

A similar scene occurs in Viktor Timakov's *Bloody Money, or Hot Summer in Magadan,* which begins with a surprisingly graphic homosexual love scene—so rare in *detektivy* as to be almost unique—between one of the bad guys and a partner who quickly turns out, with further information, to have been the man's own son, the existence of whom he had not known about.

A different, but no less effective, demonstration of criminal sexual immorality comes in Nikolay Cherginets's *The Investigation Continues.* There, the chief bad guy, Logatskiy, decides to rid himself of an inconvenient spouse by killing her during a holdup of the store where she is a clerk. Even more tellingly, another character in the same book remarks, on seeing a pretty girl on board a cruise ship, how pleasant it would be to rape her down near the engine room, where no one could hear her scream, and then stuff her out a porthole. Leonid Slovin's "Five Days and the Morning of the Sixth" seems to pose a similar scenario—a beautiful young girl is found dead alongside the railroad tracks, her head battered in—but ultimately rejects sexual violence as an explanation for her injury. By novel's end, In-

spector Denisov has figured out that the girl and her boyfriend had together leaped from a commuter train as a kind of romantic test of their
love, and she had had the bad fortune to hit a telegraph pole. In Mikhail
Chernyonok's *Losing Bet*, however, the bad guys demonstrate the evil efficiency of which Cherginets's characters had only dreamed, by tossing their
postcoital partner from the balcony of their high-rise apartment.

To be sure, the perpetrators of these acts of sexual violence and depravity are villains, so it is perhaps not surprising that they should also be villainous in their treatment of lovers. What is more surprising is the difficulty that the *detektivy* seem to have in portraying sexuality in a positive
way, even when depicting the genre's heroes. To a certain extent, of course,
the strain that police service places on family and personal life is a com-
monplace of the western mystery genres as well. In most of the western
books, however, the contest between family life and duty is generally presented as more or less an even one, recognizing that the demands of the detective's personal life are approximately as valid as are those of his professional life. In the *detektivy*, especially those from the Soviet era, there is no
contest; the balance tips severely against family life.

In many Soviet-era *detektivs*, particularly those written before the beginning of glasnost, militia wives simply don't figure at all, or if they do, they
appear as silent, supportive Soviet heroines, who endure without a mur-
mur the long and irregular hours of their militia husbands. However, as the
development of the genre permitted greater individualization of its heroes,
there was a pronounced tendency to depict wives and other women as dis-
tractions, whom the detectives were better off without. The heroes of Viktor Astafyev's *Sad Detective*, of Leonid Slovin's many novels about Inspector Denisov, and of Viktor Pronin's "Version in Snow" are all divorced or
estranged, while Arkadiy Adamov's Inspector Losev gradually loses his wife
over the course of several novels. This competition between wife and duty
is actually the central theme of a short story by Vladimir Gonik, "Edge of
the World," which was published in an annual anthology of *detektivy*. The
story itself is not a mystery, but, rather, is about the lonely duty of a Soviet
air-defense pilot stationed at a tiny base in Russia's Far North. It is impossible to know for certain why this non-mystery was published where it was,
but it is tempting to speculate that part of the reason was the unwavering
firmness with which Gonik's pilot-hero is able to let his bored and de-
manding wife slip away, rather than place the interests of his Motherland
in jeopardy. In some stories, such as Anatoliy Stepanov's "Soccer Star" or

Artur Makarov's "Five Summer Days" the heroes resolve this implicit tension between duty and family in a curious but logical way: Although full-grown adults, well established in their careers, the heroes of both stories still live at home with their mothers.

What many *detektivy* make clear, however, is that it is not so much the demands of family life that threaten the genre's heroes as much as it is sexual attraction itself. Nikolay Psurtsev's *Without Evil Intent*, for example, begins as an exploration of the temptations to put family before service. The novel's main plot revolves about the indecision of one Inspector Mokhov about what to do when he recognizes the handwriting of his wife's uncle on one of the clues in a fur-poaching case, suggesting that the uncle is a guilty participant. Mokhov's wife scarcely figures in the plot; she neither asks him to cover up for her uncle, nor demands that he think about her family rather than his duty. Indeed, she is not even aware of her uncle's sins until the novel's end, and when she does learn of them, she agrees that Mokhov has done right by exposing the uncle's crime. It is Mokhov himself who decides at the outset that he probably shouldn't ask questions, and much of the book is devoted to exploring the widening disorientation that results from that early, incorrect choice. In a pivotal scene, Psurtsev illustrates Mokhov's conflicting loyalties by having him dance with a fellow inspector's wife; even though the husband is a colleague and a friend, the physical proximity of the woman, and the sweaty temptation this evokes in Mokhov, is pointedly made parallel to the temptations that beckon Mokhov in connection with his wife's uncle. What the novel seems to argue is that, just as it is human nature—or at least male nature—to feel the sexual pull of a pretty woman, so too is it human nature to feel the tug of family ties and illicit riches. By implication, then, it is just as criminal to succumb to the one as it is to the other.

Whereas in Psurtsev's book the woman who tempts Mokhov to stray seems to be unaware of her power over the inspector, in many other *detektivy*, women are shown not only to be conscious of their effect upon men, but to be actively using this attraction to their own benefit. Anatoliy Bezuglov's "Cupid's Arrows," for example, portrays a fading Polina Volskaya-Valua and her drop-dead-gorgeous niece, Nina, who both see their beauty as a form almost of capital, which must be wisely "spent" in order to snare a rich and influential husband. A certain Lyudmila, one of the lesser villains of Nikolay Ivanov's *Tax Police*, takes an even more mercenary view of her own attractiveness. In addition to working for the tax police in order to sell their secrets to the tax-evaders her colleagues are trying to apprehend, Lyudmila protects herself by manipulating men's weakness for her beauty, which she exploits to feed her love for luxurious goods.

What is more significant about Ivanov's novel, though, is that it is nearly as hostile to another young woman, Nadya, as it is to the rapacious Lyudmila. While the latter consciously uses her beauty to ensnare both Ivan and Boris, the novel's two heroes, Nadya's effect upon the two men is even worse, despite the fact that she is an honest, goodhearted, and innocent person. Fast friends from their days in the military academy before they meet Nadya, both men fall in love with her, but she is able to feel affection only for Ivan.

The consequences of this unequally requited love are profound. Not only do Ivan and Boris fall out over Nadya, but they even are pushed to different career paths: Boris becomes a member of the tax police, while Ivan is shown to be succumbing to the siren song of private business. The two are thrown back together by Lyudmila, who is using each for her own purposes. After a brief period of bitter, renewed competition, the two men realize that their friendship is more important to them than is either woman, and so they reject both Nadya and Lyudmila. As Boris, the more heroic of the two men, concludes,

> Say what you will, but men are more natural. They have less shine, none of that make-up, glitter, and all those clever tricks. Women are a trap. For hundreds of years they have been repainting themselves, showing off their good qualities and hiding their bad ones, which still have not disappeared. (101)

It is difficult to find positive attitudes toward female sexuality in the *detektivy*. This is perhaps understandable for the novels of the Soviet era, if for no other reason than that the genre was virtually a male domain—written by men about men. As the last head of the Soviet-era Moscow Criminal Investigation department, A. N. Yegorov, put it, "Criminal investigation was and remains true masculine work, for the mind, for the soul, and for the body. It is very masculine work."[6]

Lyubov Arestova was not only just about the sole female *detektiv* writer of the Soviet period, but was also one of a very small number of writers of either sex who managed to continue publishing mystery stories in the post-Soviet era. Arestova used a female inspector in her "Supplementary Investigation," which appears to have been written about the time of the USSR's collapse, but in the greater part of her work, such as her cycle of stories about crime in Siberia, *The Last Clue*, she takes a man as her hero.

Almost as unusual as Arestova herself was Anatoliy Romov's "Man in an Empty Apartment," also published about the time the Soviet period was ending. Although Romov is male, he not only chooses a woman, Yuliya Silina, as his story's chief investigator, but even allows her to feel a growing romantic interest in the KGB officer who has been seconded to assist her with her case, since it involves the attempt to smuggle valuable coins out to the west. The closest that Romov comes to exploring Silina's sexuality, however, is to give her a periodic wistfulness about her approaching twenty-ninth birthday and the fact that she seems to have neither husband or children on her horizon. Even though attracted to her KGB colleague, Silina never permits her feelings to grow beyond a decorous, and faintly promising, warmth.

There is a similar instance in Viktor Pronin's "Version in Snow," although the sexual roles are more traditional. There, in the course of his investigation, Pronin's inspector comes across a woman to whom he is attracted, just as she appears to be drawn to him. The way in which Pronin demonstrates this couple's probity is particularly telling. Aware of their liking for each other, this estimable pair agree that they will not meet again for a month and then will part again for a further month after that meeting, before deciding whether or not their sense of mutual sympathy is worth pursuing.

The rectitude and reticence of the *detektiv* about matters of the heart is particularly puzzling in the later post-Soviet period, when the number of female authors has mushroomed. Although women like Inna Astakhova and Lyubov Arestova were among the first writers who found quick public favor in the first post-Soviet years, it was the phenomenal success of Aleksandra Marinina that really created the model for the present-day female *detektiv*. The many millions of Marinina's nineteen novels that have sold since her first publication in 1993 quickly encouraged her sister-authors and, even more, those publishers who attempted to capitalize on this unexpected enthusiasm of the Russian reader for *detektivy* written by women. Marinina continues to dominate the Russian market, but she is meeting increasingly stiff competition from writers such as Irina Zarubina, Anna Danilova, Yelena Yakovleva, Yana Belousova, Tatyana Polyakova, and—probably the most talented of the group—Polina Dashkova.

Most of the main characters of the books by these female writers are also female. Some, like the heroines of Dashkova's books, are ordinary women from various occupations—a student in *Flesh for Sale*, a translator in *No One Will Weep*, a ballerina in *Place under the Sun* —but a great many of them, including Nastya Kamenskaya, the heroine of all of Marinina's novels, are themselves *syshchiki* or *sledovateli*. Although these women pride themselves on their professional abilities, they exhibit a distinct uneasiness about the fact of their gender. Klara Dezhkina, the title character of Irina Zarubina's *Mrs. Inspector*, emphasizes her domesticity and her maternal qualities; although Zarubina stresses repeatedly that Dezhkina has a quick analytic mind and a cool head, the mannerisms that this senior law enforcement official cultivates are those of a middle-aged mom. She is forever brewing up soups or insisting that people gulp down the hot tea she carries about in a thermos. Herself a mother of half-grown children, Dezhkina is further "domesticated" by her engineer husband who, like so many men in the post-Soviet environment, is now unemployed. Dezhkina is acutely conscious of her husband's "male sensibilities" and so makes a particular point of carrying the full load of domestic chores, including fanatical baking and cooking; she also defers to her husband's authority on all issues save those that directly affect her work. The closest that Dezhkina approaches to passion is her desperate longing for a new raincoat she glimpses in an upscale Moscow boutique, but which her miserly salary does not allow her even to dream of purchasing.

Marinina's Kamenskaya approaches her femininity in a different, and even more curious, way. Marinina stresses in every novel that Kamenskaya is colorless, scrawny, and a difficult personality. Working as a kind of "human computer" for the Moscow CID, Kamenskaya is the very soul of antiromanticism; in *Small Fry Die First*, for example, she looks forward to her marriage to her longtime fiancé Aleksey Chistyakov solely for the reason that their honeymoon will give her a chance to translate a French detective novel, and so pick up a little extra money. (Kamenskaya is said to know five languages, three of them well enough to let her do commercial translation.) Her relations with Chistyakov, a mathematician, are so cool as to border on bloodless; the single basis of the bond between the pair seems to be that Chistyakov is used to her ways and is willing to cook and clean besides. Deliberately deemphasizing her femaleness, Kamenskaya nearly always dresses in jeans, baggy sweaters, and ratty tennis shoes. Interestingly,

Kamenskaya is as hostile to attractive men as she is to attractive women. In *Stylist* Marinina writes,

> More than anything, Nastya could not endure studs, men who were certain that their sexual attractiveness would help give them power over women, to make them submit to their will. She hated men who were certain that the purpose of women is to have orgasms and produce offspring and submit to the man who helps her or allows her to fulfill her lot. (51)

As Marinina repeatedly emphasizes, Kamenskaya prefers this essentially sexless state, both for herself and for her relations with her ever steady but deadly dull fiancé/husband (the two court and marry over the course of several novels). However, when the demands of her investigation require it, Kamenskaya is capable of transforming herself into an attractive woman, or even, if the circumstances warrant, into a blinding beauty. As Marinina stresses, this beauty is not only a weapon, which Kamenskaya dons the way her male colleagues might strap on a pistol, but also is a torment for the woman herself, as she feels herself turning colder, more selfish, and crueler. In Marinina's evocation of her character's sexuality, female attractiveness quickly comes to be seen as a kind of aggression, which Kamenskaya, as a law enforcement officer and as a generally higher sort of human being, uses only when and as her job requires. By implication, however, the sexuality of other, less self-conscious characters is a dangerous and provocative thing.

Although Marinina may be more explicit than many of her fellow authors in her identification of sex with aggression and power, her interweaving of love and violence are, in fact, entirely typical of the *detektiv* genre as a whole. Women in the Russian *detektivy* use their beauty. Lena, in Bezuglov's *Black Widow*, has an affair with an older professor to punish her husband for showing up late for New Year's Eve. The unnamed blonde beauty in Danil Koretskiy's "Circle of Friends" lives with a boyfriend who is "as ugly as a bulldog," solely because the man supplies her with imported clothes, wine, cigarettes, and other goods in short supply. The men fare no better. Either they are the smug, self-satisfied studs whom Marinina described, or they are lovesick fools, like the young man in Kivinov's "Made from Waste Products," who, having boasted to a young beauty over whom he moons that he will take her to Paris, is forced, for lack of funds, to hire himself out as a contract killer. Even worse off are those like the condemned murderer in Ilya Derevyanko's *Thugs*, a compulsive onanist, who confesses before his execution:

I have always been weak sexually . . . in relations with women I could never achieve the sexual act. . . . At the age of 24, I unexpectedly came to understand that I could achieve the desired result only with the dead. . . . I found citizeness K. in the forest, dragged her into the bushes and choked her to death, then committed the sexual act, with a sense of great satisfaction. . . . I coaxed 9-year-old E. into a doorway. I choked her to death, took her down into the basement, where I completed the sexual act through her rear passage. (70–71)

Property Crimes and the Crime of Property

This peculiar interweaving of love and violence has been identified by other students of Russian culture. Daniel Rancour-Laferriere probably invests the greatest significance in this Russian suspicion of love, seeing it in *The Slave Soul of Russia* as one of the cornerstones of his conviction that the Russian people are deeply masochistic. In his words,

> Sex and love *mean* violence, but the direction of this semiosis can also be reversed, so that violence *means* sex and love. Thus a Russian woman may even come to assume that a man who does not beat her does not love her, and that a man who does not have an underlying contempt for her (and all other women) is sexually impotent. (158)

Before accepting Rancour-Laferriere's reading of Russian culture as definitive, however, it is worth comparing Russian attitudes toward sex with those toward property. At least as manifest in the *detektivy*, there is a considerable degree of similarity between the way these novels regard sexuality and how they regard property.

Suspicion of material goods, particularly among the intelligentsia, is one of the most commonly remarked features of Russian life. Svetlana Boym, in her *Common Places: Mythologies of Everyday Life in Russia,* quotes Aleksandr Hertsen, who found the aspirations of middle-class Europeans to be pathetic and contemptible. In Hertsen's words, the European ideal was "a piece of chicken in the cabbage soup of every little man . . . a little house with not very big windows and a view of the street, school for the son, a dress for the daughter, and a worker for the hard chores" (68). Rancour-Laferriere quotes Tibor Szamuely, who in his *Russian Tradition* noted much the same thing.

> The intelligentsia . . . represented something in the nature of a revolutionary priesthood, a subversive monastic order. Its way of life was founded on

a genuine asceticism, an aversion to worldly riches, a scorn for the ordinary "bourgeois" creature comforts. Self-abnegation becomes second nature; the Russian *intelligent* [intellectual] was easily recognizable by his utter and un-self-conscious disregard for material considerations, his fecklessness and impracticality, his indifference to appearances and cheerfully disorganized existence.[7]

However, despite the frequency with which this persistent Russian antimaterialism has been remarked, the way in which some of the *detektivy* portray specific instances of it can still startle western sensibilities. One typical, but especially vivid, example is the investigating detective's explanation of the motivations behind the actions of Alfred, the main villain of German Kruglov's "Investigation Underway." Although Alfred has finally been nabbed by the militia for the wide-scale purchase-for-resale of scarce spare parts for farm machinery, his initiation into what Soviet law called "speculation" was, as Kruglov explains, far more modest.

> [Alfred began] with small things—he sold a motorcycle gear worth a ruble for 2 rubles, and a 6 ruble battery for 10 rubles. His first deal only brought a profit of 4 rubles, but the deal inspired him—Alfred became a believer in commercial business. . . . Things went on. Having bought four car tires in the Avtomobil store for 52 rubles, he sold them for a hundred apiece to a citizen who spoke Russian with a Caucasian accent. Eleven-ruble umbrellas went for 25. If there was a bit extra to be made, even just 20 or 30 kopeks per item, Alfred energetically pursued buying and selling. (64)

Though described in less detail, there is a similarly entrepreneurial villain in Igor Aryasov's *Three Hours to Clarify the Truth;* while working two jobs, the man also has a small private garden plot, on which he raises pigs, keeps bees, and intensively cultivates vegetables from early spring to late autumn. The purpose of all this activity is to make money, because, as the man thinks to himself, "without money you can't even dream of being independent, any more than you can see the back of your own ears" (53).

As difficult as it may be in those two books to remember that these "Horatio Alger" stories are intended by their authors to be indictments of villains, rather than the paeans to entrepreneurs that such passages might seem if they appeared in an American novel, this concept is still harder to keep in mind in the case of Raul Mir-Khaydarov's novel *Walkabouts.* Mir-Khaydarov is an Uzbek, but his attitudes toward the villainy of business in this book are very similar to those of his Soviet-Russian fellow authors. The novel is a thinly fictionalized exposé of the shadow economy in Uzbekistan in the late Brezhnev era, when the republic was a network of private—and therefore illegal—factories, workshops, and retail outlets, all of them controlled by a small group of entrepreneurs, whom Mir-Khaydarov describes as brilliant, hardworking, and punctilious. The main villain in Mir-Khaydarov's novel is Artur Shubarin, whom Mir-Khaydarov excoriates because he

- employs thousands of local people, paying them above-average wages, in better-than-average working conditions;
- understood well in advance of the local authorities that the mine on which their town's economy was based was playing out and so stepped in to take over the mine's infrastructure for his illegal factories, thus maintaining employment;
- voluntarily "taxes" his own enterprises, funneling money into the coffers of the local government authorities; and
- satisfies the appetites of the voracious domestic consumer market, which the state steadfastly ignores.

As a consequence, even Mir-Khaydarov's hero, who, while pursuing Shubarin, calls the entrepreneur "an octopus" and "a spider" (239), is forced to acknowledge that

> There are a lot of comforts in [Shubarin's home] town! If you want something fixed in your house, no problem; the tea house where painters gather is around the corner. You want a basket of flowers for your wife's birthday? Leave your address with the flower women at the bazaar, and there will come a knock on your door at precisely the right moment. Want your car repainted, or a dent fixed? Go see Vardanyan, on the edge of town. . . . You're having a wedding, and going off your head because you've never fed more than five couples before? No problem, go look for Makhmudak at the bus station around lunch time. Pilaff for one hundred, three hundred shish-kebabs, hundreds of hot pitas? Everything's guaranteed to the highest standard. (55)

It is not easy to determine from the *detektivy* precisely what it was about this entrepreneurial activity that so disturbed the authors of these books. In some cases, such as in Vasiliy Ardamatskiy's novel, *The Trial*, it seems tempting to conclude that the basis of the genre's hostility is that the black marketeers are competing with the state, to the state's disadvantage. In that novel, a senior militia official uses the following example to illustrate the dangers of the black market.

Just as soon as Bologna raincoats, imported from Italy, began to appear on the Moscow black markets, and customers were flinging themselves on the coats like hungry tigers onto a lamb, "business people" from Georgia began to think how they might make these "bolognas" themselves. Some very big brains worked on the problem. . . . That was the beginning of the Tbilisi "bolognas," which outsold the government ones. The Tbilisi "bolognas" provided a very solid profit for those clever minds, while the "bolognas" which the government bought much later filled the warehouses to the rafters, where they still are to this day. (40)

A similar kind of rationale surfaces in Psurtsev's *Without Evil Intent* when a colorful old Siberian trapper discovers that he may accidentally have provided shelter for some fur poachers. Angry with himself, the trapper exclaims,

You mean they were poachers, damn them? And I'd guess they're doing it in a big way, since [the militia] is asking about it. . . . I don't like these guys, chief. . . . Why would you want to make your own government poorer? (39)

Of course, to a western sensibility, it seems logical to ask why competition with the state necessarily means that the state becomes poorer; theoretically at least, competition could make the state more efficient. However, an incident in Bezuglov's *Criminals* demonstrates that a Russian's first response to this commercial competition is not necessarily to compete in return. In that novel, researchers at a hospital have discovered an effective homeopathic remedy, which they produce at a rate of only a thousand liters per day. Because the salesperson will allow each customer to buy as many bottles as the person wishes, each day's supply vanishes in moments, and thousands of would-be customers end up camping around the hospital for days on end. When approached by the militia, one of these frustrated customers exclaims angrily as he points to the number, 2321, written in indelible ink on his palm: "That's my place in line!" (27). The reaction of the hospital's chief administrator to this clear demonstration of his potential market is characteristic and speaks eloquently about the differences between Russian and western commercial sensibilities. Rather than increase production, the official in charge decides instead that "We better set some kind of quota for each customer" (28).

Certainly this hospital administrator's reaction justifies the conclusion that the villain Shubarin bitterly draws in Mir-Khaydarov's novel.

Commerce, entrepreneurship are not only not considered to be among the human talents, but in the mind of [Soviet] society these qualities are even considered to be activities unworthy of a real man. That's why we can't manufacture anything properly or sell it properly either, forcing our people to spend a third of their lives in endless lines. (196)

However, Shubarin's disgusted comment does not seem to delve deeply enough into a prejudice against commercial activity that other *detektivy* portray as so profound that it actually would seem to run counter to the interests of the state itself. Vasiliy Ardamatskiy, for example, based his novel *The Trial* on a group of people who purchase farm machinery parts in regions of the Soviet Union where these are in good supply and sell them in other parts of the country, where they are in desperately short supply. Although these speculators are shown to be making a good profit for themselves, there is little in their activity that would seem immoral, even in the context of the USSR; indeed, when arrested, one of the black marketeers points out that, rather than being criminals, he and his associates are "building Communism" (113). Their customers, he says, are invariably the most productive and profitable collective and state farms, precisely because their chairmen are willing to go to extraordinary lengths to gather the harvests that the state desperately needed.

The same point is taken up even more eloquently by a character in German Kruglov's "Investigation Underway," which has a plot very similar to that of Ardamatskiy's book. The chairman of a certain collective farm has been arrested for having used some of the farm's funds to purchase spare machine parts on the black market at a price well above that which the state would charge—if the state farm equipment stores had any to offer. Standing before the judge, the chairman protests in exasperation:

> Do you know what spare parts mean? They mean [fulfilling] the plan [of centrally imposed production quotas], winning [production] competitions, they mean fruit, vegetables, and grain.... They mean everything that people need. But can you get spare parts at the [state-run] Ag-Tech store? . . . This year we are going to pay the people [who belong to the collective farm] more than we did in the past. We don't have to worry about down-time in the field anymore, because we have a good supply of spare parts, for a while yet to come. That's why I took the money from the farm's accounts. (40)

Since such arguments would probably be convincing to western readers, it is worth pointing out that neither Ardamatskiy's nor Kruglov's judges are swayed by such logic. The protests by these men are understood, in Ardamatskiy's book, to be cynical and self-serving, and in Kruglov's, to be naive. Nevertheless, these arguments point to a conundrum of Soviet morality, of which at least some of the *detektiv* writers were aware. As the *sledovatel* in Kruglov's novel puts the basic puzzle,

> *Defitsit* items [goods in short supply] (no matter how unimportant they might be . . .) were a closed circle—in order not to pay extra, you had to buy in a store, but since the goods weren't in the store, you had to pay extra. (64)

This closed circle of the Soviet economy spawned an entire profession, the so-called *tolkachi*, "jostlers" or supply officers, whose thankless job it was to ensure a steady flow of necessary goods and materials into Soviet factories, mines, and state farms, by whatever means proved necessary. Such people were caught squarely in an unresolvable paradox between the necessity to meet state-imposed production quotas and the impossibility of legally obtaining the materials necessary to do so. Bezuglov's *Criminals*, which includes a number of portraits of the interlocking favors and obligations which held the elite of Soviet Russia together, gives a particularly vivid illustration of the ways in which the paradox of this closed circle could force even the most honest of men to become a lawbreaker. In this novel, one of the *sledovateli* chances upon a former colleague, also from the procuracy, who, after retirement, has taken a job as assistant director of a local scientific institute, where he is primarily responsible for supply. The *sledovatel* is astonished to see how much her colleague has aged in the six months he has been on the job. The man has grown thin, hunched, and twitchy with bad nerves. When she asks what has become of him, the man replies,

> You just can't imagine what it's like! . . . To get hold of the smallest little item, I have to shut my eyes to the rules, instructions, and the laws! I am a law-abiding man, but every step I take, I have to break some kind of law . . . I can't sleep at night any more, because I keep thinking about how many years in prison I'd get for doing this, and how many for doing that. (201)

Despite Bezuglov's evident sympathy for this *tolkach*, however, there is no doubt in his novel, nor indeed in any others of the era, that any resort to "unofficial channels of supply," no matter how selfless the motives for it, is an immoral act. As one of Adamov's inspectors in *Into an Empty Space* explains, "[black marketeering] is a dangerous evil. Today you'll pay extra to get a good-quality muskrat fur hat, tomorrow you'll buy your job, and the day after that you'll buy your freedom, if you happen to end up behind bars. The morality is the same for all these acts" (374). Aryasov's *Three*

Hours to Clarify the Truth makes black marketeering appear even more sinister. One Erik Stolts, an evil agent for a foreign power who is trying to recruit Russian informants, ruminates about why he begins by trying to buy pilfered gold: "Thief to speculator to traitor. It's one chain, it's short, and it's time-tested. Anyone who can steal gold from a factory is ready to sell technology for money" (170).

The hostility of the Soviet legal system to such "speculation" is well known. An entire division of the militia, the OBKhSS [Division for the Battle against Theft of State Property], was devoted to fighting crimes against state property. Sentences imposed for such crimes tended to be about one-third longer than those for crimes against private property and, perhaps even more telling, the 1960 Criminal Code permitted the death penalty to be imposed for crimes against private property only in cases when firearms were used; imposition of the so-called *vyshka*, or highest penalty, in cases involving state property depended only upon the scale of what the state had lost. The *detektiv* genre was also enlisted in this battle against the private use of public resources. A wide variety of crimes against the state featured in the Soviet *detektivy* including, in addition to the examples already cited, plots such as Anatoliy Udintsev's "Search," in which two fugitives from a prison labor camp get weapons, clothes, and food by breaking into a rural store; Adamov's *Search Underway,* in which a ring of thieves use forged documents to steal state-owned powdered lemon concentrate; and Arestova's "Regarding the Disappearance of . . ." in which the manager of a radio and television store keeps the more desirable equipment to sell under the counter for higher prices.

What is less clear, however, is precisely why it was that the Soviet system, and the *detektiv* authors whom it published, were so hostile to this spontaneous privatization of state resources. Western observers have been inclined to understand this hostility as ideologically motivated, in that usurpation of the public sphere aggrandized the private sphere, thus threatening the state's claim to totalitarian control. In the earlier and more halcyon days of the *detektiv,* Soviet authors understood the mechanics of black marketeering in very much the same way as do those western observers, save of course that the value signs were reversed. The goal and purpose of the communist system, after all, was that the state would provide to all; any spontaneous diversion of goods or resources was in effect illogical, since the diverter would essentially be depriving himself or herself. This state provision for private needs was spelled out explicitly in the early 1960s in Lev Ovalov's *Secret Weapon* (published in English as *Comrade Spy*). More properly a spy thriller than a *detektiv*, this novel purports to be the fictionalized account of a real attempt by the CIA to kidnap a Russian acoustical expert and force her to work for the United States. While they have her imprisoned, her captors attempt to woo her with the material benefits of defection, which she rejects scornfully.

> "All those fine things you offered me—the institute, the cars, the house, the money, the resorts, the beautiful clothes—are they supposed to represent the acme of human existence? You really aren't very well briefed on my personal life. Just remember everything I had in Moscow. Our institute is such a good one that *you're* interested in *our* discoveries, and not vice versa. As for the automobile, when I need one, I can get one. Whether it belongs to me personally isn't all that important. And I certainly don't need my own five-bedroom house. My daughter and I get along very well in our apartment. And more than once, during vacation, we went to the Caucasus Mountains and the Crimea, which are at least as good as your resorts. As for the fine clothes, that's just silly. For that matter, it's from *us* that *you* people get your fine furs." She laughed bitterly. "I don't know what your experience is, or how long you lived in Russia. But you certainly don't understand Soviet Russians." (123)

As the circles of private use of public resources grew ever wider during the Brezhnev era, much of the force of this simple ideological argument was lost. The greater frequency with which the *detektivy* attempt not only to depict black marketeering, but also to explain why they hold it to be evil, suggests that the system was increasingly perceiving the need to move beyond ideological explanations for its hostility and to posit in their stead some kind of deeper moral reasons. It is highly suggestive of the Russian mentality that the most common explanation that the *detektivy* offer for why black marketeering is bad is the suggestion that possessions themselves are bad. Indeed, this antimaterialism was made explicit in the foreword to Koretskiy's first novel, *The Karate Principle*. There Yu. A. Kostanov, a senior procurator, "explains":

> The main point in Koretskiy's work . . . is his exposé of the corrosion of the soul, of aspirituality and what it breeds—"thingism" [*veshchizm*]. If rather than having ideals by which to live a person has instead pants with a foreign flag sewn onto a certain well-known place, Japanese stereos and videos, cars, deluxe cooperative apartments, etc. etc. then to a significant degree that person has lost his essence as a human being. (3)

Hostility to this "thingism" may well be the single most ubiquitous feature of the *detektivy*. The surest and most reliable of shorthand indicators of a new character's moral worth, for example, is the description of how he or she is dressed. In Bezuglov's *Criminals*, one of the villains is glimpsed for the first time, emerging from a chauffered Volga. He is

a man of about thirty-five, in cream-colored slacks and a light-brown safari shirt, wearing light summer loafers which resembled house slippers, but at the same time looked very expensive, obviously from the Beryozka store [where sales were conducted only in dollars, which ordinary Soviets could not legally possess]. His look was completed by his precisely cropped crewcut, his fashionable Italian glasses with smoked lenses, his Japanese briefcase with an electronic lock, and a massive Seiko watch on a metal band. (33)

Another of Bezuglov's novels, *Black Widow*, which won a mystery competition sponsored by the militia, introduces its major bad guys in the following way:

[They were] two men and a woman, the latter wearing a garish dress and dripping jewelry. The younger of the two men was wearing a blue velvet suit, a red lurex shirt, and a huge gold ring glittered on his finger. The other man . . . was wearing soft leather boots, riding breeches, and what looked like a Cherkess jacket, save that it had no cartridge loops, the jacket belted in by a heavy, silver-studded belt. (119)

This hostility to flashy clothing is evident even in the earliest of the *detektivy*, such as Ivan Lazutin's *Militia Sergeant*, first published in the mid-1950s. There a young man, who has fallen afoul of the militia, is being bailed out by his mother, the spoiled and brainless wife of a well-to-do professor.

A wide-brimmed straw hat with colored feathers, brightly painted lips, a colorful gauzy dress, with golden rings and jewels jammed onto her plump fingers, all of this flowed one into another, giving off various colors and recalling a gigantic jellyfish, which in the bright light of the sun gives off all the colors of the rainbow. There was something overbearing, to the point of obtuseness, in the face of this woman, no longer young, who appeared to have abused cosmetics for a great many years. Barely noticeable elongated scars on her face said that Viktoriya Leopoldovna had even made use of plastic surgery in order to stay young. (39)

The author's obvious distaste for this woman is even more suggestive than is Bezuglov's dislike of ostentation, because Viktoriya Leopoldovna is clearly shown in Lazutin's novel to be only a fool, rather than a villain. It is precisely that slippery slope between foolishness and villainy, however, that many of the *detektivy* seem to fear. Thus, for example, in Psurtsev's *Without Evil Intent*, the inspectors entering a young woman's apartment are appalled to discover that "the interior of [her] home was luxurious, as if from the pages of some advertisement. The furniture in the living room had curved legs, all of it white and airy, seven pieces at least. The fluffy, springy carpet was strewn with various colorful pillows and low tables, on which stood glittering crystal vases" (4). Such luxury immediately makes the militiamen suspicious. One asks in rhetorical disgust, "Why don't we have the right to ask people like her what they used to pay for all this? She didn't do it with tips from the beauty shop, did she?" (5). As might be expected, their suspicion very quickly proves justified, for the young woman turns out to be part of a fur-poaching ring.

What is most interesting, though, are the many *detektivy* in which even legal, aboveboard possession of things of value seems to carry a moral taint. Several of the *detektivy* suggest openly that, just as physical beauty seems an unfair temptation for any one person to enjoy above another, so, too, is it unfair for one person to possess more physical objects than another. In these novels, even though the militia are called in to investigate the theft of personal property, their sympathies clearly run against the victims. In Bezuglov's *Black Widow*, for example, a young couple, the Yartsevs, though only newlyweds, already possess a large apartment in the center of their provincial city, a car, and considerable jewelry. All of this luxury has come to them either as gifts or by inheritance. Included among the latter is a large diamond ring that Lyudmila Yartseva had inherited from a grandmother. Heedless of their wealth, the pair flaunt their good fortune, living grandly and well. By degrees, each is drawn off into affairs; the pair reach the point of divorce; and, as if emblematically, the valuable ring disappears, stolen by one of the "doubtful" acquaintances who has gravitated to their openhanded lifestyle. While never quite saying so in so many words, the novel clearly implies that the Yartsevs are at least partially responsible for their own misfortunes.

Ivan Shevtsov, in *Theft*, is even more suggestively acerbic about the pre-revolutionary diamond pendant that one of his secondary characters, Ilya Norkin, inherits from an aunt. As the manager of a state-owned fur store, Norkin owns other luxuries in abundance—a car, fancy furniture, a comfortable country home—but it is the diamond pendant that draws the attentions of the novel's real villain. When the pendant disappears, the militia are required by law to search for it, but they do so with obvious reluctance, since Norkin already seems to have more of life's goodies than he has a right to. One of the older investigators in the novel laments that

> before the war . . . it was considered a great honor to be acquainted with a famous artist, or a painter. . . . But now if you boast that you have a poet . . . for a friend, nobody bats an eye. But if you say that your friend works as a salesclerk in [a department store] or in a fish or meat store, then everyone is begging you immediately, . . . introduce me! introduce me! (39)

Although most of the *detektivy* made quite clear the harm that such acquisitiveness was, in their estimation, inflicting on Soviet society, perhaps the most interesting novels were those that further argued that materialism also devours the individual. In Astafyev's *Sad Detective*, one of the novels that signaled the beginning of Gorbachev's new policy of glasnost, a militia investigator tells the story of a woman he had met outside a prison, where she has been visiting her husband.

> [When first married they] worked a great deal, and loved one another . . . things were good. Their children grew and the time passed unnoticed, working and worrying. But [the woman] began to notice the automobiles around their apartment building, and the dachas in the country, and the apartments of their friends and acquaintances, with all the carpets and crystal and tape recorders and fashionable clothing and handsome furniture. . . .
>   So she too wanted those things, and began to urge her husband to change jobs, to get something better. He resisted. She threatened divorce, that she'd take away the children. So the husband changed to a better paying job, and first thing he starts bringing home extra money. Enough for a color television! The second time he brought enough for a rug, and the third time . . . he didn't come home. And now she would have to wait years for him. (33)

Essentially the same kind of story is offered in Psurtsev's *Without Evil Intent*, in which a young woman finds herself dragged into crime in part because she fears the violent temper of the villain with whom she has been living, but even more because she has found herself addicted to the luxuries of the good life. Berating herself, she wails,

> When I was with him I could permit myself things that others couldn't let themselves have. You saw how I used to dress, how I lived, how much gold I had. You saw that? That was all because of him! I'm an idiot! An idiot! Trash

for hire! I know I should have left long ago, run away. I couldn't make up my mind to do it though, because I was afraid of losing my shiny jangly things.

Perhaps the clearest illustration of the implications of this view of the dangers of materialism, however, come in Arestova's "Last Clue." There, one of the characters, who is about to be arrested for black marketeering, suddenly realizes that it is his love of comfort and fine things that has drawn him into criminal activity and thus, as he expresses it in his moment of epiphany, "his own things were his enemy!" (195). When the militia discover him the next morning among the rubble and shards of the apartment he has destroyed in a drunken rage, one of the officers remarks, "They should show this in the movies. . . . This is one side of the thief's life that unfortunately usually stays in the shadows" (200).

It might be argued that this equation of material possession with villainy was conditioned by the Soviet economy, the extreme shortages and failures of which, by the end of that system, had nearly succeeded in creating a society without material goods of any sort. Only a person who was willing to violate the law might own anything, since there was no legal way for people to get things. As Tim McDaniel put it in his *The Agony of the Russian Idea*, it was only through what he calls "the private use of public resources" that people could hope to survive. He writes:

> The saleslady would take the best cuts of meat to give to the doctor who was about to perform an operation on her child. The factory foreman had hoarded spare parts to be exchanged for better food for the factory cafeteria. In the economy of shortages, positions allowed people monopolistic control of resources that could be bartered for other scarce goods. Despite the formally state-run system of distribution, individual entrepreneurship on a universal scale gave the lie to any claims of top-down regulation based on the plan. Negotiation, bargaining, and informal exchange were ubiquitous. . . . This whole system had enormous implications for social stability: it gave everyone a stake in the system and also made everyone complicitous in formally illegal activity. (141)

By the logic of this argument, however, Russian hostility toward material goods ought to have disappeared, or at least diminished, with the end of the communist system. When there was no legal means to acquire, for example, a Seiko watch or Italian sunglasses, then, obviously, the character who possessed such things was clearly going to be morally compromised; however, when such items, and millions more besides, are as available in

Moscow as they are in London or New York, this equation between possession and evil should no longer be valid.

Very strikingly, however, this hostility toward material possessions is
even stronger in the post-Soviet *detektivy* than it was in their predecessors.

Andrey Kivinov, for example, is one of the most talented of the new Russian mystery writers, and is himself a working policeman who now also
writes for one of Russia's most popular TV dramas, *Cops* (*Menty*). In many
of his stories, his characters express exasperation with the *victims* of crimes
of property. The following outburst from "Backup Plan" is characteristic.

> In the winter [thieves] steal overcoats off coathooks, in the summer they steal
> tires and bicycles. And in such quantities that [the militia] barely have time
> even to take the complaints, with no time left for investigation or solutions.
> People are stupid, too, doing stuff like leaving their things around without
> anyone watching over them, or bringing total strangers into their houses, or
> flashing their money about. . . . I'd like to see a line in the legal code, that if
> it's your fault that something got stolen, then it's you that has to go look for
> it. (511)

Kivinov's hostility against property extends even to "Citizen Chuchurina,
who had had her knitted cap stolen in a cafeteria two years previously and
who since then had come to bother [the militia criminal investigator]
about it about once a month" ("Nightmare on Stachki Street," 17).

Hostile as Kivinov seems to be to material possessions in general, he also
differentiates between those who possess a great deal and those who possess little. In "Gone with the Wind," the first sign that the victim of a robbery may prove himself to be a villain is the man's indifference to having
been robbed of "My VCR, a Sharp, a leather coat, money, and maybe 70
thousand [rubles]." Learning that it will be several days before the over-
taxed militia experts will be able to take fingerprints at the crime scene, the
man says airily, "Maybe then it isn't worth raising a fuss. For me the loss is
nothing. The bump on the nose [which the thief gave me] is an insult, but
it'll heal. You people [in the militia] have more work than you can handle
as it is" (116–17). Offended that this robbery victim might have so much
that he can shrug off the loss of items that are beyond the dreams of a
poorly paid militiaman, the investigator decides to investigate the victim.

A similar confusion about who is being guarded against what comes up
later in the same story. Kivinov's hero runs into the colleague mentioned
above, who, whenever his district's crime-solving statistics drop so low as

to make them look bad before the higher authorities, goes to a newly privatized supermarket, where, as the militia investigator explains, "all this stuff is private property now," making it easy to pad the militia's crime solution statistics with hapless shoplifters. The fact that the militiaman's zealousness is only for purposes of improving departmental statistics, rather than for protecting private property, is made abundantly clear as the same fellow confesses that he refuses to arrest shoplifting bums, especially if they eat their "loot" right in the store. Pointing to one such bum, this militiaman says, "I figured out that he can eat a half kilo of cheese in five seconds. But I don't pick up guys like that. People have to eat. Anybody who could have bought it instead of stealing, though, then it's my holy duty to pick 'em up" (128).

Shitov's *Cathedral without Crosses* gives an even more intriguing view of the tangled Russian attitude toward property because the novel is intended to be a celebration of the entrepreneurial acumen of its central character, the *vor v zakone*, or "made guy," Goncharov-Shmakov. As explained in the previous chapter, Shitov uses his hero to demonstrate that a Russian can become as good a businessman as an American. Indeed, Goncharov-Shmakov proves to be better than his western competitors precisely because material riches for him are no more than the means to an end, rather than a goal in and of themselves. Shitov consistently differentiates his hero from the lesser thieves about him, who squander their money on cars, jewelry, and other possessions. Goncharov-Shmakov does permit himself the purchase of several houses in Russia, and of large rings for his wife and mistress, but the only other expenditure that Shitov seems regularly to grant his hero is hosting elaborate banquets in expensive restaurants. By the end of the novel, even this degree of excess pales on Goncharov-Shmakov. Shaken by the discovery that his longtime mistress, Larisa, has entered an Orthodox convent, Goncharov-Shmakov passes some of his money to his now-grown son, and then conveys the rest to the church, because

> In order to be rich, some people commit crimes, evil deeds, and treachery, while others sacrifice their freedom, independence and love. They are all unhappy, since they act against their own conscience and general human morality. God forbid that we should fall among their number. (383)

This is precisely the same point made in 1987 by Amirkhan Azlarkhanov, the thoughtful ex-procurator who is the hero of Raul Mir-Khaydarov's *Walkabouts*. As this doughty hero comes to learn the full depths of corruption in Uzbekistan, he sighs: "How many ways and means there are to buy a man—with money, a position, a woman, a car, fashionable clothes, a rare book, a dacha, antiques, jewelry, sporting goods . . ." (243).

Murderous Sympathy

If, as the preceding suggests, it is the general view of the *detektivy* that sexual attraction "causes" such crimes as rape, prostitution, and adultery, and the attraction of objects "causes" theft and black marketeering, it is then perhaps not so surprising that the genre's attitude toward murderers, if not murder itself, is that the crime is "caused" by factors other than a desire to murder or a will to evil. In the words of Inspector Borodin, the hero of Dashkova's *Nursery*, "Over the course of many years he had learned one cruel truth—that in order to become the victim of even the most accidental and unmotivated killing, the victim had to offer himself up for it, at least a little" (32). This is the logic by which murder, more than any other of the crimes that are pictured in the *detektivy*, bears out the words of Psurtsev's inspector, that "crime is a tragedy not just for the victim, but also for the criminal" (77).

As noted in the preceding chapter, murder was a comparatively rare event in the Soviet-era *detektivy*, for a variety of reasons. The strong constraints of ideology and censorship against the depiction of killings thus makes it all the more striking how often the murders that do appear in these books prove to be either the unintended consequences of the commission of other crimes, or the necessary follow-up to an earlier crime. In some instances, the person who eventually must turn to murder is shown to have been irredeemably evil from the beginning. In Leonid Zalata's "Wolf Berries," for example, the villain, who kills a young woman in order to prevent her from telling the authorities about the illegal turtleneck factory he has set up, proves at the climax to have been a member of the Nazi occupation *polizei*. As the chief investigator in the novel muses, "Somehow [he] could not get into his head that these kinds of cuties [like the criminal] could be loved, that they would have families and children, and that the hands of a criminal might give a sincere stroke of fondness" (100).

In other instances, the murderer is even depicted as subhuman, almost animal. In Arestova's "Search in the Taiga," a dim-witted Siberian hunter decides to rob an expedition of geologists of their clothes and supplies in order to sustain his own stay out in the taiga. Unable to think of any other method of relieving the expedition of their boots and food, the Siberian hunter simply comes to the camp when most of the geologists are gone and shoots the one geologist still there. Since this hunter is the only possible suspect, the sole question of interest in the story is how the militia will track him in the vast Siberian forests, making this less a *detektiv* than a variation on a hunting story. This comparison is made all but explicit at the story's end, for when he is captured, the murderer is described as howling "like an animal." A senior inspector in Adamov's *Evil Wind* ranks killers of this sort even lower, calling them:

> human amoebas, [who] aren't interesting to study, because they are too primitive. The kind [of criminal] that feels like getting drunk, so they drink, feels like stealing so they steal, feels like putting a knife in someone so they put a knife in someone, and if the guy dies, well, it's that kind of a business. All of that is just so much dust to an amoeba. (38)

By far the greatest number of Soviet-era *detektivs*, however, depict murders as the follow-on results of other crimes. Prishelets, the blackmarketeering businessman of Ivan Shevtsov's *Theft*, has to turn to murder, first to rid himself of some contract thieves whom he had used as part of a swindling scheme, and then—this time unsuccessfully—to rid himself of his assistant, who had engineered the first murder. A similar necessity occurs in Anatoliy Matsakov's "Nasty Weather," which opens with the discovery of an apparent accident victim on a communal farm deep in the Belarussian countryside; after considerable investigation, the death proves to be a murder committed by the man's neighbors, who are trying to cover up their attempt to extort money from him. Similarly, in Arestova's "Regarding the Disappearance of . . . ," murder becomes necessary in order to cover up the large-scale diversion of state-owned radios and tape recorders into private sale. The same motivation drives the murderer in Viktors Lagzdins's *A Night at Elk Farm*. Despite the fact that the novel clearly and apparently selfconsciously follows the model of the western "locked room" mystery, the motive behind the murder proves at the climax to have been the villain's need to keep it concealed that he has been stealing platinum from the electronics factory at which both he and his victim had worked.

While the *detektivy* do not accept such explanations as acceptable reasons for murder, they do suggest a surprising amount of sympathy for the criminals who have been swept along by their earlier crimes to the commission of murder. In the words of Captain Mokhov, the chief investigator in Psurtsev's *Without Evil Intent,*

> I've noticed that I hate these scum [criminals] until their crimes are solved and I've arrested the guilty parties. Until then I see them as some sort of abstract purveyor of evil. . . . But when [the criminal] is caught, I start to work with him, to dig around in him . . . and pretty soon I start to notice that my attitude toward him has changed. (77)

The senior investigator in Adamov's *Evil Wind* makes essentially the same point, when he tells his junior that

> I have seen all kinds of people, some who have stepped outside the bounds just for a moment, and some who have gone seriously wrong, and some who have simply become animals. It's my job, after all. And I've never met a one, even the ones who have sunk the lowest, the most desperate of them, who could honestly say to me, "I'm happy. I don't need anything else." I know that things are bad for all of them, no matter how much bravado or show they put on. And all of them do evil things. (38)

Viktor Astafyev even identifies this strange sympathy as the root cause of all of Russia's ills. His *Sad Detective* is a curious work, for it represents the appropriation of the *detektiv* genre by an author who was not normally a junk fiction writer, but who, rather, had much higher aspirations. Published in January 1986, *Sad Detective* was, for its day, a shockingly frank discussion of the rot that had eaten its way into Russian society. Unlike the Adamov and Psurtsev characters, the hero of Astafyev's story does not himself feel any sympathy for criminals, but he does acknowledge that his lack of sympathy is very atypical of Russians:

> Working in the militia had squeezed all pity for criminals out of him, that universal but poorly understood and inexplicable Russian pity which has preserved for all eternity in the flesh of Russian man an unquenchable thirst to sympathize, to strive for the good, and yet in the same flesh, in a "sick" part of the soul, in some dark alley of the soul, there lurked an irascible, blindly inflammable unthinkable evil. (33)

The purpose of Astafyev's novel is precisely to explore why it is that the Russian people harbor this "unquenchable thirst to sympathize." The militiaman in the story, who has been unwillingly retired from the force after being badly wounded in the line of duty, turns in some desperation to writing in the attempt to understand, in his words,

> [why do] Russian people always pity prisoners and [are] so often indifferent to themselves, or to their neighbors, invalids of war and work? Ready to give their last piece of bread to some convicted bonebreaker and bloodspiller, to snatch out of the hands of the militia some rabid hooligan who just a moment ago was storming around.... The criminal lives well, freely, even vigorously among such a good-hearted people, and certainly he has lived well in Russia for an age. (10)

As we have seen, there is a lot more murder in the post-Soviet *detektivy* because, not surprisingly, there are also a lot more motives for murder than there were in their Soviet-era predecessors. The changed conditions of Russian life have allowed the *detektiv* genre to move its plots much closer to those of its western counterparts. Some examples of western-style murder plots were offered in the first chapter, but there are many more. Dashkova's *Place under the Sun*, for example, revolves around the disposition of the controlling block of shares in a lucrative casino following the owner's murder, while Marinina's *Stylist* supposes the need to conceal a publisher's manipulations of his printing runs and the defrauding of his authors and translators. The St. Petersburg militia inspector and author Kivinov provides a whole array of motives for murder in his short stories. In "Chance Companions," for example, a band of criminals working out of an auto repair shop steal cars to order from their repair customers, ridding themselves of the inconvenient first owners by murdering them; in "Seductive Dreams," a certain Albert gains control of now valuable apartments in prime parts of Petersburg by using lovelorn student nurses to overmedicate the decrepit old women who have inhabited them throughout the Soviet period; in "Absence of Proof," the killers begin as burglars who use a beautiful young woman to entice their victims into evenings of drink and carousing in saunas, during which their apartments are robbed. But, just as in the stories from the Soviet period, the logic of this crime leads these burglars inexorably to murder.

As this last example may suggest, the introduction of many new reasons why one person might be moved to kill another has not much changed the genre's inclination to see murder as "a tragedy not just for the victim, but also for the criminal" (Psurtsev, 77). This is perhaps clearest in stories like Kivinov's "Made from Waste Products" or Marinina's novel *Small Fry Die*

First, in each of which the desperate desire to gain money leads the central characters to turn to the only profession for which they think they have any skills: contract killer. Marinina makes the consequences of this choice particularly graphic by having the first "target" the novice assassin gets a contract to kill turn out to be the unknown sniper who has gunned down a mafia chieftain's grandson. This intended victim, because she had chosen the young man as a random victim to advertise her services, happens to be herself.

Dashkova's *Place under the Sun* is nearly as sympathetic to the character who seems, until the novel's end, to be the murderer. This red herring is a beautiful, but obviously insane, young woman who had been having an affair with the murder victim. Oddly enough, much of the plot revolves around the efforts of the victim's widow to overcome official certainty that they have captured the real murderer, since she does not believe that the supposed killer could have done what she is accused of doing. Even more tellingly, once the real murderer has been exposed, the widow is almost as sympathetic to her as she was to the supposed, but false, murderer. The real murderer—who has killed three people, attempted to kill a fourth, and has falsely implicated a fifth in the murders—still gets to plead her justification:

> Listen, have you ever had the soles fall off your only pair of boots when it's only November, and you've got the whole winter ahead of you, and you haven't got so much as a penny? Has your stomach ever ached with hunger? . . . To get my own, to get what I need, I'm ready to gnaw anybody's throat . . . and that's normal. I want a lot of money. I love it when I have a lot of everything, expensive, pretty, the very best. I love it when I can fly wherever I want to in the world, go business class and sleep in five-star hotels. (451)

This sympathy for criminals who have been seduced by what another *detektiv* writer, Nikolay Ivanov, has called "the taste of the golden calf" (*Tax Police*), is probably most pronounced in the works of Kivinov, which show a persistent indifference, bordering upon numbness, to murder. Kivinov's investigators pursue the killers with intelligence and passion, yet, at the same time, with considerable fatalism, exhibiting a surprising lack of conviction about their role as militiamen. To a certain degree, this fatalism is a reflection of the deep disillusionment in the workings of the law that Kivinov's detectives all feel. In none of Kivinov's stories is there any reason to suppose that the fact that a murderer has been apprehended means that he will also be punished. Another part, though, of Kivinov's apparent indifference toward the many murders that his investigators encounter is the undeniable logic that a great many of the murders in the new Russian environment are simply a modern twist on the old Russian theme of *kto kogo* (who does whom); many of the victims of murder in Kivinov's world could equally easily have been the perpetrators, and vice versa, had they been a little quicker and a little smarter. Many of Kivinov's murders are portrayed essentially as a cost of doing business in the chaotic conditions of the new Russia. In the story "Track of the Boomerang," as we have seen, it is business itself that drives the characters to murder. In that story, two men, closest of friends since childhood, open a business just as Soviet laws first change to permit them to do so. Their business flourishes and the two men become wealthy, thus becoming increasingly conscious of how much more they now have to lose. Dissatisfied with one another's business decisions, the two lifelong friends come quickly to hate each other so deeply that each takes out a "hit contract" on the other, with the result that, as the radio puts it, "an hour apart, in different parts of the city, the two directors of the major business concern 'KandS' were shot" (353).

As that plot suggests, the most compelling reason for the world-weary indifference of Kivinov's characters to murder is that they see the murderers and their victims equally to be symptoms of processes in society. As one of Kivinov's inspectors explains at the end of "Chance Companions,"

> You know what? This is a virus . . . a virus of murder. Human life has ceased to be of value. Our larger organism is infected with this virus, and there's no immunity. And there's no doctor to cure us either, except for us ourselves. It's an era of cruelty. Why? I don't know. . . . Maybe it's a punishment of some kind? But for what? Our people used to be the kindest of all. Maybe there's a war going on? (229)

Conclusion

The vocabulary of Kivinov's hero is quite different from that of the Soviet heroes of the 1950s, but it is remarkable the degree to which the sentiment remains unchanged, that crime represents a society that is at war with itself. In spite of the enormous political, economic, and social changes that Russia has undergone in the past fifteen years, the new *detektiv* sees crime in Russian society in essentially the same terms as does Ivan Shevtsov's

Theft, published in 1988. The hero of that novel, Inspector Dobrosklontsev (whose name means, approximately, "well-intentioned"), takes a short vacation to visit his native village, near the Field of Kulikovo. That battlefield is a major monument of Russian nationalism, for it was there, in 1380, that Dmitriy Donskoy achieved the first Russian victory over the Mongols. Standing in the middle of the battlefield, Dobrosklontsev muses,

> [here] where every holy thing that was sacred to every Russian man was to be found, he felt as if he were pulling free from the quicksand of busy urban life . . . he suddenly realized that it was only in . . . those heaps of stones and glass, concrete and steel, that it was possible for [criminals] to exist. On a clean field of battle the war against their like would have been won. (204–5)

Shevtsov does not place this meditation on the Field of Kulikovo by accident. Igor Bunich, a post-Soviet novelist, states explicitly in his *Absolute License* that, before the arrival of the Vikings in the ninth century, Russia "had a sociopolitical structure which . . . had no kings, khans, emirs, princes, or leaders. Everyone was equal, and they governed themselves collectively . . . in those [prehistoric] years when everybody was hacking and killing everybody else, when the clang of sword and whistle of arrows was never stilled even for a second, in the region of Rus all was quiet and calm" (272). Not all of the *detektiv* writers are as forthright as Bunich, but most of their novels, both Soviet and post-Soviet, suggest that crime is somehow an alien phenomenon in Russian society.

As the examples in this chapter demonstrate, crime in the *detektiv* tends to be depicted as an omnipresent danger to which the criminal succumbs because of weakness, or because of bad decisions made earlier. Both in the Soviet era and in the new *detektivy*, it is conceded that abusive sexual behavior can be evil. But sex itself, or at least sexual attractiveness, seems to share some of the blame, for if one human being did not attract another, sex crimes would be impossible.

The crime fiction from both eras accepts the premise that society must punish those who appropriate material objects that belong to others, but in the new capitalist Russia, as much as in the socialist Soviet Union, the *detektivy* also imply that any person who values objects more than people is morally suspect, whether that person is the original owner of the object or its thief.

The most striking difference from the conventions of the western genre, however, appear in the *detektiv* genre's pronounced sympathy for murderers. While novels of both the Soviet and the post-Soviet era de-plore murder, they also generally see murder as something into which characters are forced by greed, fear, or weakness, thus rendering the murderer nearly as pitiable as the victims. In the post-Soviet era, there are many more dead bodies, but the genre implies strongly that this is because the temptations and confusions of society have also multiplied exponentially. The overwhelming explanation that the genre offers for Russia's explosion of crime is not that humans have grown more evil, or that the country now has the surfeit of consumer goods, short skirts, and weapons that make robbery, sex crimes, and murder more possible, but rather that society has betrayed both criminal and victim by suddenly changing all of its rules. The sense of helpless disorientation that results is articulated by one of Kivinov's heroes in "Chance Companions," re-plying to a colleague who suggests that the best solution is to go get drunk:

> No, Mishel, vodka won't chase the blues away, and the bottle won't solve any problems. . . . The worst of it is that there's no end in sight. How many mur-ders are there, and how much theft? Makes you want to throw up your hands. We solve one crime, and there's ten new ones come in. It's like the ceiling crashing down on us, and we're trying to cover our heads with our hands. . . . It's society that makes criminals, and it's us that's supposed to get rid of them. But what can we do? Has anything changed in the cops in the last five years? Anything at all? Not a fucking thing has changed. There's peo-ple out there on every street corner, shouting, "Where's the militia? Where's the militia?'" A better question is, "Where are YOU?". . . Society makes its own criminals, so it should destroy them too. . . . Is it the militia that turns a man into a murderer? No, it's society does that. So if there's a lot of murders, that means that society is fatally wounded. The militia isn't the cure-all. Like the drug addicts say, it's too late to be drinking mineral water, if you've al-ready shit out your kidneys. (178)

Notes

1. Quoted in Gagarin, *Russkiy syshchik* (Moscow: Otechestvo, 1994), 364.
2. *Russkiy syshchik,* 364.
3. *Kommentarii k ugolovno-ispolnitelnomu kodeksu* (Moscow: Ekspertnoe byuro M, 1997), 412–14.

4. *Kommentariy k ugolovnomu kodeksu Rossiyskoy Federatsii* (Moscow: INFRA M-Norma, 1997), 300–302.

5. *Kommentariy k ugolovnomu kodeksu*, 550–51.

6. *Moskovskiy ugolovnyy rozysk: Istoriya v litsakh* (Moscow: MVD, 1998), 504.

7. As quoted in Daniel Rancour-Laferriere, *The Slave Soul of Russia: Moral Masochism and the Cult of Suffering* (New York: New York University Press, 1995), 46.

CHAPTER THREE

Good Guys and Bad Guys

ONE OF THE FUNDAMENTAL ASSUMPTIONS of the mystery genre is that there are "good guys" and there are "bad guys." Normally, those who chase criminals are understood to be morally superior to those whom they chase, although the western genres are also rich in examples of the reverse. No matter which way the equation runs, the conventions of crime fiction require that its books and stories in some way take up the question of why some people are good and others bad. The Russian version of the genre is no exception. Indeed, in many ways, the question of what constitutes good behavior and why is even more central to the *detektiv* than it is to its western cousins. The inclination of the *detektiv* genre to see crime as a symptom of social ills, rather than as the actions of individuals, however, raises an obvious complication, which Arkadiy Adamov's Inspector Losev points out in *Swamp Grass*: "Our militia comes from the people! . . . How can the militia be better than the people?" (68).

The *detektiv*, even more than its western cousins, takes as a given that its inspectors and investigators are morally superior to those whom they are chasing, but it also supposes a much higher degree of similarity between hunters and hunted. Indeed, both in the Soviet era and afterwards, it is not unusual to find passages in which what obviously are meant to be positive characters are shown to be thinking thoughts similar to those expressed by one of Andrey Kivinov's heroes in "Rat Hunting": "When [the criminals] are going about their business, I get furious, so bad I could explode. But once they get taken down, all that anger in me melts away somehow. [The criminal proves to be] just an ordinary kind of a guy, exactly like me" (623).

What Kivinov means in context is that his hero is able to identify with the criminal as a human being, but it is also true that many post-Soviet and—what may be more surprising—Soviet-era *detektivy* show their positive characters going well beyond empathy for criminals, to the point of becoming like them, at least in the technical sense that they themselves also violate laws. To be sure, there are scores of perestroika-era and post-collapse novels that feature corrupt or venal militiamen or members of the procuracy, but those novels make perfectly clear that these are crooked cops who, at the very least, are wrong, even if not necessarily evil. The truly surprising thing about the Russian genre, though, is how many characters who are clearly intended to be positive heroes are shown to be casually violating laws.

Such law-breaking by the good guys is particularly striking in *detektivy* from the "high Soviet" period, when positive characters were required to be unblemished examples of rectitude, providing models of behavior that good Soviet citizens might emulate.

To be fair, many of the instances in which positive heroes violate the laws of the state they are supposed to be serving are ones in which an investigator has to cut corners or make a judgment about conflicting or unclear laws in the higher interests of catching a criminal. This conundrum is articulated particularly well in Adamov's *Evil Wind* where Inspector Losev decides to open a letter his chief suspect has received. Heading off possible objections from the rest of his investigative team, Losev says,

> This is a just battle, moral in the highest degree, isn't it? You will say that this kind of battle cannot be fought with immoral methods, and that to dig around in a man's life without him knowing about it is immoral. Always? Every time? No matter what the circumstances, I ask you? But as we know, there are no abstract truths; truth is always concrete. What is good? What is evil? Can't the one become the other in certain concrete circumstances? The wound of a bandit's knife is evil, but the wound of a surgeon's knife is good. . . . If our study of human life is based on those principles and those goals about which I have been speaking, then [opening this letter] is good, not evil. It is moral, and no one can convince me otherwise. (175)

As eloquent as Losev's explanation may be, the fact remains that his failure to secure the recipient's permission, or the sanction of a procurator, before opening the letter, meant that he was in formal violation of Soviet laws in place since 1960.

Similar pragmatic flouting of Soviet laws by state law enforcement officials is common in the Soviet-era *detektivy*. A different Inspector Losev, this one the hero of a number of stories by Leonid Slovin, uses any method he can to gather information, including, in one story, accepting the offer of tea from a suspect's wife because this allows him to take advantage of her absence in the kitchen to rifle through her husband's desk, copying phone numbers from his address book ("Five Days and the Morning of the Sixth"). Inspector Pakhmonov, in Lyubov Arestova's "Regarding the Disappearance of . . ." takes similar advantage when in another suspect's apartment, poking around in lieu of the legal search for which he would have to get sanction from the procurator but for which he does not yet have sufficient grounds to ask. Trying to discover the source of some stolen gold jewelry, the inspectors in Nikolay Cherginets's *The Investigation Continues* take a taxi ride with a driver whom they suspect to be a fence (largely because he is a gypsy) and pretend to be potential jewelry buyers. Apparently justified when they finally browbeat the driver into offering to set up an illegal purchase of stolen goods for them, the aggressive methods the inspectors use look to be a clear instance of entrapment. Another scene from the same novel seems of even more questionable legality: Wanting to force another driver to reveal who had been his passenger on a certain day but not wishing to take the risk that their inquiries might alert their suspect to the fact that they are interested in him, Cherginets's inspectors pretend to be inspectors from the GAI (the State Highway Inspection—the equivalent of the highway patrol) who are investigating an accident that did not occur. They use this phony accident as the pretext to require the driver to reveal the identity of his passenger as a putative "witness" to an event that never occurred.

As questionable as such practices may seem, at least they might be justified on the grounds that the militia are flouting one set of laws in order to uphold another. In a great many other novels, however, the heroes of *detektivy* flout laws for much less compelling reasons. In Cherginets's *The Investigation Continues*, an operative trying to infiltrate a gang of suspected bank robbers establishes his criminal *bona fides* by stealing a third party's watch at the beach—and the text never mentions whether he ever returns it. In Leonid Medvedovskiy's *Interrupted Journey*, a young woman disappears about two-thirds of the way through the novel; she is not herself a suspect, but is presumed to be withholding information about an acquaintance who is. Thinking she may have been kidnapped by the perpetrators in order to keep her silent, the investigators mount an intensive search. The young woman is finally discovered being held prisoner in a shed out in the countryside. Rather than rescue her, however, the militia decide to let the young woman spend another night as the kidnapper's prisoner in order to "teach her a lesson" for not having told them the full truth during the earlier interrogation. By western standards, this decision would seem to make the militia accessories after the fact for the young woman's kidnapping. It should in fairness, however, be pointed out that the laws of the Soviet republic in which Medvedovskiy's novel is set (not named, but apparently Latvia) were such that the militia were actually not under any legal obligation to look for the young woman in the first place. By a quirk of legislative incompetence, the republic's statutes about kidnapping only applied to underage children, so that the woman's captors in fact were doing nothing illegal in abducting the woman from her home and keeping her locked in a barn. It was only when they attempted to silence her more permanently that they violated local law.

Given that agency's reputation for efficacy, it is not surprising that even the KGB, the most sacrosanct of the Soviet law enforcement agencies, played loose with the niceties of existing laws. In Yuzef Printsev's "Wedding Postponed," for example, the security organs capture a high-stakes antique smuggler by getting one of their operatives, a beautiful young woman, to pose as a hard-currency whore and antiques speculator. In short order, this woman becomes the suspect's chief deputy, then his mistress, and finally his fiancée. In the process, she moves well beyond information gathering to actual provocation, trying to goad her "beloved" into ever more flagrant violations of Soviet law. Although Igor Aryasov's novel *Three Hours to Clarify the Truth* does not feature such flagrant examples of the KGB flouting procedure, one of the characters, a certain General Alekseyev, the senior official in charge of a team of operatives, offers a particularly frank articulation of why the security organs might overlook their own infractions while serving higher interests. Using the metaphor of a boxing match, Alekseyev says, "In my opinion, in any fight, big or little, you shouldn't try to win on points, but rather by knockout, or by a huge margin. Then no judge can help your opponent" (83).

The high ideological purposes of the *detektiv* in the late Gorbachev era may be seen in the afterword to Aryasov's novel, which describes the book, and others like it, as being on the "front lines . . . of the struggle for the minds, hearts, and souls of Soviet people" (285). If anything, the ideological intensity is even higher in Raul Mir-Khaydarov's *Walkabouts*, which, as has been mentioned, is a broadside attack on underground private business in Brezhnev-era Uzbekistan. Such loftiness of purpose makes it all the more striking that the book's hero, who dies at the novel's end and so becomes a kind of saint or martyr of Soviet law enforcement, is in fact in violation of state law for most of the story. Once Amirkhan Azlarkhanov has been forced from his post as state procurator (to be sure, his expulsion is politically motivated and highly unfair), he has no standing in Soviet law that would justify his elaborate infiltration of the villain Shubarin's illegal industrial empire. Azlarkhanov becomes Shubarin's most trusted lieutenant and confidant, privy to the most illegal of the man's dealings. Yet, he has no means or ability to do anything about Shubarin's violations of Soviet law because he is, in fact, a private citizen. Although Mir-Khaydarov stresses that Azlarkhanov is scrupulous about not taking money or other favors from Shubarin, the ex-procurator's duties as a self-appointed infiltrator require that Azlarkhanov accept at least some of what Shubarin offers and close his eyes to the other violations of Soviet law that he witnesses. At the very least, this makes him an accessory to Shubarin's crimes, and would seem also to put him in violation of Soviet laws requiring that citizens inform the appropriate authorities of crimes of which they chance to gain knowledge.

Mir-Khaydarov's book also provides a particularly clear example of another kind of official disregard for existing laws, which is all the more troubling because of the high indignation with which the novel condemns the illegal capitalism it is exposing. After Azlarkhanov has been illegally forced from his post as procurator, but before he becomes Shubarin's confidant, he takes a job as the legal consultant for a small local jam factory, which, like nearly everything else in the Soviet Union at that time, was state-owned. Bruised by his unfair dismissal, and grieving for his wife, who has been robbed and killed by the dissolute but untouchable son of a local bigwig, Azlarkhanov welcomes the position as a quiet, stress-free haven. The major enticement of the job for him, however, is that it demands no more than about an hour a day of actual work, thus letting the exprosecutor use the bulk of his workday to research and formulate proposals to reform the Soviet criminal code, which he plans to put forward in a book. Neither Azlarkhanov nor Mir-Khaydarov seems to be aware that, by using the jam factory's desk, typewriters, and paper supplies for his own private purposes, to say nothing of the time for which he is being

paid, the heroic ex-prosecutor is, in fact, stealing, robbing the state as unambiguously and straightforwardly as is the villain whom Azlarkhanov
has sworn to unmask and bring to justice.

Mir-Khaydarov's inability to understand that his hero is pilfering time
and supplies from his employer is especially noteworthy because the novel
is very much a part of the glasnost-era campaign against official incompetence and indifference. This was the period when popular fiction was har-
nessed to Gorbachev's attempts to change the fact that, in the USSR (as one
of Mir-Khaydarov's lesser villains puts it), "no one ever gets prosecuted for
not accomplishing anything, but we prosecute people all the time who ac-
complish something" (140). Mir-Khaydarov's exposés of the sloth, venality,
and incompetence of Soviet officialdom are so bitter and so perceptive that
the novel's attack on capitalism often seems to be an appeal, in fact, to introduce capitalism, disguised as an attack. Since that kind of maneuver was
one of the Aesopian ways in which banned ideas could be smuggled into Soviet discourse, it is difficult to be certain whether Mir-Khaydarov genuinely
considers Shubarin to be a villain (even if the man is described as constantly
watching a bootlegged copy of *The Godfather* for tips on how to behave).
Whatever Mir-Khaydarov's intention, though, Azlarkhanov's indifferent execution of his duties at the jam factory inevitably comes to mind when
Shubarin complains bitterly that, while he may steal from the state, he at
least provides employment for thousands of people who might otherwise be
unemployed, while the do-nothing, incompetent state officials who will
condemn him to death if he is caught are also taking from the state, but
without providing anything in return, not even the proper performance of
the jobs for which the state is paying them. As Shubarin says,

> One thing offends me—I have destroyed nothing in this life, have torn noth-
> ing down, have spoiled nothing, have reduced nothing to dust. All I have done
> is build and multiply, I have done good [*sozdaval dobro*—which can also be
> translated as "created property"] in the most direct sense.
>
> And no matter where you look, there's a black host of examples of peo-
> ple who've done the opposite. You can list the names of all those who have
> destroyed this kolkhoz or that, or a sovkhoz, or a factory, or a kombinat, or
> an institute, or a newspaper, or a shop, who in the end have destroyed the
> earth, who are destroying the rivers and lakes, cutting down the forests,
> manufacturing televisions which explode, causing houses and hotels to
> burn down . . . but to them it's all like water off a goose. Not a single one of
> them has been subject to that terrible punishment [i.e., the death penalty],
> even though, if you were to count it up, the losses caused by all of us private

workshop owners can scarcely compare with the destruction that those people have caused. (202)

The law enforcement heroes of other *detektivy* show a similar disregard for the distinction between that which belongs to the state and that which belongs to them. In Cherginets's *The Investigation Continues,* one of the *uchastkovyye* has an arrangement with the clerk of a book kiosk on his beat by which the hard-to-find children's books that come to her stand will be kept under the counter for him to purchase for his little daughter. The *uchastkovyy* in charge of the railroad station in Adamov's *Swamp Grass* has a similar arrangement with the administrator of the railroad cafeteria, who keeps the best food for him, because, as the policeman says to his superior, "A great deal is given to him of whom a great deal is demanded!" (15).

At least Inspector Losev, the hero of Adamov's novel, recognizes his colleague's behavior as a form of theft and chastises him for it. Near the end of Aryasov's *Three Hours to Clarify the Truth,* General Alekseyev, the senior KGB official in charge of investigating the diversion of state gold into private hands, learns that his granddaughter has fallen seriously ill. Immediately, Alekseyev telephones the chief administrator of the city's best hospital, a friend, to make sure that his granddaughter gets a private room and the care of the hospital's best specialists. Not only does Aryasov's novel not remark upon what is a clear abuse of the general's position, but the afterword to the novel by G. Ananyev, who appears to be a spokesman for the Soviet law enforcement organs, singles this incident out as a demonstration of the general's qualities as a human being, and thus, by extension, as a positive representation of the entire KGB. Ananyev says, "It is symbolic that General Alekseyev connects [his granddaughter's] recovery with the liquidation of a dangerous group of criminals" (286).

Toward the end of the Soviet era, it first became possible for authors to suggest that, as Slovin puts it in *Bulletproof Vests,* "In the work of the militia, where it seemed like the main danger ought to come from murderers and thieves, what [the investigators] mostly had to watch out for wasn't armed criminals, but their own bosses" (257). Once censorship collapsed, and after the circumstances of Russian life changed dramatically, Russian crime fiction became filled with pictures of law enforcement officials who were on the take, or otherwise corrupt. Valeriy Maslov's *Made Mafia,* for example, begins with the city procurator—the senior local law enforcement official—being pulled from his car and beaten by militiamen, who later in the novel prove to be under the control of a local corrupt politician.

Dmitriy Petrov's *Setup for a Sucker* shows the entire law enforcement establishment of the provincial city in which the story is set to be so corrupt that, by novel's end, it is the book's main villain whom Moscow appoints to be regional procurator, thus ending any hopes the hero might have of exposing the man's crimes. In Dashkova's *Flesh for Sale*, the hero, a colonel in the GRU, or military intelligence, ultimately fails in his attempts to rescue the heroine from the clutches of a Chechen guerrilla because most of his colleagues in the intelligence services are in reality paid informants for the Chechens. It is because at least one, and possibly more, law enforcement officials are corrupt that the hero of Marinina's *Small Fry Die First* chooses to violate department regulations by going underground when he is falsely accused of corruption. Understanding that he is being set up by an unknown colleague, and knowing he will not be able to clear himself of the charges if he is in a holding cell, the hero runs away because he can not otherwise fight a corrupted system.

It is important to stress again that these are all examples of corrupt official behavior that the *detektivy* unambiguously condemn. To be sure, many of these novels do explore in some detail the reasons why so many law enforcement officials are unable, as Colonel Gordeyev, the eminence grise of Marinina's novels, expresses it, "to resist the pressure of the material stimulus ... sad as this is to confess" (*Stolen Dream*, 231). Without exception, the post-Soviet *detektivy* that in any way depict the militia show Russia's law enforcement establishment to be seriously underfunded, working under conditions bordering on the impossible. In the words of Colonel Gordeyev, from the same novel,

> [The criminals] shoot at us when and as they consider it necessary, while we must account for every shot, writing up reports by the ton! They have money, people, weapons, cars with powerful motors, the very latest technology, while all we have is a briefcase that was manufactured sometime before the [Second World] war and experts who have had to teach themselves whatever it is they know. We don't even have enough money for gasoline. (341)

Working conditions in Nikolay Ivanov's *Tax Police* are even worse: one of the main characters has as his office the women's toilet, converted to an office by the simple expedient of ripping out the stools (30). Perhaps because he is a militiaman who has now left the service, Nikita Filatov is extremely forthright, and extremely bitter, about the financial miseries that post-Soviet law enforcement professionals must endure; the investigator's lot is, in Filatov's words, "A beggar's wage, which sufficed only to eke out the month on the edge of poverty. Years and years of counting on a pension which would prove even more ridiculous than his full salary, the mumbling of his children as they reluctantly answered questions about what their father did for a living . . . cheap vodka, random acquaintances, human misery, and endless human nastiness . . . " ("4:15 Moscow Time," 270).

Even though the genre is unanimous in its agreement that, as the epigraph to Filatov's collection of short stories, *Electronically Tested*, puts it, "You'd have to be a complete idiot to work in the militia right now!" the *detektiv* nevertheless is severely unforgiving of law enforcement officials who succumb to material blandishments. This is especially clear in a work like *Stolen Dream*, where author Marinina stacks the deck as much as possible by describing her turncoat investigator as a sympathetic, conscientious, highly concerned widower, who is juggling a miserly salary and the unreasonable demands of his job as he attempts, single-handedly, to do a decent job of raising his beloved twelve-year-old daughter. Unable to make ends meet, he reluctantly exchanges what he considers to be minor information for cash. Exposed later as a traitor, he explodes, "Maybe I am a fool and a swine, maybe I am a weakling and despicable, but I want my daughter to grow up healthy and as happy as possible. You think that's a crime? Do I really not have the right to want that, and to try to achieve it? You think that's sick, and against public morality?" (277).

In spite of the impossibility of the man's position and the understandable reasons for which he has succumbed to corruption, the answer that Marinina's book gives to the unhappy inspector's questions is unequivocally "yes." An equally vivid answer to the predicament Marinina's novel poses is given in Yelena Yakovleva's *All Joking Aside*, where a former investigator who has gone over to the private sector is found to have withheld evidence that might damage his client. Discovering this, his former colleague, and one-time good friend, snarls, "Get the hell out of [my car] before I punch you in the face, like I'm itching to do. I'm giving you two days to evolve back up from an ape into a human being. If that doesn't happen, then I don't know you" (232).

That said, it must be confessed that the post-Soviet *detektivy* have lower expectations of their good guys than did their Soviet counterparts. In Kivinov's story, "Seductive Dreams," for example, the heroes manage, after long struggles, to stop a villain who has been coercing lovelorn student nurses into killing off old single women so that he can gain control of their desirable St. Petersburg apartments. After confiscating the villain's bankroll, the investigators decide to reward themselves with a pizza, which they pay for with a twenty dollar bill peeled from the villain's wad. Their theft of evidence then turns into fraud when the bill proves to be a photocopied counterfeit, but the investigators console themselves with the thought that the pizzeria is unlikely to go broke from the loss of this one pizza, as well as the implied justification that they deserve some kind of reward for their efforts (413). A similar, but less deliberate, kind of misuse of evidence appears in Filatov's "Electronically Tested," when the hunting knife that is crucial as evidence in an assault case proves to be missing, because the investigators had used it to open a tin can while they were drinking vodka in one of their offices and had later misplaced it.

While it is clear that the authors view these minor abuses of authority as nothing more than peccadilloes, the many instances in which the positive characters of the new *detektivy* are shown to be violating one set of laws because of the strictures imposed upon them by other statutes are more disturbing. Unlike their Soviet-era predecessors, which had to be far more circumspect about suggesting that the criminal law process could in some way be flawed, the post-Soviet *detektivy* are deeply concerned with the ways in which the formalities of criminal procedure impinge upon what the heroes of these novels, and their authors, consider to be the proper execution of their jobs. Some of the most vivid examples come from the stories of Kivinov, no doubt because he is a working criminal investigator and, thus, has a store of real-life absurdities upon which to draw. In "Rat Hunting," for example, the hero puts a sleeping potion into the tea he offers to the secretary of one of the suspects, so that he will be able to search her office while she is unconscious.

In Kivinov's "Nightmare on Stachki Street" the investigators find themselves on one side of a door, with the main suspect's accomplice on the other. The woman refuses to open up, and they have no warrant, which means that they are powerless to proceed, because "A positive result from [breaking down the door] could only be guaranteed if the killer was sitting on the other side writing out a confession. Any other possibility would threaten [the investigators with] an administrative inquiry about their unauthorized entry into the apartment, with the full arsenal of possible sanctions [for the investigators] up to and including what in soccer is called 'being ushered from the field of play'" (40). In this instance, the investigators walk away frustrated, unable to dream up a pretext on which they might plausibly circumvent the procedural rules which prevent them from advancing their case.

In "Chance Companions," another of Kivinov's stories, two drug addicts attempt to choke a cab driver to death in order to rob him. The driver passes out, and the addicts steal the cab. The investigator catches the thieves, but the procurator indicts them only on a charge of petty hooliganism (a catch-all Soviet-era crime defined by the new Criminal Code as "the flagrant violation of public order, expressing clear disrespect for society, accompanied by the use of force . . . and also the destruction or threat of destruction of the property of another" [Article 213]), and then releases the pair. The outraged cab driver is convinced that the militia have been bribed, but the real reason for the procurator's decision is that the pair had found only 4,500 rubles in the cab, and the Criminal Code of the time specified that "larceny" begins at the loss of 5,000 rubles (177). An even clearer example of the bitterness that Kivinov's heroes feel about the laws they are supposed to enforce comes in the story "Baby Doll," where the main character recounts what had happened to one of his colleagues:

> Last summer [the militiaman] had chased off a herd of drunken fools, wounding the most active of them with his service pistol. No other "means of action" were demonstrated [by the drunks], and Casanova [the nickname of the militiaman] wasn't "shooting in order to preserve social order" [the legal justification for use of deadly force] which would be justification for the use of his weapon], but instead only to save his own life. So, naturally, his use of the gun was ruled to have been unnecessary, and they took away [his] gun and opened a criminal case against him. True, he wasn't fired from the organs [the militia]; they said they'd wait for that until the end of his trial. The authorities paid almost no attention to the cop's explanations, or to the testimony of the girls who had witnessed the whole thing, and so [the militiaman] was . . . prepared for the worst. (53)

Despite the fact that this operative is likely to be fired, perhaps even jailed, he is still luckier than the operative in another of Kivinov's stories, "Nightmare on Stachki Street," who gets a lethal stab wound while trying to arrest a suspect. As the unlucky detective lies on his deathbed, his superior begs him to sign a statement saying that the wound had come from having stumbled against a protruding nail, because no one has actually seen the stabbing. The militiaman's death would thus saddle the department with yet another unsolved crime, further damaging their crime-solution statistics. Better, the chief implores, to pass the incident off as an accident, to which, surprisingly, the injured militiaman agrees.

Filatov, also a militiaman at one time, has a similarly jaundiced view of Russia's legal system. In "4:15 Moscow Time," the legal system in St. Petersburg actually grinds to a complete halt, because the city's judges have gone on strike. Without the judges to sanction the actions of the procuracy, the procurators cannot sanction the opening of criminal cases, which leaves the militia powerless to do anything at all. Although one of Filatov's characters observes sympathetically that there is some justification for this strike, since judges earn less than the secretaries in the new private commercial banks, Filatov's impatience with Russia's legal system is clear. He makes a similar point in "Electronically Tested," where his hero thinks in disgust that

> It was as though no one in the glorious organs of internal affairs was working for any kind of final result . . . it was the process itself which was important, and the numbers in the statistics. . . . Lawyers work for money. Good money! And the criminal knows perfectly well what he is risking his freedom and even his life for. But what about the militiamen? They are doing it all for their salary, the promise of a good pension, and a bang-up free concert on Militia Day, the 10th of November. (39)

Perhaps the most graphic example of the ways in which the *detektiv* genre permits its heroes to break the law, however, comes in Kivinov's "Chance Companions." The hero and his partner are out on the street in the dead of night, working a case. They see a young woman, unescorted and alone. In order to teach her that her behavior is dangerous, the two criminal investigators pretend to be drunks from the Caucasus; after grabbing and pulling at her a bit, one of the pair pulls out his service revolver. The young woman flees in terror, after which the hero remarks, "Well, maybe now she won't go out alone at night alone and won't end up a victim of the eternal passions!" (208).

Law versus Justice

This incident illustrates neatly one of the fundamental tensions of the *detektiv* genre, that between *zakon*, or "law," and *spravedlivost*, which usually is translated as "justice," but which etymologically might better be rendered as "righteousness." This tension has become explicit in the post-Soviet version of the genre, but it may be sensed even in so early a novel as Ivan

Lazutin's *Militia Sergeant*, first published in the 1950s. In an incident similar to that of the Kivinov story, the protagonist, militia sergeant Nikolay Zakharov, spots a well-dressed arrogant young man who tosses his cigarette butt onto the ground. Precisely to "teach him a lesson," Zakharov forces the young man to his hands and knees to pick the butt up, berating and deliberately humiliating him in front of the gaggle of admiring girls who surround him.

Although one incident is from the Khrushchev era and the other from that of Yeltsin, both demonstrate the distinction that Russian law enforcement officials, and presumably also a significant portion of the reading public, understand to exist between behavior the law allows (or, perhaps more precisely, does not forbid) and behavior that is correct and proper. The dilemma appears too in Arestova's "Last Clue," where the militia have to release their prime murder suspect after she has been held for the statutory seventy-two hours (even though three separate witnesses have positively identified her voice as that of the killer), simply because the suspect refuses to confess, and the procurator refuses to accept the voice identifications as sufficient proof of guilt. Arestova makes her opinion of such legal niceties plain when the released suspect goes on to threaten another killing in order to cover up her first one.

Obviously, such examples are not far removed from incidents that might be found in western cousins of the *detektiv*, in the sorts of novels that also explore inadequacies in how existing laws are enforced. In the Russian novels, just as in the western ones, situations are created that require that law enforcement officials indulge in a certain bending—or even breaking—of the laws, in order to see that justice is done. In the Russian versions of the genre, however, the law enforcement official is as likely to be shown bending the law to help a criminal as he or she is to be doing so to catch one. For example, one of the heroes of Kivinov's "Petersburg Present" is interrogating a drug addict who begins to go into withdrawal; sympathetic, the investigator lets the young man inject himself with illegal narcotics right there in the office (291). Even odder is Kivinov's story "Kisses, Larin," in which the hero permits a repeat offender whom he has just captured, but against whom he has no particular animus, to use his office for a private visit with his girlfriend, obligingly waiting out in the hall while the pair have intercourse on his desk.

Examples from other *detektivy* show that *spravedlivost* extends beyond turning the occasional blind eye. In Filatov's story "4:15 Moscow Time,"

Major Filimonov, a very senior militia official, drives the story's hero, Vinogradov, and his colleague Dagutin back to Dagutin's apartment after a gru-
eling but misdirected interrogation at the precinct station. (In this story,
Vinogradov has quit the militia and is working, very discontentedly, for a
private security firm.) Having discovered before they were taken in for interrogation that a third colleague has been killed, Vinogradov and Dagutin
decide to observe the Russian custom of drinking to the memory of their
fallen comrade. They invite Filimonov to join them; he refuses at first, both
because he is on duty and because he is driving (Russian law forbids driv-
ers to have any alcohol at all in their systems). However, once he learns that
the other two are drinking to honor the memory of their fallen friend, the
major not only joins them ("That's something sacred, it is!" he says), but
makes a point of draining his glass to the bottom, as custom requires. "You
could tell that Filimonov was a worthy man. Behavior like that should be
rewarded, so Dagutin, not harboring his grudge, held up the bottle. 'Again?'
he asked" (266).

Even in the Soviet period, when the literary respect for law had to be
much higher, this quality of *spravedlivost* could intervene in an event, transforming what seems plainly to be a violation of the law into something benign, or even positive. A case in point is Anatoliy Bezuglov's *Criminals*, in
which a *sledovatel* has to pursue a case involving an elderly local woman
who had been a partisan during World War II. The old woman has threatened a local administrator, first with a pistol, and then with a rifle, because
the man had sent a bulldozer to raze her house. At first, the *sledovatel* believes that the woman is being prosecuted properly, because she has not
only used illegal weapons to threaten a government official, but has even
fired the weapons, all apparently to protect her property. Another elderly
neighbor explains, however, that the woman is indifferent to her property
but, rather, is trying to prevent desecration of a nearby mass grave in which
several of her partisan comrades had been buried, victims of the Nazis. Indeed, it was to protect the common grave that the woman had built her
house there in the first place, because, as her neighbor exclaims, "That's a
sacred place!" (193). Strikingly, the *sledovatel* agrees and drops the case. As
if to make the point even stronger, the progress of the novel later confirms
that it is the official who is a villain, rather than the old woman.

As unlikely as it may seem to westerners accustomed to thinking of the
Soviet Union as a police state, the qualities of official discretion shown in the
examples above were in fact considered to be the highest goal of Soviet law

enforcement. Ye A. Smolentsev, at one time the vice president of the Supreme Court of the USSR, notes in an afterword to Vasiliy Ardamatskiy's novel *The Trial* that "Soviet law is by nature humanitarian and just (*spravedlivyy*). For us, punishment for a crime is not revenge or the lowering of human worth" (127). Essentially the same point is made in the foreword to a collection of reminiscences about Moscow criminal investigation, in which the best of Russia's militiamen are said to be people who have

> devoted their lives to the battle against evil, cruelty, and trickery . . . people of duty and calling, who have risked their health and lives, have forgotten about comfort, about their own spiritual and cultural growth, about their near ones, their wives and children, all to see that Justice (*Spravedlivost*) should triumph. (*Moskovskiy ugolovnyy rozysk*, 5)

To judge at least by those memoirs, the lengths to which real law enforcement officials would go to seem "just" were sometimes remarkable. V. D. Roshchin, who was assistant head of Moscow Criminal Investigation in the immediate post-Soviet years, recounts in one such memoir how a confessed murderer once began expressing doubt that Roshchin could handle the pistol he was wearing. To prove that he could, Roshchin set up an empty bottle on a stump, walked some paces away, and then shot it. Roshchin then set up a second bottle and handed his loaded service weapon to the confessed killer, to allow the man to show his skill also, which the man did more than amply by blasting the bottle into the air with his first shot and then shooting it again while it was still in the air. After this demonstration, the killer handed the pistol back to Roshchin.[1]

The explanation Roshchin gives for this extraordinary violation of police procedure, and common sense, is that the murderer has agreed to show the militia where he has buried the bodies of his two victims, not for purposes of evidence, but rather to enable the victims' families to give them a proper burial. Because this demonstrates to Roshchin that the criminal has what he calls "the remnants of a human soul," the Moscow investigator feels the obligation to treat the criminal in a way that, by Roshchin's estimation, permits the killer to retain his sense of being a human being. That principle is advanced explicitly by Gafa Khusaynov, a famous Moscow investigator from the 1970s, who in the same volume of reminiscences says, "I always proceeded from the idea that everyone, even the great sinners, were people. They have the right to demand human treatment of themselves, and then they will respond in kind" (*Moskovskiy ugolovnyy rozysk*, 501). In fact, in an equally startling anecdote from the same volume, the extent to which criminals might "respond in kind" is clarified when a famous Moscow cat burglar of the 1970s, known by the nickname Vengrover, is described as accidentally breaking into the apartment of a sleeping militia investigator. Appalled at the monastic simplicity in which the investigator lives, Vengrover is reputed to have left a large sum of money on the bedside table of the poor-but-honest investigator (510).

What such anecdotes illustrate, both in real life and in fiction, is that the distance between *zakon* and *spravedlivost* for many Russians can be so great as to make the two notions polar opposites. Indeed, at least one Russian legal theorist of the post-Soviet period characterizes the entire history of world jurisprudence as a battle between two antithetical legal traditions, one deriving from law, and the other from justice.[2] Essentially the same point is made in a dust-jacket blurb by one of the first post-Soviet *detektiv* writers, Andrey Izmaylov, who asks, "They say that where there is no law, there is no justice . . . but is that always so?"[3] Perhaps the fullest exploration of the distinction between the two notions that exists in the Russian mind is the one given by the scholar Aleksey Shmelyov:[4]

> We call a person *just* who is occupied with the distribution of benefits (or punishments) and who gives to each as he needs or deserves. A teacher may be *just*, but not a student; a judge, but not a defendant. When a journalist writes that a judgement was *severe but just*, he wishes to say that the pronounced punishment corresponded to the weight of guilt. . . .
>
> Many peoples hold that *honesty* is extremely important in life, but it is particularly highly valued in Protestant culture. . . . In distinction to *honesty*, the demand for *justice* can be seen to hold something which is more peculiar to Russians than to other peoples. We are ready to consider *justice* as more valuable than abstract and soulless *legality*. The question, "How shall I judge, according to the law or according to justice?" is scarcely translatable into other European languages. And when Russians speak foreign languages, they sometimes experience difficulties because those languages lack words which correspond precisely to the Russian word *justice*. In place of justice such speakers must resort to "honesty" or "legality."

There are several reasons for the widespread Russian mistrust of law. In the Soviet period, censorship and other considerations restricted authors to complaints about ways in which the powerful of this world might circumvent the laws, but in the post-Soviet *detektivy* the complaint is even more straightforward—that the powerful of this world are now *writing* the laws, solely for their own benefit. In "Static," Filatov's investigator-hero says to his partner, "What makes Yeltsin and Grachyov [at the time Minister of Defense] any better than [the New Russians]? They're all bandits and thieves, except the Yeltsins are bigger thieves, and more brazen. . . . It's still not clear who's more dangerous for Russia, [organized crime] or those assholes in the Kremlin" (317). As he sadly concludes somewhat later in the same work, "The laws are bad, no one will argue with that" (353).

Kivinov is even more direct, arguing in "Gone with the Wind" that laws are nothing more than the musical score the powerful write down so that public officials may create the kind of "social music" the mighty few enjoy most. In the words of Kivinov's investigator,

> They let go the ones they should arrest and arrest the ones they could let go. It's like there's a band director somewhere, pointing his baton—that one over there, this one over here . . . the one who's writing the music is the composer. If someone orders a march, [the militia, procurators, and judges] will play a march. If they order a waltz, a waltz they'll get. Who is ordering the music? The one who pays for it. That's the whole mechanics of the thing. (84)

If anything, Kivinov's vision of the mechanics of law-making in Russia has grown even more cynical with time. In "Baby Doll" Kivinov's hero scoffs at a doubting fellow-investigator, "The Christian-Democrat party in Italy is founded almost entirely on mafia money. So the laws in the parliament there are made almost entirely by people who are useful to the mafia. Money makes money. Cattani or somebody like him can shit around if he wants, but nothing changes. The same thing [is true here]" (231).

At first glance, the conviction of Kivinov and others that laws are designed by the powerful to protect that which is theirs may seem like an outmoded reflex from the recent Marxist past. It was a tenet of the early Soviet years that, as Lenin put it in his *State and Revolution,* "The fundamental social cause of excesses which violate the rules of social life is the exploitation of the masses, their want and poverty. With the removal of this chief cause, excesses will inevitably begin to 'wither away.' We do not know how quickly and in what stages, but we know that they will be withering away" (Connor, 221). Lenin based his conviction in part on Marx, who also understood western law to be a consequence of the capitalist system that had evolved to regulate economic transactions, and to protect the private property that lies at its heart.

As fully as it may have been informed by Marxism, though, Lenin's conviction that the western-style legal tradition should "wither away" also had a specifically Russian dimension, which may be found in many other Russian thinkers and writers. This dimension is apparent in another place in *State and Revolution,* where Lenin elaborates his opposition to formalized laws by explaining that "Any law [or "right"—tellingly, the word *pravo* may be translated in either way] is the application of *identical* dimensions to *various* people, who in fact are not identical, and are not equal to one another; thus any 'equal law' is a violation of equality and an injustice" (Connor, 222). Western observers, particularly those who are hostile to the Bolsheviks and Russia's socialist experiment, might see Lenin's words as nothing more than an ingenious sophistry designed to justify the proletarian reign of terror that the revolution unleashed. While political expediency may have been part of what lay behind Lenin's argument, Lenin was not the only Russian who objected to laws precisely because they created arbitrary rules into which specific individuals must be fit. It is difficult to conceive of a figure more remote from Lenin, spiritually, politically, and philosophically, than Fyodor Dostoyevsky. Yet, in *Notes from the House of the Dead,* Dostoyevsky voices virtually the same objection to Russia's legal code of his day as Lenin did to that of his.

> I remember there was one thought which . . . was to haunt me throughout the whole of my time in prison. This was . . . the problem of the inequality of punishment for the same crime. It is true that it is impossible to compare one criminal with another, even approximately. For example, there may be two criminals who have both killed a man: all the circumstances of each case are taken into account; and in each case the punishment determined is practically the same. But note what a difference there is between the two crimes. One criminal . . . may have slit a man's throat just like that, for no reason at all. . . . The other criminal has killed to defend the honor of his fiancée, his sister, his daughter, against a debauched tyrant. One man has killed because he is a vagrant . . . defending his life and his freedom . . . another slits the throats of little children just for the hell of it . . . to savor their terror. And what happens? Both men are given penal servitude. (75–76)

That Lenin and Dostoyevsky should find common ground in the notion that uniformly applied law is unjust derives in part from the history of Russian law, which is quite different from that of the west. Where, in the west, law has, for the past several centuries, been increasingly understood to define and defend the "natural" rights a citizen possesses simply by the fact of his or her birth, the tradition that has prevailed in Russia is that of so-called positive law, which understands laws to be the way in which the ruler, or the state, grants permission for subjects of the state to perform certain acts. In such a system, anything not specifically permitted is technically illegal; there is no such concept as an "innate right" that the law is intended to defend. This is made specific in a recently published textbook on the subject of information security:

> As is known, law [*pravo*] is the conjoined whole of generally obligatory rules and norms of behavior that are established or sanctioned by the state in relation to defined spheres of the life and activities of state organs, organizations, and the populace, or individuals. (Yarochkin, 133)

Among the consequences of this understanding, as Svetlana Boym points out in *Common Places: Mythologies in Everyday Life in Russia*, is that "the Muscovian legal tradition did not pay attention to the rights of the servant of the state. Moreover, the 1649 Code of Laws does not recognize the value of a human being as such; it lacks the concept of a person who could inflict or suffer from insult or dishonor. Everyone, including the clergy, is described according to their occupation and place in the state hierarchy" (80).

It is a chicken-and-egg problem to question whether positive law has made Russia what it is, or whether there is something innate to the Russian character that finds positive law attractive. Whatever the answer to that question, there are several aspects of it that depend upon the profound differences in the development of western and Russian thought. As Timothy Ware reminds his primarily western readership in *The Orthodox Church*, the superficial similarities between western and eastern Christianity are deeply misleading:

> Western Christians, whether Free Churchmen, Anglicans, or Roman Catholics, have a common background in the past. All alike (although they may not always care to admit it) have been profoundly influenced by the same events: by the Papal centralization and the Scholasticism of the Middle Ages, by the Renaissance, by the Reformation and Counter-Reformation. But behind members of the Orthodox Church—Greeks, Russians, and the rest—there lies a very different background. They have known no Middle Ages (in the western sense) and have undergone no Reformations or Counter-Reformations; they have only been affected in an oblique way by the cultural and religious upheaval which transformed western Europe in the sixteenth and seventeenth centuries. Christians in the west, both Roman and Reformed, generally start by asking the same questions, although they may disagree about the answers. In Orthodoxy, however, it is not merely the answers that are different—the questions themselves are not the same as in the west. (9)

The consequences of Russia's separate development are not solely theo-logical; there are many other arenas of Russian life in which "the questions themselves are not the same as in the west." Western historians of both law and philosophy agree that it was the conjunction of the splintering of the-ology and the rise of mercantile capitalism that led to the development of both the western conception of the individual and the highly elaborated body of laws that—to the western way of thinking at least—defends that individualism. Brian Morris, for example, finds that in John Locke (who wrote at approximately the same time as Moscow was promulgating the seventeenth-century code of laws to which Boym refers above):

> Mechanistic science, bourgeois political economy and empiricist philosophy form an essential unity and express an underlying pattern. With respect to nature a "one-sided atomism," with respect to social life, a "metaphysics of in-dividualism," with respect to the human mind a focus on discrete and self-sufficient "ideas." All conceptions are consonant with the conditions of mer-cantile capitalism, which was then beginning to emerge in Western Europe. (Morris, 45–46)

This dependence of modern western law upon the emergence of capital-ism has been noted both by those who are hostile to it and those who judge that twinned development to be one of the greatest achievements of hu-mankind. Soviet theorist Yevgeniy Pashukanis elaborated a so-called Commodity-Exchange Theory of Law, which argued that, in bourgeois so-ciety, all laws, including criminal laws, derive from the act of commercial exchange. This act is the intellectual source of such phrases as "paying for one's crime" or "repaying a debt to society," and also gives rise to the grad-uated punishments specified for various transgressions, creating a kind of price list of criminal activity. Essentially, the same argument is made, but with the value signs reversed, by conservative capitalist economist Friederich von Hayek, who saw western-style law as arising from the re-versability of commercial transactions. Because people in a trade culture one day might be buyers and the next, sellers, it was necessary to create mu-tually agreed-upon rules that would minimize uncertainty for both parties, no matter which role they were playing. [5] It was only with such a "complex of rules" that, in the words of legal philosopher Lon L. Fuller, man might be rescued "from the blind play of chance and . . . put . . . safely on the road to purposeful and creative activity" (9). It is worth noting that both Pashukanis and Hayek predict that law would disappear from societies that no longer practice commercial exchange of commodities, although the former sees this as a condition to be desired and the latter to be a disaster.

By contrast, the economic model that prevailed in Russia until the advent of socialism, and that in many parts of the country seems to have returned today, is that of the so-called natural economy, which Tim McDaniel characterizes as "universal access to the land; household production largely for use; exchange through barter; with limited monetarization and a large degree of local autonomy" (97). As McDaniel notes elsewhere in his book *The Agony of the Russian Idea*, this natural economy was inherently paternalistic and collectivist and administered through the community elders. Putting a premium upon consensus, this economic model defended the interests of the community against individuals. It was precisely this paternalism the nineteenth-century philosopher and disaffected social critic Pyotr Chaadayev saw as the characteristic that took the place of law in Russia:[6]

> For us [Russians] it is not the law which punishes a citizen who has done wrong, but a father who punishes a disobedient child. Our taste for family arrangements is such that we lavish the rights of fatherhood on anything that we find ourselves dependent upon. The idea of lawfulness, of right, makes no sense to the Russian people.

Whether it is innate to the Russian character, or a product of what McDaniel describes as the motive force behind the Russian "idea," that is, the instinctive rejection of notions and values imported from the west, there is a persistent strain in Russian thought that sees the attempt to create an impartial, universally applicable legal code to be not only impossible, but alien. During the eighteenth and nineteenth centuries, most of Russia's periodic attempts at legal reform were instigated by German-born professors or their students.[7] These reforms inevitably came to frustration because of the insistence of even the most liberal of tsars to reserve for the throne the power of absolute monarchy—which by definition is antithetical to a code of laws. In the Soviet period, as Pashukanis argued, communism will know nothing of legal rights and duties because with communism economic exchange will be abolished, as will all the legal and political conceptions that derive from it. Even in the post-Soviet period, as one of Russia's prominent legal theorists explains,

> The conception (and paradigm) of the development of jurisprudence in [post-Soviet] Russia remains unelaborated and in many regards unclear and

ill-defined . . . in the chaotic flood of contemporary publications and proposals for the directions in which post-Soviet jurisprudence might evolve
there are several directions which are quite different from one another con-
ceptually. In our view, these may be separated into the following groups: a
liberal-democratic direction; the former Marxist-Leninist direction (somewhat modernized in vocabulary); and a traditional direction (an anti-western
one, harking back to pre-revolutionary Russian jurisprudence in its nativist-
Slavophile interpretation).[8]

Who Decides What Justice Is?

If this theorist is correct, the greater part of jurisprudence in Russia remains governed by impulses that tend more toward *spravedlivost* than toward rule of law. Since even the new Criminal Code offers great scope for
what Russia's General Procurator Eduard Pobyalo called "judicial discretion,"[9] there must of necessity be some mechanism by which, to use
Adamov's image, it is possible to tell whether the knife is being wielded by
a bandit or a surgeon. Ardamatskiy's Soviet-era *The Trial* asserted that "Not
every criminal is necessarily a bad person" (101), while Marinina's post-
Soviet *Stolen Dream* showed its heroine telling students of criminal law,

> It is only in the textbooks that the criminal is bad and the victim worthy of
> sympathy. In fact there are criminals that could make your heart burst with
> pity, while there are victims sometimes who are, to say it mildly, unpleasant,
> who don't evoke any sympathy, and some who long ago should have been in
> prison. (182)

What neither novel makes clear, however, is the method by which good
criminals can be differentiated from bad criminals, or, come to that, bad
victims from good.

Because the *detektiv* is so often addressing readers who essentially share
the same set of values as the genre, novels normally do not explain why
characters are good or bad, but rather simply telegraph their moral worth
by providing them with certain attributes, or placing them into a particular setting. Some of these "valuative attributes," such as luxurious clothing,
expensive furniture, or a general interest in material possessions have been
mentioned in the previous chapter. In the post-Soviet novels, as much as in
the Soviet-era ones, the character who dresses too well, or who wants to
own something "unnecessary" will invariably prove to be a villain.

There are other shorthand ways in which the *detektiv* signals good guy or bad guy, some of which may seem strange to western readers. For example, there is a very strong prejudice in the genre against people who enjoy restaurants. Inspector Levashov remarks in Viktor Pronin's "Version in Snow" that

[he] had noticed many times before the magical effect of the word "restaurant" on people who wanted to make an impression, be noticed, show off. And his boss had talked of the mysterious influence of this word on people who were inclined to break the law. The crime statistics were always higher in the vicinity of a restaurant than they were in other public places. (265)

As early as 1955, the villain in Ivan Lazutin's *Militia Sergeant* rhapsodizes to a companion,

What do I love? I love a lot of things, but what I love most are cool summer evenings. I love the lights in restaurants. A soft breeze blowing through the open windows. Wine on the table, a lot of wine! A band, playing something a little bit melancholy . . . a slow, floating tango, let's say. God, my heart feels good at times like that. I love it! Just one night like that is worth giving up whole years. (11)

More than three decades later, Mir-Khaydarov outlined the same correlation in *Walkabouts* between restaurants and criminality.

So what if nearby people have to replant after the spring downpours or after frost has killed the cotton, and people in the villages eat poorly . . . and thousands and thousands of students, even school kids, were working on farms far from their homes, and there were floods, earthquakes, famine, hurricanes, fires, shock-work months, voluntary Saturdays, voluntary Sundays, droughts, revolutions, local and regional wars—here [in the restaurants where the mafia gathered] it was always a holiday of the satiated life, and no doubt to people in the city it seemed more prestigious to be a regular at the Lido [restaurant] than to be, for example, an honorary member of the European Geographic Society. (16)

The genre's dislike of restaurants continues into the post-Soviet era. In Ivan Shitov's *Cathedral without Crosses*, for example, one of the ways that the author continues to stress that his unusual hero is a criminal is to show him throwing large sums of money about in restaurants and night clubs, including one in New York called The Tired Cowboy, which is said to have a cafe on the ground floor for students, a restaurant with a striptease show on the second floor for middle-class patrons, and a third-floor room for "clients of substance," where there were "tastefully hung models of decorative birds . . . the twinkling of artificial stars in the 'heavens,' soft music, [which poured] from the stage where the orchestra helped to free the restaurant's visitors from the worries and cares which tormented them" (347). In Marinina's *Small Fry Die First,* it is the fact that he keeps a personal restaurant for his gourmandizing that signals the appearance in the plot of the most senior, and most dangerous, of the novel's villains, while in Petrov's *Setup for a Sucker,* the efforts of the novel's central character and his wife to open a small privately owned restaurant next to their town's railroad station pulls both of them into a hell of rape, adultery, and murder.

The same bias is reflected in reality. In memoirs published to commemorate the eightieth anniversary of the formation of the Moscow Criminal Investigation Division, one of the authors speaks of two Moscow mafiosi who had originally been cadets in an elite military academy. However,

> They got interested in discotheques, they danced like crazy, especially break dancing. They were attracted to the gay, carefree, sweet life, and not to stern military service. They received their lieutenant's bars, but gave them up immediately, choosing to go into commerce instead. Next they mastered the life of night clubs. Yakov took up roulette and Igor billiards. And women and wine of course. Later they began travelling around the foreign resorts, got rid of their Russian-made cars and got foreign ones, wore fashionable high-quality clothes. All this demanded money, money, money. (MUR, 615)

The need for "money, money, money" is of course the reason why restaurants seem so sinister to most of the authors of the *detektivy.* The genre offers that same advice by inference in scores of other novels. As noted in the previous chapter, in the Soviet-era books, even if they are technically the victims of crimes, the people who had positioned themselves at the "pinch points" of the Soviet economy were uniformly viewed with suspicion, precisely because of the way that riches seemed mysteriously to accrue to them, even in the rigidly controlled socialist economy. Most of these people were managers of retail shops, overseers of distribution, and *tolkachi* (the "fixers"of the Soviet economy), all professions that western readers might anticipate. There was one other profession, perhaps more surprising, that frequently figures in the *detektivy* as a career chosen by bad guys— dentistry. Dentists are incidental villains in Ardamatskiy's novel *Trial* and in Shitov's *Cathedral without Crosses,* while in Aryasov's *Three Hours to*

Clarify the Truth, an early secondary villain, who serves to introduce the main plot, as well as the novel's main villain, are both dentists. In Printsev's story "Wedding Postponed," villain Leonid Belkin moves from dentistry to gold purchasing to hard currency speculation. In Adamov's *Evil Wind*, the dentist ends up a murder victim, but only because he is suspected of having dealt in the preparation of black market gold caps and crowns; and in Kivinov's "Seductive Dreams," a dentist becomes an accomplice to murder by supplying drugs to a man who uses them to murder old women in order to privatize their apartments. In Bezuglov's *Criminals*, the only man whom Asa Danilova, the beautiful but amoral villainess, finds worthy of her affections is, of course, a dentist. Even Ivy Litvinov, who was intimately familiar with Soviet conditions, chose a dentist as her major villain in *His Master's Voice*.

Tempting as it may be to ascribe the genre's antidental bias in the Soviet years to the generally low quality of Soviet dentistry, the real reason for the high frequency of villains with dental training is that dentists were about the closest thing to privately employed individuals that the Soviet system permitted. Even honest dentists had the opportunity to make an income several times larger than that earned by ordinary workers. "Do you know how much those false teeth bring in?" an inspector asks in bitter incredulity in Ardamatskiy's *The Trial*. "A thousand rubles a month at least!" (25). For purpose of comparison, at that time, a doctor's monthly salary would have been about 200 rubles. More important, though, was that dentists were virtually the only Soviet citizens who were legally permitted to buy and sell gold, because of its utility for making dental crowns; thus, it was easy for them also to work gold on the side.

Even at its most simpleminded, though, the *detektiv* never implies that all dentists, or all restaurant patrons, are criminals. Rather, the genre uses characteristic occupations and locations to suggest the symptoms of criminality. The problem of what constitutes criminality itself has been much harder for the genre to solve, in part because Russia's Marxist heritage still makes people suspect that crime is a product of economic conditions, and in part, too, because Russians persistently sympathize with those "unfortunates" who have fallen afoul of the country's law enforcement agencies. For all the sympathy that the genre may show to certain criminals, however, most books manage to delineate those who are plainly are meant to be seen as villains.

Some authors do so by making their evildoers subhuman, as Arestova did in her "Search in the Taiga," discussed in the previous chapter. Arestova's rather simplistic explanation for evil has an element, though, that is seen in fuller form in other *detektivy*. As Nikolayev, the arresting officer in Arestova's story, handcuffs the murderer, he says, "The taiga won't hide the likes of you. . . . You loved yourself too much" (59). This element, of loving one's self more than one loves others, or what Anatoliy Udintsev in his story "Search" identifies simply as "the itch to eat and drink a little better than everyone else" (224), appears in nearly every *detektiv*. In Cherginets's *The Investigation Continues*, a group of men who had met while serving sentences for burglary "graduate" after their release to armed robbery, which leads to a nearly fatal assault on the guard at a rifle range where they are attempting to steal weapons, and then to the murder of the militia investigator who begins tracking them after the assault. Like many novels, this one depicts murder as an inevitable, if unintended, result of having once taken the decision to step beyond the law, but it specifically differentiates the leader of this criminal band, a certain Logatskiy, from the others, because he begins to enjoy outwitting the militia. Cherginets's plot deliberately parallels Logatskiy's growing confidence in his own cleverness with the seriousness, and the cruelty, of the crimes that he commits, culminating with Logatskiy knowlingly leading the detective who has been following him into a fatal trap. Although members of the band help Logatskiy kill the militiaman, Cherginets makes it very clear that only Logatskiy is a true killer, while the others become dangerous only because of his influence on them. Indeed, in some ways, Cherginets seems to argue that coming under the influence of a man like Logatskiy is one of the risks that an ordinary criminal might run, once he chooses to step beyond the law.

This link between the man who has put himself beyond society and the will to murder is made even more explicit in Ivan Shevtsov's *Theft*, where the chief indictment leveled at the villain, Prishelets, is that he loves to have power over others. As he explains after his arrest, in his statement to the militia,

> This is my weakness. . . . I love when I have lackeys around me. It is pleasant to give orders, to feel my superiority over those cattle, those two-legged goats. I love to watch them bow and scrape and humble themselves, how they are ready to buy and sell each other for 25 rubles. (262)

The villain in Printsev's "Wedding Postponed" has arranged an elaborate plan to steal an airplane in order to escape to the west because he has a burning desire to open a law firm of his own. Even though frightened that he is about to be caught, the villain pushes ahead with his plan because

> If he were to refuse now to take part in [his own scheme], he would not only destroy his dream of having his own law practice but also lose any chance to make it to the "free world." He would also lose something that he had grown accustomed to during the months of preparation for his plan—his superiority over the ordinary members of his conspiracy, and the incomparable feeling of power and license, when the slightest of your desires or orders is carried out without a murmur! (67)

Artur Shubarin, the villain of Mir-Khaydarov's *Walkabouts,* expresses virtually the same sentiment when he boasts,

> I feed my sense of contempt handsomely by keeping many of the local administrators dependent upon my handouts. If Ikram [another bad guy] loves to watch the dancing girls wriggle about in front of him, to get him to give them big banknotes, what gives me pleasure are the "dances" of corrupt administrators, who all come racing like so many gypsies to get the same thing as those half-naked dancers are after. (203)

Although Mir-Khaydarov, Printsev, and Shevtsov all try to make clear in their novels that their main characters are evil by the standards of any culture, it is nevertheless difficult for western readers to appreciate that, to Russian readers, it is precisely this desire to be set apart from others, and to have arbitrary power over them, that makes the villains of these works evil. Thus, Shevtsov remarks of his villain in *Theft* that

> To Prisheltsev [all his accomplices and underlings] were no more than the means of production, with whose help he could produce a profit. As people, with their own thoughts, ideas, tastes, and views, they were of no interest to him, although he knew perfectly well their characters, human weaknesses, and emotional strings on which he might play. (113–14)

The conviction that individualism not only leads to vice, but is *itself* a vice is stated even more directly by Vil Lipatov, one of the "grandfathers" of the *detektiv*. In "Elk Bone," one of Lipatov's several stories about village detective Fyodor Aniskin, the crime under investigation is moose-poaching, not murder, but the "cause" of his crime is what in the west would be called individualism. The first sign of this individualism—which has led, as the story makes clear, to his other crimes—is that the poacher has for many years crossed out the name of the sole candidate during elections, thus ruining the unanimity of the village's vote. As Aniskin says, once it has become clear that not voting has led ineluctably to moose-poaching,

> I could have arrested you a million times before, and you would have ended your life in a camp, but I believe in Soviet power and I put my faith in it completely. There was no prison that was worse than your life, Dmitriy. Nothing could be more terrible than to be one-hundreth of one percent, while the people are the rest. You died thirty years ago! (79)

Western readers would expect to find such sentiments in Soviet-era *detektivy*, but may be surprised to find that, rather than disappearing in the post-Soviet novels, the dislike for individualism has grown even stronger. Some of the criticisms that are leveled at individualism are essentially the same as they were in the Soviet period. Thus, for example, the major villain in Marinina's *Stolen Dream* is characterized in the following way:

> Arsen was not ambitious, he didn't chase glory or money, and he didn't want power. All his life only one thing interested him—to manipulate people, to tug on his secret strings which he held in his hands and which other people didn't even suspect, watching with pleasure as their careers and fates changed. (244)

The judgment in Ivanov's *Tax Police* is even harsher. There the villain is a Russian-Jewish émigré to America, who has come back to invest his money in the newly capitalist Russia. In addition to being given the suggestively offensive name Kozyolskiy (or "goatish"), this villain is described as having the following convictions:

> Kozyolskiy thought that everyone who received wages was nothing but a lump. Only the person who paid out money wasn't a lump. Like the picture or not, but that was the reality. In business you can't step aside for anybody, otherwise tomorrow morning the cleaning lady will be wanting to sit in the president's chair, giving the orders. (176)

In the post-Soviet *detektivy*, though, the indictment of individualism has grown wider. It is not just that individuals by definition wish to pull away from the whole, or even that the desire to be different inevitably presumes the desire also to distinguish oneself from the others, which leads easily to the desire to manipulate others, and order them about. Many of the new *detektivy* see the dangers of Russia's new political and economic system to be that its underlying tenet of individualism *by definition* sets everyone in society against everyone else.

Some of the *detektivy*, for example, understand the new political and economic order of Russia to mean that anything can be a commodity, including human beings. Inna Astakhova's novel *Ordered to Forget the Past* is about criminals who abandon the overcrowded field of illegal narcotics to take up the even more lucrative traffic in immigrants, smuggling their miserable cargoes through Russia into Europe on faked papers for huge sums. Human beings are the commodity in both Igor Khristoforov's *Russian Slave Girls* and Dashkova's *Flesh for Sale*; in the first, it is Russian girls who are captured for sale to harem keepers in the Caucasus, while in the second, it is demobilized Russian soldiers, who are drugged and sold as slave laborers in Chechnya.

Other writers see the relationship between humans under capitalism more directly still. Mention has already been made of Filatov's "Static," in which one investigator at a stakeout speculates that the man whom they are watching may be carrying human organs in his backpack, either to sell for transplants, or perhaps simply to sell as meat. Perhaps the most straightforward characterization of individualism and capitalism as inherently evil, though, comes in Igor Vinnichenko's *Honeymoon*. Set in a provincial city, this novel involves the investigation of a Satanic cult that proves only to be a cover used by a commercial enterprise to disguise the fact that it is kidnapping derelicts, runaway children, bums, and society's other castoffs in order to sell their body parts. When he finally understands the crime he has been investigating, the hero exclaims,

> It was queer suddenly to feel myself to be no more than a bag stuffed with valuable goods. My talent, my imagination, my relations with others, the accumulation of my life's experience, and my immortal soul were of no commercial value, while my guts, my liver, my kidneys, and other such trash all had a fixed market price, payable in hard currency! (147)

Vinnichenko's conviction that "True satanism has become utterly respectable today, and even attractive—Every man for himself! How is that not a motto for the road to hell?" (135) makes explicit an assumption that seems to underlie nearly all post-Soviet *detektivy*: that crime has blossomed in Russia because the collapse of the old order has sanctified a dog-eat-dog form of individualism. As Tim McDaniel observes in *The Agony of the Russian Idea*,

> [Russian people ask themselves] Isn't capitalism a struggle for the survival of the fittest? Since, as the people were told constantly, they could not count on

the government, wasn't it logical, as Yeltsin's senior adviser Sergei Shakhrai stated, that above all people must think of themselves. . . ? (185)

Conclusion

As the *detektivy* demonstrate, Russians have a strong sense of good and evil, but the terms of the two concepts are such that they can seem confusing, even contradictory, to a reader with western sensibilities. Although the genre does not appear to give a full carte blanche to its positive heroes, condoning any and all kinds of activity, the kinds of acts it permits its heroes can look very strange by western standards. As noted, heroes may lie, steal evidence, pull strings, commit fraud, and physically threaten citizens. In one of Andrey Kivinov's stories, "Kisses, Larin," it even seems to be all right that the hero compromise one of his informants—who, to be sure, is a hardened jailbird—in such a way that he is murdered by his fellow gangsters. By contrast, villains seem to be evil no matter what they do. In addition to being vilified for crimes such as murder, theft, and robbery, the bad guys of various *detektivy* are excoriated even for dressing well, enjoying restaurants, and simply for working hard. Some bad guys, such as Artur Shubarin in Mir-Khaydarov's novel *Walkabouts*, with his far-flung network of factories and shops and his hundreds of employees who might otherwise be without work, or the industrious janitor in Aryasov's *Three Hours to Clarify the Truth*, who works two jobs and keeps a small farm besides in order to have extra money, might be heroes in the west.

The key to understanding this apparently disjointed code of morality lies not in individual acts, but rather in the purpose for which an act was undertaken, or the intent that lies behind it. If the purpose of an act is to serve private ends or advance individual interests, then the *detektiv* will view it with suspicion and probably condemn it outright, no matter how apparently benign the act may be. Conversely, as long as the purpose of an act is to serve "the people" or the disembodied state, the genre accepts it as good—even if property is stolen or people killed.

It is tempting, of course, to understand the principles behind this Russian conception of good and evil as deriving from Marx, because it was precisely Marx's criticism of capitalism that this economic system "reifies" human beings, by which he means that a person in a capitalist system "treats others as means, reduces himself to the role of means, and becomes the plaything of alien forces."[10] As with other distinctive features of Russian society, though, there is also a strong correlation between the *detektiv*'s critique of the moral implications of individualism and Russian Orthodox theology. The religion that shaped and informed Russia for nearly a millennium accepts, on the one hand, that all humans are sinful and error-prone, yet still bear the likeness and image of God, and, on the other, defines as the one insuperable sin the separation of the self from the community. As Timothy Ware puts it in his book on Orthodoxy, *The Orthodox Church*, "In the Church there is neither dictatorship nor individualism, but harmony and unanimity; men remain free but not isolated, for they are united in love, in faith, and in sacramental communion" (23). It is for this reason that Vinnichenko is able to argue, as he does in *Honeymoon*, that "Satan is absolute solitude."

Despite the apparent clarity of this yardstick, though, there still remains a certain ambiguity about the distinction between law and justice. Although the *detektiv* plainly argues that the distinguishing characteristic of the genre's Russian heroes is their commitment to justice—*spravedlivost*—the primary tool the genre permits these heroes in pursuit of that justice, for all the liberties they are permitted, is still law—*zakon*. However, because the genre seems so clearly to agree with the way in which the post-Soviet textbook *Juridical Psychology* by V. L. Vasilyev defines "justice"—that it is "the measure of the possibility for self-realization of a personality in given social conditions, meaning the achievement of social harmony" (129)—it is the failure of all people to treat one another "justly" that causes crime. Thus, the laws that humans devise to protect themselves against these mutual acts of injustice are inherently flawed because they are symptoms of the same diseased social system as are the kinds of behavior they are constructed to prevent.

For all the valor that Soviet-era heroes may demonstrate in battling bad guys, and all the weary sense of duty that post-Soviet heroes exhibit in their losing battle against the rising tide of Russian crime, the *detektiv* suggests strongly that, in the end, good guys and bad guys are simply two sides of the same coin. As Colonel Gordeyev, the "voice of reason and experience" in Marinina's novels, puts it at the end of *Stolen Dream*,

> In our work it is impossible to maintain moral purity. The truth has to be looked in the eyes, because idealistic fairy tales are only good for idiots. . . . The mafia of course is immortal, but quality detectives haven't faded away

either, so far. And they aren't going to either. . . . [to which Nastya Kamen-skaya's fiancé adds] "And from a mathematical point of view, you will always exist parallel to one another, never intersecting. Never. They won't break you, but you won't crush them either. (444)

Precisely the same point was made a decade earlier, in Viktor Astafyev's *Sad Detective*:

The purpose of those who have put on the uniform is the same as it is for all people, that they should plow and sow, reap and build. However, these mon-sters continue to rob and kill and raise hell, so that evil has to be countered with a power which can not itself be called good—only a power which builds may be called "good." A power which neither sows nor reaps, but which still eats bread, and with butter on it at that . . . has long ago lost the right to call itself a constructive power. (13)

Notes

1. *Moskovskiy ugolovnyy rozysk* (Moscow: MVD, 1998), 567.
2. V. S. Nersesyants, *Yurisprudentsiya* (Moscow: Norma-Infra M, 1998), 3.
3. On the back of A. Kivinov, *Strakhovochnyy variant* (St. Petersburg: AOZT-Valeri-SpB; AOZT MiM-Delta, 1995).
4. *Itogi*, 21 April 1998, 67.
5. As cited in Lon L. Fuller, *The Morality of Law*, rev. ed. (New Haven: Yale University Press, 1969), 24.
6. As cited in Daniel Rancour-Laferriere, *The Slave Soul of Russia: Moral Masochism and the Cult of Suffering* (New York: New York University Press, 1995), 31.
7. Nersesyants, 118.
8. Nersesyants, 155.
9. *Itogi*, 1 October 1996, 53.
10. As quoted in Fuller, 26.

CHAPTER FOUR

Punishment and Rehabilitation

IN THE WESTERN VERSIONS of the mystery genre, the elements of punish-ment and rehabilitation following a crime are not usually explored in any detail. The detective does his or her work, the miscreant is identified, and the reader closes the volume, assured the villain will suffer in some way for what has been done. Whether or not the miscreant will rejoin society at some later date is a matter of indifference, to the genre and its readers alike.

The *detektiv* is no exception in regard to punishment, for it, too, usually chooses not to show what happens to criminals after they have been ar-rested. When a particular *detektiv* does make reference to the aftermath of a crime, it often is with a weary dismissal like that which may be heard in Arkadiy Adamov's ending to *Evil Wind*.

> Zurich [the villain] is going to fight [prosecution] with all he has. He will lead [the procurators] in circles, lie, try to provoke them, slander others, will try to drag more and more new people into the orbit of the investiga-tion, some of whom, of course, he'll be forced to [name] . . . and others he'll drag in just to confuse the *sledovatel*. And he'll change his testimony a hundred times, and write endless complaints, and toward the end maybe he'll even start philosophizing about how he made use of the "shortcom-ings and mistakes of the system." And all this has to be done so that he will take a proper "vacation" from his "work," [i.e., will go to prison] so that he won't interfere in the future with efforts to correct those shortcomings and mistakes. (272)

In most ways, this passage reflects the official stance of Soviet jurisprudence. The confidence of Adamov's Inspector Losev that Zurich the villain will eventually be sent to prison, regardless of his efforts, and those of his lawyers, to slow and confuse the process, is, of course, a product of Soviet censorship. The system requires that the legal establishment be portrayed in a positive light, but it is equally a fact that the Russian legal system is designed to produce convictions once a case has actually been brought, as was explained in chapter 1. This certainty is probably also the product of experience, which would have taught its participants that a legal system that was bent upon conviction and that prized confession as a central element of that process, had a number of means at its disposal that it could use to secure both.

In another regard, however, Adamov's investigator seriously violates one of the most central tenets of Soviet jurisprudence, thus highlighting the most important way in which the *detektiv* was meant to differ from the western versions of the genre—even if it often did not do so in fact. Losev's cynical doubt that his villain will in any way be changed by his experience behind bars contradicts the avowed purpose of the Soviet prison system. Characterizing Zurich's eventual sentence as a "holiday," no matter how ironically, suggests that Adamov's character believes the villain will return to his villainy as soon as he is released. As we have seen, such a possibility violates what Ye A. Smolentsev, one-time vice president of the USSR Supreme Court, called the entire goal of Soviet law enforcement: "to correct and reeducate the criminal" (Ardamatskiy, 127). Even in the post-Soviet environment, where "the process of the administration of punishment has been de-ideologized," as one commentary on Russia's new 1997 Criminal Code puts it, "achieving the goal of punishment—the correction of the condemned—does not consist only in the proper observation of juridical prescription, but also places a strong stress on moral education."[1] It is because of this continued faith that the goal of incarceration is rehabilitation that Russia uses its prisons to hold people before they come to trial, but then sends them after conviction to so-called corrective labor camps.

Punishment and Crime

As surprising as this may seem to westerners accustomed to thinking of the USSR as a prison state, in the 1970s the average corrective labor camp sentence in the Soviet Union was only about three and a half years.[2] In part, this low average was due to the fact that, until the legal code was changed in 1997, no prison sentence could be longer than fifteen years. Sentences could not run sequentially, and the only sanction stiffer than fifteen years in a hard labor camp was the death penalty, which could only be applied for eighteen specific crimes.[3] The 1997 code retains the death sentence, but also increases the maximum sentence to twenty years, while making possible sequential sentencing, up to a total of thirty years. Although the death penalty remains on the books, its application has been in temporary abeyance since the days of Gorbachev.

Probably even more important for keeping the average prison sentence low, however, was the great frequency with which prisoners were released because of group amnesties or administrative releases granted to individuals. Indeed, to judge at least by the *detektivy*, it appears that the commanders of individual prisons have the authority to release prisoners as they see fit. It is impossible to tell from available evidence how responsibly such decisions are made, but a newspaper article about criminals who had been granted amnesty in 1993 and 1994 makes it seem either that the camps rehabilitate people quickly, or that the commanders are extremely trusting. Among those granted amnesty, and their crimes, were:

- G. V. Kim, 33, convicted of organizing a gang that committed fourteen robberies and three murders in two months;
- G. A. Mikhaylov, 33, convicted of killing his boss in the factory where he worked; subsequently killed two fellow prisoners while in jail;
- P. E. Stakhovtsev, 49, a former senior official in the militia, convicted of armed robbery and responsible for two murders;
- V. V. Brovkin, 29, who had raped and killed two girls, ages 11 and 6; and
- B. S. Moiseyev, 56, who had used an ax to kill his girlfriend, and their 10-year-old son and 12-year-old daughter.[4]

The *detektivy* further suggest that criminals can be released even without amnesties and permitted to take short "vacations" on the outside if sufficiently powerful figures are interested in arranging such furloughs. In Raul Mir-Khaydarov's novel *Walkabouts,* for example, the heads of both of the criminal gangs that figure in the book use incarcerated criminals to do their dirty work on the outside, in one case for a period of six months (235). At least under the old Criminal Code, this "work release" arrangement had obvious advantages to both parties. The fifteen-year cap on sentencing meant that criminals need not fear any further legal repercussions for their actions, while their powerful patrons were always protected by the alibi that the alleged perpetrator was officially serving time in prison when the crime or crimes occurred. It was not just because sentences were short that the investigator in Adamov's novel speaks derisively of the Soviet prison system. More important is that there was not much relation between the magnitude of the person's crime and the retribution he was to suffer.

Nearly all *detektivy* imply in some way that punishment is unlikely to fit the crime in the Russian penal system. In some novels, this lack of faith is shown by the simple fact that some people receive longer sentences for lesser offenses than do other people who have committed what logic—or at least western logic—would suggest are more serious crimes. For example, in Vladimir Shitov's *Cathedral without Crosses*, a prisoner complains that he had received a ten-year sentence for stealing a peasant's suitcase, while another character, the novel's hero, got only eight years for stealing two kilograms of gold (135). Discrepancies of that magnitude, troubling as they may have been, were even greater in the Stalin years, when the model for the current Russian correctional system was created. One writer examining the relationship between the evolution of the labor colonies in Stalin's years and their present condition noted that in the early 1950s (when the maximum sentence was 25 years)

> One [inmate] paid bribes on the black market to rent an entire railroad train and received a 25-year sentence. Another had stolen a piece of wire, and got exactly the same sentence-'Theft of socialist property' in both cases. A lot of people were getting jailed for stealing wire then, because it was good for fixing shoes. Steal two truckloads of potatoes or two million rubles—twenty-five years. The guy who had murdered three people just walked around laughing—him they had given a sentence of ten years. (*Poyedinok No. 16*, 278–79)

Much more important than the suspicion that there is little relationship between crime and punishment, however, is the sense that certain groups of people can evade the law entirely. This was noted with particular bitterness by Mir-Khaydarov's crusading ex-procurator, in the novel *Walkabouts:*

> The procurator opens a case, conveys the materials to the court, and it would seem he has done his duty right up to the end, but there's no result. The court gets pressure from Party organs, and Soviet organs, from the People's Control, from Party Control, and next thing you know all that's left of the procu-

rator's demands is dust—this guy can't be touched, he's someone's brother, or someone's brother-in-law, or a deputy in the parliament [which in the Russian is the euphonious phrase "*brat, svat, deputat*"], or a Hero of Socialist Labor. One fellow whom prison is just aching to swallow up manages to wriggle off the hook, and then a second and a third, all of them with good protection and a solid rear guard, until they simply stop paying any attention to the procurator, because they think that laws aren't written for those who have power. (50)

In a great many *detektivy*, especially those that come from the late Soviet years, and even more those from the post-Soviet period, it seems that the characters not only are convinced that the law will not punish the powerful, but even worse, that any contact with the law on the part of the less powerful is likely to end poorly for that person, regardless of whether or not he or she has actually done anything. A vivid example of this is given in Andrey Kivinov's "Gone with the Wind," in which the militia discover that one of their suspects is living under a false name, using a passport and other documents which he has stolen. The man explains that he has been forced to assume this false identity because his record as a convict makes it impossible for him to get work or obtain the legal permission necessary for him to live in St. Petersburg. He explains further that his conviction had been unjust to begin with: One evening, he had been walking his girlfriend's German shepherd and had been attacked by a mugger, who attempted to steal his fur hat. The dog had chased and knocked down the mugger, ripping the man's ear in the process. Once the militia arrived, the mugger had insisted that the dog walker had been drunk and had only set the dog upon him because he was scolding the fellow for public drunkenness. The mugger proves to be the son of an important official, so the dog walker spends five months in Kresty Prison while awaiting trial, after which he is given the maximum possible sentence of eight years at hard labor (118). What may be the most revealing part about this tale, however, are not the inversions of justice that Kivinov suggests are possible in the Russian judicial system, but rather that the investigators to whom the man tells this story are inclined to doubt in the particular that his account is true. Meanwhile, they have absolutely no doubt that the statement is true in a general sense. As one investigator remarks to another, "I don't know, maybe that story about the dog is a lie too, but in principle that sort of thing is possible" (123).

The picture of the relationship between crime and punishment emerging from the *detektivy* suggests a system that is arbitrary and unpredictable in the extreme, both in the Soviet era and now, in post-Soviet Russia. To judge at least by the *detektivy*, people who are caught up in the Russian judicial system seem about equally likely to become punished by the system as to have their trammeled rights restored or defended. At least one western legal scholar has argued that this kind of arbitrariness is an inevitable consequence of a legal system that places rehabilitation above punishment. If the general purpose of incarceration is moral education, rather than retribution, there is little incentive for the judicial system to be overly scrupulous about crime and criminals, especially if the maximum possible period of reeducation is not especially onerous. In one scholar's words, "If the worst that can happen to the defendant is that he should be given a chance to have himself improved at public expense, why all the worry about a fair trial?" (Fuller, 165).

Students of the Soviet criminal justice system have suggested that a similar imprecision characterized most of Soviet law enforcement. Soviet censorship practices generally permitted public discussion of crime only as part of highly publicized campaigns of law enforcement, which usually did not have the goal of catching or stopping specific wrongdoers, but rather the broader purpose of instructing the public at large about what activities the state disapproved of. Since the goal of such campaigns was the improvement of society in general, the individuals chosen to illustrate such moral lessons, and the specific acts they had committed, were less important than was the overall lesson. As Maria Los notes in her study of Soviet law, the sporadic law enforcement campaigns of the post-Stalin years "do not seem to touch the core of the problem [of crime] and, in fact, do not even attempt to do so. Their main function is symbolic; moral campaigns are cheaper and ideologically more acceptable than economic and political reforms. They are designed to convey to the population the impression that some prevalent sources of evil are being dealt with" (165). As Los points out, though, the regime was less concerned with identifying and eliminating specific lawbreakers than it was with offering up representative examples for purposes of public education: "During these waves of mobilization of anticrime efforts and sentiments, there are always some people selected and sacrificed to fuel the campaign, to promote an image of the effectiveness and diligence of the criminal justice system and to demonstrate that the threat coming from those selfish individuals is very real and accounts for current malaises" (192).

Los appears to assume that the imprecise, "edifying" approach to law enforcement she is describing was a feature of the Soviet dependence upon propaganda, which sought to explain the persistent economic failures of the system by suggesting that the country was riddled with secret evildoers. In many ways, though, the Russian law enforcement system has grown even more imprecise since independence than it was in the Soviet period. There has, for example, been a great deal of public posturing about the many gangland and contract killings that have afflicted Russia since independence. These, however, have brought almost no arrests or convictions, even in such high-profile murder cases as that of senior member of Parliament Galina Starovoytova, gunned down on the stairs of her apartment building in November 1998 or of American businessman Paul Tatum, gunned down at a busy subway station in central Moscow in 1997. No doubt the extremely low rate of solution and conviction for such crimes is explained in part by the professionalism of Russia's paid assassins, who leave few clues, and also in part by the inadequate resources of training, equipment, and personnel that Russia's outclassed militia must endure. Such explanations do not serve, however, for such prominent, well-publicized crimes as the attempted overthrow of Gorbachev, in August 1991, or the attempted coup against Yeltsin, in October 1993. Some of the perpetrators of these widely publicized acts were convicted and even imprisoned, but none served long sentences, instead being freed by pardons or in amnesties. Indeed, one of the most prominent figures in the October 1993 coup attempt is Aleksandr Rutskoy, who subsequently was elected governor of Kursk *oblast*, thus making him, among other things, responsible for law enforcement in his region. Members of Russia's Duma are constitutionally protected against criminal prosecution. This has allowed, for example, at least one member (Col. Albert Makashov) to openly violate Russia's laws about making racially incendiary statements and is rumored to have protected many others against investigation of their financial and other dealings. Indeed, this freedom from possible prosecution is said to be a major inducement prompting wealthy lawbreakers to run for parliamentary office.

The impunity with which some members of Russian society seem able to flout or ignore the law is matched by the culpability that other members seem to bear simply because of their existence. Law enforcement and other officials deny it, but there is considerable anecdotal evidence that Moscow and perhaps other big cities have dealt with the growing numbers of Russia's newly homeless by periodically rounding them up and dumping them in the countryside, far beyond the city limits. Russia's battles against separatists in Chechnya, which compound a general public suspicion of "people of Caucasian nationality" (rendered in Russian by a phrase that can also mean literally "*faces* of Caucasian nationality"), have encouraged officials indiscriminately to demand identity papers and residence permits of Russian citizens based solely upon their appearance, rather than upon any other kind of probable cause. At times, this has been the justification for wholesale expulsions of dark-skinned peoples, regardless of whether or not they had legal permission to live and work where they were found. Indeed, although there is some argument about it, most Russian legal experts agree that Russia's continued reliance upon the *propiska* system, a Stalin-era practice that attempts to limit the population of big cities and popular locales by requiring that residents obtain legal permission to reside in a particular place, is itself a violation of the 1993 Russian constitution. However, Russia's officials continue to rely upon this system as a principle foundation of public control.

Similarly, Russia's Criminal Procedure Code, in effect since the 1960s, is also in formal violation of Russia's Constitution. The latter decrees that investigation and incarceration are under the supervision of the judiciary, while the former, which controls how things are actually done, keeps those procedures under the purview of the procuracy, just as was true in Soviet, and even in tsarist, times.

Perhaps even more unsettling than official disregard of the law is that many Russian law enforcement officials continue to enforce laws that no longer exist, or that they know are soon to disappear. It was reported in 1996, for example, that, even though the new Criminal Code had been drawn up, and the date when it would come into effect had been announced, the militia were continuing to investigate acts that would soon cease to be criminal, most prominently those involving dollars and other hard currency. In 1995, Soviet-era currency laws were used to convict 3,322 people for illegal use of hard currency; they were part of the larger contingent of 36,552 Russian citizens who were sent to jail between 1993 and 1996 for acts that ceased to be criminal on January 1, 1997. Among them were persons prosecuted for violations of statutes concerning "socialist property," a term applied by the Russian courts as late as 1994.[5] Equally suggestive, little has been made public about the fates of individuals who were sent to prison at the end of the Gorbachev era for such Soviet-era crimes as "speculation" or "indolence" (*tuneyadstvo*), suggesting that at least some of those arrested for crimes against the socialist order continued to be punished for their crimes long after the socialist system itself had disappeared.

It is not difficult for westerners to understand how the arbitrary nature of such a system might encourage its citizens to view Russia's judicial system cynically, particularly once the Soviet system collapsed. Thus, some students of Russia have seen it as both logical and inevitable that post-Soviet Russia would suffer a proliferation of criminal bands. In the words of Tim McDaniel, "Uncertainty about the future is one of the sources of the mafia's strength in contemporary Russia. Confronted by the prospect of a hostile new society unwilling to protect them, many young people surrendered themselves to these groups that gave some sense of belonging and provided immediate material benefits" (185).

What may be harder for westerners to understand is why there has not been more pressure to change the arbitrary workings of the Russian judicial system, especially in the post-Soviet years when such citizens' initiatives should—in theory at least—be easier than they were in the Soviet period. Some of the dimensions of the answer to this conundrum have already been touched upon. The widespread Russian conviction that laws drawn up by humans will be imperfect, and hence unjust, is surely part of the reason, as is a wider uncertainty about what the core values of Russia now are, and should be. As commentators like McDaniel have noted, whatever its other failings may have been, the communist system at least had the virtue of moralizing the arbitrary actions of the legal code. The goals and aims the Soviet system claimed to be pursuing were so inarguably lofty, and of such general human benefit if they were to be achieved, that specific errors or misapplications of the laws seemed a small enough price to pay for the attempt. The more chaotic and ill-defined market economy system that has replaced communism does not seem to have a consistent set of core values, or, perhaps more precisely, has not been able to explain why capitalism, once adopted, should be constrained by law, custom, or morality. This Russian inability to justify the laws and practices by which westerners are accustomed to softening and controlling the competitive struggle that capitalism imposes is reflected in the great number of *detektivy* that explore the question of how a person without money is supposed to survive in the post-Soviet commercial culture. These novels agree that it remains wrong for someone to kill another person for material gain, but they seem uncertain of why, or at least of how to articulate it. Even Aleksandra Marinina, who shows no nostalgia for the Soviet system in her works, and who has personally benefited substantially from the coming of a western-style economy to Russia, nevertheless remarks in one of her books,

> [Kamenskaya, the heroine] was totally unable to understand why a man who knew three foreign languages was able to live in such a comfortable and pretty house, while another person who knew five languages [i.e., Kamenskaya herself], and who furthermore was doing good for society with her hard, dirty, but oh-so-necessary work [as a criminal investigator], why that second person was forced by her income to live in a tiny little crowded apartment with a combined toilet and shower. She did not for a moment allow that her [now-rich] former lover was not an honest man—he was neither a thief nor a con man. And his money was clean, honestly earned. Just, there was a certain, well, incorrectness perhaps, in the way that our life today is constructed. (*Stylist*, 170)

If You Live with Wolves, Best Learn How to Howl

The most startling reason the *detektiv* suggests for the Russian citizens' disinclination to create a more consistent and predictable criminal code, however, is that most Russians do not appear to see a strong distinction between lawbreakers and themselves. To a certain extent, this is the "Russian sympathy" of which Viktor Astafyev complained in his *Sad Detective*. It is also related to the ways in which, as has been explained in chapter 2, the socialized economy of the Soviet Union forced even honest, well-intentioned citizens into the necessity for eternal compromise. The result of that constant struggle against shortages was perhaps put most succinctly by Andrei Sinyavsky, a dissident writer whose conviction for "anti-Soviet activities" in 1968 gave him the opportunity to observe Soviet society from both sides of the prison bars. As Sinyavsky put it, "In the broadest sense . . . every Soviet citizen is, by definition and necessity, a criminal."[6] The mechanisms of this universal criminalization have been explored more fully by other commentators. Tim McDaniel, for example, explains in *The Agony of the Russian Idea* how

> de facto every position under developed socialism gave rights of private use of public resources: in other words, it allowed for corruption, and in a certain sense depended upon individual initiative. But perhaps corruption is not the right word, for the practice was so universal and accepted that it has to be regarded as part of the conservative self-perpetuation of the system. . . . In the

economy of shortages, positions allowed people monopolistic control of resources that could be bartered for other scarce goods. Despite the formally
state-run system of distribution, individual entrepreneurship [took place] on
a universal scale. . . . Negotiation, bargaining, and informal exchange were
ubiquitous. . . . Although economically irrational, this whole system had
enormous implications for social stability: it gave everyone a stake in the system and also made everyone complicitous in formally illegal activity. (141)

During the Soviet period, westerners tended to be highly sympathetic toward most Russian lawbreakers, assuming that it was either the country's
ubiquitous economic shortages or its attempts to impose ideological
thought control that drove most Soviet citizens to skirt or violate their nation's laws. The implication of this sympathy is that a nation's right to impose laws upon its citizens is, at least to a certain extent, dependent upon
that nation's ability to provide its citizens with an unspecified, but large,
supply of goods and services. If it is unable to provide these, citizens are then
to be tacitly permitted to provide for themselves what the state cannot, even
if they circumvent laws and established morality in order to do so.

To western readers, the tendency of the Soviet-era *detektivy* to depict the
USSR as an overly generous but loving mother who is being plucked bare
by a small band of greedy entrepreneurs and other people with western
business instincts thus seems either naïve or crudely propagandistic. It is
difficult, for example, for a western reader to share the authorial scorn that
Ivan Shevtsov intends to lavish upon his Prishelets, in *Theft*, by having the
fellow gloat that

> For his skills and character, the USSR was an absolutely ideal country, almost
> what one might call the Promised Land. Here he had flourished without es-
> pecial effort or risk. There [abroad] he did not see any open room for his ac-
> tivities as a "free entrepreneur," as he liked jokingly to call himself. Over there
> even the mafia has strict laws. Here [in the USSR] though there is almost no
> competition, just open land and unplowed virgin prairie. (131)

What westerners failed to appreciate in their sympathy for the Soviet
Union's budding entrepreneurs, however, was that a citizenry grown accustomed to skirting or flouting laws—even unjust and illogical laws—is also
going to grow ever more unlikely to respect state authority of any sort. The
progressively corrosive quality of corruption was, however, clearly understood by at least some Soviet authorities. In 1990, a commentator wrote in
Soviet Militia, the professional journal for Soviet law enforcers, that "In

conditions [of constant shortages] the market gradually turns everything into something to be bought and sold . . . jobs, ranks, laws, personal integrity, even social justice."[7]

There is a passage in Adamov's *Into an Empty Space* that illustrates eloquently why the instinctive western sympathy for those who connived and contrived to get around Soviet-era laws was probably misplaced. The words are those of a powerful criminal boss, whom the hero, Inspector Losev, has agreed to meet over dinner in a restaurant, thus providing neutral ground on which the criminal can try to persuade the inspector that he and his band are in fact not doing anything bad and should be left in peace. The villain explains that

> Everyone wants to live his life in his own way. . . . [Some] want to serve society, refusing themselves many things personally, or doing without. There aren't many of these people right now. Romantics and idealists, these are limited and nearsighted people. The majority of people . . . an enormous majority . . . these are materialists, energetic, practical people without sentiment. They understand that the most important thing right now is material comfort, which is the only thing that they are willing to work for. And I don't mean work for the sake of their grandchildren and great-grandchildren, but for themselves, so that life gets better not in a century, but today, right now. Better for you personally, and not necessarily for everybody. . . . There are different kinds of people in this last category . . . one of them, let's say, grows early cucumbers or tomatoes in his plot and then is the first to get them to market, while a second has a knack for repairing all kinds of electrical things . . . and a third is an ambitious demagogue who pursues his own advancement, travelling abroad and giving lots of orders, while a fourth kind shortweights customers and sells bad goods, and a fifth kind studies our planned economy, our system of supply, and figures out ways to get rich. (438)

It is the collapse of the Soviet system, and its replacement with a more western-style economy, that makes Adamov's passage so instructive. The requirements of the market economy reverse the moral value signs on most of the activities this villain cites. All of them were violations of Soviet law at the time he was making this argument; working harder to be the first to bring vegetables to market, or translating a knack for fixing small appliances into a livelihood, are elegant illustrations of the very meaning of a market economy. Even the "ambitious demagogue who pursues his own advancement," if described in more positive vocabulary as the builder of a business empire, is a figure whom western social and economic models would celebrate.

However, the fact that short-weighting remains a crime, and thus morally reprehensible even in a market economy, highlights the way in which permitting citizens to violate one set of laws can lead them to violate others. To westerners, the Russian inability to see a distinction between the "good" entrepreneurship of planting early cucumbers and the "bad" entrepreneurship of short-weighting may seem no more than naivete, but in fact it derives from the absence in Russian legal practice of two other features of western law. Most legal philosophers appear to agree that human commercial behavior is generally governed by what economists call the economics of marginal utility, by which is meant that humans make decisions based upon the greatest possible utilization of their economic resources. Thus, in the case both of ambitious vegetable marketing and of surreptitious short-weighting, the economic actor is seeking the greatest possible return on available resources. However, as legal philosopher Lon Fuller explains, marginal utility has come in western practice to be tempered by the economics of exchange.

> Before the principle of marginal utility nothing is sacred; all existing arrangements are subject to being reordered in the interest of increased economic return. The economics of exchange is, in contrast, based on two fixed points, property and contract. While it permits interested calculation to reign everywhere else, such calculation is excluded when the question is fidelity of contract or respect for property. Without self-sacrificing deference toward these institutions, a regime of exchange would lose its anchorage and no one would occupy a sufficiently stable position to know what he had to offer or what he could count on receiving from another. (28)

While it can easily be shown that Russians do not understand the principle of contracts in precisely the same way as westerners, it can be taken as given that the principle to which Fuller alludes is sufficiently well accepted in Russia that it can serve as a bulwark against the excesses of marginal utility; not so, however, with the Russian attitude toward property. As has been demonstrated both here and elsewhere, the Russian attitude toward property is highly ambivalent, in particular resisting the notion that property rights should take absolute precedence over human need. In the Russian context, people who choose to make property more important than people are immoral precisely because they have "lost their anchorage," and thus are pushing their own advantage under the economics of marginal utility.

To the great majority of Russians who still would not agree that property rights stand higher than people, the economic activities that the mafia chieftain outlines in Adamov's passage are easily understood to be part of a single moral continuum, even in the changed economic conditions of post-Soviet Russia. It is probably for the same reason that, as chapter 2 has detailed, none of the new *detektivy* portray business activity as even morally neutral, to say nothing of positive. Rather, business leads child-hood friends to murder one another (Kivinov, "Track of the Boomerang") or forces a beautiful young woman to become the mistress of a publisher she actively loathes (Marinina, *Stylist*) or causes otherwise honest investi-gators to lie, conceal evidence, and go against their own consciences (Yakovleva, *All Joking Aside*). Marinina, the reigning queen of the new genre, attempts at least a positive nod toward Russia's new economy by making her heroine's half-brother into a successful banker, but she is nev-ertheless unable to restrain her heroine's distaste for her half-brother's power. The general disposition of the *detektivy* toward the business activi-ties that have become so prominent a feature of the post-Soviet environ-ment, and which westerners find so positive, may be summed up in words from another of Marinina's novels, when her investigator-heroine confesses that she "doubted whether there are *any* commercial firms nowadays that work totally honestly" (*Stolen Dream*, 36).

Implicit in Marinina's comment, of course, is the Russian distinction be-tween legality and justice already discussed. The fact that it is legal does not, to the Russian mentality, make business righteous. At least in the esti-mation of the genre, the laws of new Russia remain as complicated, entan-gling, and contradictory as were the laws of the Soviet era. As one of Kivi-nov's heroes remarks, "Take a look, our law is made up of nothing but contradictions. And it's made up like that on purpose! And that's why it never changes!" ("Track of the Boomerang," 231). This same confusion also infects less cynical characters. Nikolay Ivanov includes among the few pos-itive characters of his *Tax Police* a gruff, uncomplicated inspector much like the standard positive hero of the "high Soviet" *detektivy*, who now finds it all but impossible to work:

> Morzharetov had never thought so much about his work. In field work, in the MVD [the militia, or police], to set out a net for a criminal, then drive him into a trap, to save someone from danger, how much thought and analysis does that require? Just work, as is worthy of your name and your rank. But now there were these incomplete laws, you had to figure out the balance of forces in the government, which changed at least once a quarter, and only then could you begin to make your plans. (79)

The issue the new *detektivy* find most morally complex is the necessity to have money that Russia's new economic and social structures impose upon its people. Although none of the new *detektivy* are prepared to state that wealth is definitionally bad, none of them offers positive visions of ways in which wealth might be acquired, and most of them illustrate the various pitfalls into which people desperate to get money might stumble. Mention has already been made of works such as Kivinov's "Made from Waste Products" and Marinina's *Small Fry Die First*, each of which features sympathetic characters who are forced by economic exigencies to become contract killers. Similar characters figure in Anna Danilova's *I'm Coming to Find You*, in which a pretty young woman becomes a prostitute and drug peddler because this is the only profession she can find that offers steady work and doesn't require elaborate training, and in Marinina's *The Bright Face of Death*, in which two young women take for granted that they should trade their bodies for the opportunity to travel to Turkey.

What all of these novels share, in essence, is the same aversion to bourgeois life as that articulated by Karl Marx when he identified the chief attribute—and to him chief flaw—of western life to be that, when man "treats others as means, [he] reduces himself to the role of means, and becomes the plaything of alien forces" (Fuller, 26).

The Legal Need Not Be Just, So the Just Need Not Be Legal

Western readers may easily sympathize with individual characters who are forced into crime by financial exigency, much like the actress in Yelena Yakovleva's *All Joking Aside*, who has had all her jewels and clothing stolen by her maid, but who then pleads with the militia that the thief be released, because the woman would have stolen only because she needed the money. That sympathy, however, is still very different from the Russian sympathy of which Viktor Astafyev complained in *Sad Detective* as early as 1986. As we have seen, Russian experience and conviction adds to the broader human sympathy for an unlucky or unhappy person the more specific ingredient—that the main distinction between a criminal and a citizen is simply that the latter has not yet been caught. Thus, in the new system as in the old, the state's imposition of a punishment for a crime looks arbitrary to most Russians, another calamity brought down upon a fellow sufferer, rather than the due retribution of an impartial and equitable system.

The Russian tolerance for crime is best illustrated by the rapidity and completeness with which society has been taken over by well-organized criminal bands, who by some estimates may control as much as 80 percent of Russia's economy. A large portion of these bands are the *vory*, or thieves, who collectively are known as the *blatari*, or *blatnyye*. The latter terms are usually also translated as "criminals" or "thieves," but they derive from another Russian word, *blat*, which connotes extrasystemic influence or power. *Blat* is something that powerful people possess and may dispense to less powerful supplicants who seek from them the goods, services, or other benefits for which they otherwise would have no access. The full meaning of the word may be appreciated through one of the criminal world's slang terms for earth's sun: *blatnoy sharik*, or "ball of *blat*."[8]

The *blatnoy mir*, or "thieves' world," thus combines both criminality and power. Although it has to a great extent merged into the mixture of corrupt government officials, new businessmen, and outright criminals that Russians now call the mafia (the word has become so thoroughly Russified that its Italian origins have almost been forgotten), the *blatnoy mir* originated well before the collapse of the Soviet Union. Historians know of well-established gangs of thieves and other criminals who worked Moscow and other big cities at the end of the nineteenth century,[9] and some historians would even trace them as far back as the thirteenth century, and the invasion of the Mongols.[10]

Unlike the newer criminals of the mafia, or the dim-witted amateurs-of-opportunity who feature in most Soviet-era *detektivy*, the *vory* of the traditional *blatnoy mir* are members of a strictly controlled, well-defined subculture within Russian society who identify themselves to one another, and to the outside world, by elaborate systems of behavior. These include vivid homemade tattoos, coded to signal not only a man's prison record and his relative status among his fellow *vory*, but also to show his criminal specialty. Importantly, these specializations are strictly adhered to, enforced by the draconian "thieves' law." Thieves also have a separate language called *fenya* (or *ofeniya*), which uses the grammatical structure of Russian but has virtually an entirely separate vocabulary stock. The origins of *fenya* are a matter of considerable debate among linguists and criminologists, but most agree that the vocabulary includes words from Ukrainian, Polish, Turkic, and western European languages.[11] Other sources include Yiddish, Romany, and the jargons of other Russian subgroups, especially sailors.[12]

Although the *vory* came into existence because their activities were criminal, it is important to understand that criminality as such is only an incidental, rather than a necessary and defining, feature of these bands. In the words of one prison camp memoir: "You think thief [*vor*] means someone who stole something, but that's wrong. It's possible not to steal anything, and still be a *vor*, or you can steal your entire life, but not be considered a *vor*."[13] Available evidence suggests that the world of the thieves and that of ordinary Soviet citizens remained fairly well separated until the middle of the 1970s, when the thieves began to penetrate into Soviet power structures. According to one official account of this process of criminalization, it was prompted by jealousy among the thieves, who noted the increasingly lavish scale on which corrupt Soviet officials and administrators were permitting themselves to live. The thieves determined to force these corrupt officials to share their illegal proceeds, on the principle that "You're a thief and I'm a thief, but you are living in luxury without particular effort or risk, while I have to work hard and be at risk, all to earn bread and bread-beer (*kvas*), often enough in 'places not so far away' [i.e., in prison]."[14] As explained by Soviet experts from the militia, this period of forced "contribution" was rapidly replaced by the realization that the traditional criminal world and Soviet power structures could serve one another to enormous mutual advantage, particularly since the kinds of favors that state and party administrators might do for the *vory* were frequently functions they were supposed to perform anyway, but for purposes of advancing the state's interests, rather than their own. If something the *vory* wanted of the administrators did happen to be formally illegal, the administrators often had the power simply to change the laws. This fusion of *vory* and corrupt Soviet administrators created what one group of Soviet legal experts called a "paracriminal world."[15]

Equally important, however, the romance and swagger of the thieves' world also began to capture the Soviet public imagination, perhaps in part because rigid censorship and the dull uniformity of public entertainment in the late Brezhnev years made the thieves' world seem attractive by comparison. Movies such as Vasiliy Shukshin's *Red Berries of the Snowball Bush* and the wildly popular underground songs of the talented actor and songwriter Vladimir Vysotskiy began to bring not just the vocabulary but also the ethos of the *blatnoy mir* into mainstream Russian society.

Once it could take public notice of the growing popularity of the thieves' world, the Soviet literary establishment was—not surprisingly—against the phenomenon. Anatoliy Udintsev's hero in "Search" explodes when he finds one of the two escaped prisoners for whom he has been searching in the taiga, murdered by his supposed partner.[16] Gazing at the disfigured corpse, the chief investigator barks, "I wish I could show this to the fools who hang around stairwells and courtyards, bellowing their thieves' songs! To say nothing of showing it to the people who are crippling the souls of the young with romantic nonsense about thieves!" (260).

If the growing frequency of thieves' jargon in daily Russian language was any indicator, such disapproval had little effect on the growing popularity of at least the outer attributes of the *blatnoy mir*. When *fenya* first began to appear in the *detektivy*, the attitude of both writers and the militia they depict seems to have been much like that in Lyubov Arestova's "Last Clue." There a young militiaman, wishing to appear tough, dashes off a bit of thieves' jargon, for which he is immediately scolded by his superior.

> Alik, have some care with the jargon there. We don't much like it around here. . . .Why should an investigator know jargon? So that the criminals can't fool him, so that he can know where he is in any situation. . . . Stupid investigators throw those kinds of empty words around, to show off. And so they descend to the level of the thieves, when they should be above them. (96)

Unfortunately for those who would have had the militia defend Russian grammar while also defending Russian society, thieves' jargon offered too many advantages to be kept out of the *detektivy* for long; *fenya* is a salty, colorful, and highly evocative language, particularly adept at expressing the nuances of the gritty underside of Russian life. Increasingly, thieves' jargon seems to have become the language in which the militia and the criminals communicated with one another, so that any author of *detektivy* who continued to have his characters speak classical Russian inevitably seemed inauthentic. Indeed, as Nikita Filatov acutely notes in his post-Soviet story "4:15 Moscow Time," reality and fiction began to imitate one another, as the real militia strove to appear more like the militiamen who figured in books and films. Filatov's character Vinogradov, a former militia inspector now turned private eye, thinks, as he is questioned by a tough-guy cop, "I wonder who they imitated before there were movies and TV? Stage actors? . . . And what about ordinary people? How did they talk to each other without [crime films and TV movies] to imitate?" (215). In another story in the same collection, Filatov suggests that matters may even have reached the point that, as Vinogradov muses, "Even the thieves

aren't as hot to use thieves' jargon as are the operations teams of our glo-
rious militia" (16–17). Much the same point is made in "Four Sheets of
Plywood" by Yevgeniy Kozlovskiy. At one point, Alina, a crackerjack journalist, and Bogdan Mazepa, the ace detective whom she is interviewing,
begin to quarrel about where they should have lunch. Mazepa suggests a
private (non-state) restaurant, where the service will be better "because
they have to shave bucks off the beam" (*babki nado strogat*).

> "I just hate it," Alina's pent-up anger boiled over, "when the cops [*menty*] use
> jargon!"
> "Not me," Mazepa parried, "I love it when lady reporters use words like
> '*menty!*'" (371)

However, accounts of the internal structure of the thieves' world make it
seem probable that it was much more than the criminals' vocabulary that
made the *blatari* appealing to the broader mass of the Russian public. Valeriy
Chalidze compares the structure of the typical criminal band to that of the
artel.[17] The artels were the typical economic units into which Russian peasants
organized themselves when they left the estates to which they belonged, moving to the cities or elsewhere in Russia to earn the money to pay their tithes or
quit-rents (or, as Dostoyevsky discusses in *Notes from the House of the Dead*,
when fate threw them into prison); normally these artels were small groups of
men, most of whom (though not necessarily all) came from the same region,
who lived together, engaged in a common economic purpose, and shared the
costs and benefits of their living and labor on a communal basis. Decisions in
the artels were taken communally, tempered by deference to the authority of
older and more experienced members. Even when there was a single acknowledged leader, he directed the artel as the first among equals, with the ultimate goal always being the greater well-being of the group.

The anatomy of the typical criminal band makes the reasons for
Chalidze's comparison plain. Criminal bands are established on regional or
territorial lines and are vertically structured, but without a rigid command
system. In general, there seem to be only three layers in such gangs—a
small collective of leaders, a larger number of gang members, and an in-
definite number of apprentices, hangers-on, and "wannabes." Authority is
conferred on the senior criminals by mutual assent of the gang members,
and also requires the affirmation of the senior thieves from other bands.
Curiously, one of the terms used for such senior criminals is *avtoritet*, the
same term that sociologist Oleg Kharkhordin uses to denote figures like

Aleksandr Solzhenitsyn and Andrey Sakharov in their roles as moral leaders of informal dissident circles in the Soviet era. Quoting another Russian sociologist, Kharkhordin distinguishes between the English notion of "authority"—which he terms "power of a legitimate type," suggesting that it is state-sanctioned—and the Russian *avtoritet*—"a phenomenon of a purely informal order. In its pure form it is based exclusively on the respect a concrete individual pays to another concrete individual."[18]

As noted, the various members of groups have criminal specialities, each of which is hallowed by tradition, and bears a jargon name that does not seem to have changed at least since the time of the revolution. The criminal leaders do not appear to direct the activities of members, beyond requiring that they stay within the confines of their specialities, and observe the main points of the "law": they may not have families; they may not work for the government; they must treat other thieves "honorably" (i.e., according to the thieves' law); and they must contribute to the common fund, or *obshchak*. Violation of these rules seems to be punished swiftly, but all accounts speak of the insistence that punishments be shaped by "justice"—the same *spravedlivost* discussed in the preceding chapter. In an article about corruption published in *Soviet Militia*, the authors observed dryly that "the word 'justice' is to be heard no less frequently in the mouths of thieves (*vory*) than it is in the mouths of politicians during an election campaign."[19] The aptness of their observation is demonstrated by remarks about Anatoliy Bykov, who in 1998 was a powerful business and political figure in Krasnoyarsk, but by 1999 was in jail in Hungary under indictment for racketeering, and by 2000 was back in Krasnoyarsk, apparently still in possession of most of his ill-gotten fortune. Noting that he would help those who came to him for assistance—including giving an old woman a new stove—an admiring constituent said of Bykov,

> You know, he is just [*spravedlivyy*]. He doesn't stick his nose into things that aren't his affair. . . . Or into little businesses either. He lets them develop without bothering them. But what is his is his. He won't let anyone near what's his. People respect him in the region because he is strong and just.[20]

What guarantees that the sanctions the thieves impose on one another are "just" is that decisions are taken communally, in conferences of senior criminal authorities. However, sources seem divided as to whether the *vory* view the fruits of their labor as individual or collective property. Chalidze, whose evidence is based upon the mid-1970s, speaks of criminal bands dividing all of the proceeds of their members' activities more or less equally, with some consideration given for the additional effort one or more members may have contributed to pulling off a particular crime (47). More recent observers suggest that individual criminals have responsibility only to contribute a significant portion of a crime's "take" to the gang's *obshchak*, after which the disposition of the remainder of a crime's profits is at the discretion of the perpetrator. One thing that does not seem to be permitted, however, is for a gang member to view such profits as capital, to be saved or invested. The ethos of the *blatari* is as anti-material as that of other parts of Russian society, and so thieves are expected to blow their money as quickly as possible on clothes, women, and restaurants.

The purposes of the *obshchak* seem originally to have been narrowly defined, primarily to meet the needs of gang members who were in labor camps (including paying necessary bribes). Since the *obshchak* could not be used to support thieves outside of prison—a strict requirement of the "law" was that a thief must live on the proceeds of his craft—the common funds seem to have become large pools of cash. Once changes in Russia's laws of economic activity made it possible, those funds proved ready sources for investment, allowing the criminal gangs to move quickly into the joint ventures and import-export activities that marked Russia's first steps toward capitalism. According to at least some students of Russian crime, the huge amounts of cash in the *obshchaki* also were useful for paying the bribes necessary to move not only individual decisions, but, increasingly, Russia's legal structures in ways that were beneficial to the *vory v zakone*—the "made guy" criminal authorities who coordinated and oversaw the criminal bands. In the words of militia experts who studied this criminalization of late Soviet society, "the cooperative movement proved a 'golden vein,' a Soviet Klondike, for organized crime."[21] It is important to stress, however, that while the *obshchaki* may increasingly have come to function like investment funds, their ownership and the benefits they generated appear to have remained collective, rather than individual.

Although there is some evidence of female *vory*, the thieves' world is overwhelmingly masculine. The ethics of their law does not forbid thieves to take wives, but primary allegiance and affection is owed to the band and its members, rather than to a wife or children. Indeed, a wife or female companion is viewed as a "resource" who might be offered to a fellow gang member, put up as stakes in a card game, or passed to a fellow thief when the "husband" is sent to prison.

Although none of the available sources about the *blatnoy mir* seem to address the question directly, most factual sources, as well as the fictional depictions of this world in the *detektivy*, suggest that the thieves also tend to share the attitudes of the wider Russian populace when it comes to choosing the victims of their crimes. State property, or that of large impersonal corporations, seems to be targeted more frequently than that of individuals, and rich individuals are victimized more often than poor ones. As previously explained, experts hypothesize that corrupt Soviet officials brought the *vory* down upon themselves in part because of the grand scale on which they had begun to live, but even more because the thieves perceived this wealth to be unearned, which therefore made it "just" that this wealth should be shared. Conversely, popular accounts, at least, maintained that *vory* were reluctant to steal from those who earned their living by the sweat of their brow, especially if they had little. As the previous chapter describes, there are even accounts of *vory* who feel such pity for the poverty of their victims that they leave money, rather than take it. Such legends help explain the ambiguous regard in which Russians have tended historically to hold thieves. They may hate small thieves, especially if they themselves are victims, but they tend to revere and mythologize large-scale successful thieves, provided that such thieves take from people who possess more than they can have acquired through their own labor, and share it with those who have already had part or all of the fruits of their labor taken from them by overlords, masters, and tsars. Such a formulation recognizes the persistent Russian tendency to distinguish between property to which people are viewed as having some right—most prominently the immediate land they personally till, but in a larger sense the objects that they have created by their labor, or that they use to earn their living—and those other kinds of property that seem to adhere to the rich without reason or justice, such as landholdings too large to be worked, income based on interest or stock shares, and other forms of "undeserved" wealth. A crucial element of the stories about Russia's famous criminals—the legendary Solovey Razboynik ("Nightingale the Brigand") or the historical brigands Stenka Razin (of the seventeenth century), and Emilyan Pugachyov (of the eighteenth)—is precisely that these criminals were returning to Russia's poor the property that the rich had earlier snatched away from them, rather than taking the property for their own enjoyment. Indeed, one of the most famous legends about Stenka Razin is that, when his men complained that the brigand appeared to enjoy his new bride, a captured Persian princess, more than he did them, Razin obligingly chucked the poor girl into the Volga.

In short, while specific features may seem objectionable to most Russians, the basic characteristics of the *blatnoy mir* are essentially those that a great many Russians still consider to be important to a just and properly run society. Power among the *vory* is diffuse but local, administered by structures that are hierarchical, yet still communal. Thieves' "laws" are simple and strictly enforced, but "crimes" against them are considered as unique events, adjudicated collectively to seek "just" solutions, following principles that place the preservation of group harmony above the satisfaction of individual claims or complaints. The thieves have contempt for material things, yet suffer no material privations, enjoying a brief but raucous life of wine, women, and song. Their way of life rewards ingenuity and daring, yet their lives themselves are clearly understood to be subordinate to the whims of chance, thus freeing thieves both of the burden of planning in advance and of accepting responsibility for failure afterward, should fortune choose not to smile upon them. The similarity of so many features of the *blatnoy mir* to those that a large part of the wider Russian public supports and desires thus makes understandable, even logical, the otherwise startling fact that, at least according to a survey conducted in 1997, a full 80 percent of the Russians polled admitted that they trusted the criminal world more than they did the militia or the state.[22]

The Social Purpose of the *Detektiv*: Russia's Two "Big Questions"

It has already been remarked that the *detektiv* flourished particularly at the end of the Gorbachev era, when the genre seemed especially well suited to exploring, and thus explaining, the many failures of everyday Soviet life. Since, as Tim McDaniel points out, "Poor performance was not rooted in weak organization or lack of resources, but in sabotage by enemies" (96), the reflex of Russian thought is not to ask "What is going wrong?" but rather to demand to know "Who is guilty?" Thus, the *detektiv*, with its general structure of depicting a crime, then searching for that crime's perpetrator, was a perfect vehicle for attempting to answer this very Russian question of "*Kto vinovat?*" ("Who is guilty?") for the poor work, venal self-interest, and other failings that had brought the USSR to the sorry condition in which the late 1980s found it.

While not explicit, or even necessarily articulated, the only conceivable purpose of seeking to find out "who is guilty" is to answer the other traditional "Big Question" of Russian literature—"*Chto delat?*" or "What is to be done?" At its most programmatic, of course, the answer to this question must take the didactic form of the worst kind of ideological novel, as is exemplified by Nikolay Chernyshevsky's eponymous novel of 1863. In a broader sense, however, all crime fiction—in Russia and elsewhere—is, by implication, a way of illustrating how life on this planet might be improved. While few crime novels, and probably none of the better ones, actually make fully explicit the morals on which they are based, the genre exists precisely to illustrate the consequences of violating laws and principles that the authors (and their readership) hold dear, and thus to suggest that one way to avoid these consequences is not to commit the acts.

By its nature then, crime fiction everywhere is in the business of moral education, a fact about the genre that is multiplied many times in Russia, where both readers and writers are in the habit of understanding the purpose of literature to be educational and uplifting. As Igor Vinnichenko put it in his novel *Honeymoon,* "Even reading *detektivy* can sometimes be good for the soul," an overt social purpose for the genre that is echoed by publisher Stanislav Gagarin's claim that a "milkmaid from Vologda" (the Russian equivalent of "a housewife from Topeka") has written to him to express her hopes that her two sons will receive a proper moral education in reading Gagarin's books.[23]

As has been noted, though, the moral "map" underlying the *detektiv* can seem contradictory, even baffling. In the *detektivy,* good guys lie, cheat, steal, and even kill, while bad guys do things like work two jobs, manufacture goods consumers want to buy, and wear nice clothes. The key to understanding such apparent contradictions, however, is to see the larger purpose for which the actions were committed. At least the *detektiv* genre, and presumably the Russian readership, will consider actions committed for an individual end or benefit to be bad, while actions committed for some larger communal purpose—even if these violate laws or have tragic consequences—are going to be seen as good.

The question this formulation begs, however, is how to distinguish between genuine social heroes and the characters like Mir-Khaydarov's Shubarin and the *tolkachi* or "fixers," of whom Ardamatskiy, Bezuglov, and Shevtsov wrote in the mid-1980s, who claimed to be skirting the state's laws in order to serve the broader social good of "the people." As chapter 3 has demonstrated, for most of the Soviet period, and even for the imperial period which preceded it, the question of who genuinely had good social intentions and who had individual, and therefore bad, intentions for the acts they committed was usually decided on a formal, rather than an intrinsic basis. Only those whom the state empowered to act—the militiamen, the *syshchiki,* and the *sledovateli*—could be considered "communal," while those who acted on their own initiative were individuals and thus reprehensible, even when pursuing what they perceived to be the interests of the state. The earnest *tolkachi* of the early Gorbachev era are the best illustration of the primacy of the state over even the best-hearted of private intentions. As novels like Ardamatskiy's *Trial* and Bezuglov's *Criminals* show, the fixers' individual attempts to resolve the paradox of having to steal from the state in order to meet the responsibilities which the state has placed upon them become evil precisely because they are individual.

However, the growing realism of the Gorbachev era increasingly made it clear that a state uniform did not automatically make its wearer into a good person, thus posing more sharply the fundamental question lying beneath the moral structure of the *detektiv.* How is it possible to distinguish genuinely social-minded motivations from individualistic ones? The search for answers to this question became even more urgent (for most Russians at least) after 1991, when the Russian world was essentially stood on its head. "Speculation," "parasitism," and "greed" now became "entrepreneurship," "individual initiative," and "ambition." Benefits of citizenship like health care, education, and recreation now became commercial commodities, to be purchased by those who had money, and foregone by those who didn't. Formerly high-status jobs such as teacher, poet, army officer, and law-enforcement official now became low-paid (or, all too frequently, unpaid) objects of derision, while the black marketeers and speculators of the recent past suddenly became celebrated and powerful oligarchs. As novels such as Dmitriy Petrov's *Setup for a Sucker,* Leonid Monchinskiy's *Especially Dangerous Animal,* Valeriy Maslov's *Made Mafia,* and myriad others demonstrated, the fact that a person was a law enforcement official seemed now almost to guarantee that he was a villain, rather than a pillar of virtue. Indeed, expectations of law enforcement officials had fallen so low by the end of the 1990s that Polina Dashkova could intend it as praise that a senior militia official "had committed a number of sins, but no more than were to be expected for his position in the service" (*Golden Sand,* 285). Meanwhile, as Andrey Kivinov, Aleksandra Marinina, and many others have illustrated, ordinary citizens found themselves unable to resolve the paradoxes between the serving of self, which capitalism requires, and the communalism, which the Russian moral impulse continues to uphold.

As most of the novels cited in this study demonstrate, that paradox remains essentially unresolvable. There are innumerable villains in the post-Soviet *detektivy*, but there are also large numbers of more ordinary sinners—people who have been forced into crime by financial exigency, by their failure to understand the nuances and contradictions of the new capitalist system, or by their simple moral confusion. Indeed, as this chapter has already suggested, a great many of Russia's citizens see themselves as little different from criminals, or the criminals as little different from themselves. In such an environment, the simple moral equation of "Thou Shalt Not Do X" seems inadequate, because it does not answer the next question that the complexities of life seem certain to present: What happens if you already did X?

As noted, part of the answer to that question is the exploration of punishment. An equally important part, however, is what happens *after* punishment. In a moral environment with clear demarcations between good and evil, it is relatively simple to see the villains and transgressors as fundamentally different from good people, and so not raise the question of whether, and under what circumstances, a transgressor might rejoin the larger body of society. As has already been discussed, it was this straightforward morality that underlay most Russian mystery fiction of the 1960s through the mid-1980s. As authors gained the possibility to explore the nuances of crime and guilt more honestly, however, the weighing-up of the guilt and innocence of those who fall beyond the law became increasingly important.

The final question of the *detektiv* thus becomes essentially that of rehabilitation—how the lawbreaker or the transgressor may retain and build upon the good within him or her, and so rejoin society. Logically at least, the communally minded principles for distinguishing good from bad would seem to make the issue of social rehabilitation relatively straightforward—villains would be returned to society once they understood that individualism is evil, and so turn to serving "the people." Jeffrey Brooks finds essentially that pattern in his analysis of the "penny dreadfuls" that appeared at the end of the nineteenth century, much like the explosion of *detektivy* at the end of the twentieth. As Brooks explains in *When Russia Learned to Read*, in those *pinkertony* the criminals who step outside the boundaries of acceptable social behavior are shown earning the right to rejoin society by performing some heroic social service. However, this is not the same kind of exculpation one might find in a western pulp fiction mystery. As Brooks points out: "When Western European and American outlaws decided to return to society, they sought pardon—not from the state of some other representative of official authority, but from the community of their fellow citizens" (198). In the Russian versions of these genres, "there is no unofficial court of appeal. Only the state and church had moral authority to pardon the rebellion of Russian fictional bandits . . . they could earn a full pardon by patriotic feats, such as heroism during wartime, or, occasionally, through acts of religious penitence such as pilgrimages" (171).

In its earlier and simpler days, the Soviet *detektiv* followed the same pattern, illustrating or suggesting how a criminal might eventually rejoin society by serving the state. Valery Chalidze cites as typical an incident from Lev Sheynin's book *Notes of a Criminal Investigator*, in which a gang of thieves are shown helping the militia recover a watch that has been stolen from a visiting official of the French Communist Party (50). Even by the 1970s, however, suggestions that a criminal might redeem himself had become quite rare in the *detektiv*. In part, that may have been due to the increased faithfulness with which the genre was beginning to reflect Soviet reality, particularly once glasnost had begun. As Chalidze points out, redemption through service to the state would have been far more common in books than in life because one of the strictest tenets of the thieves' law was that members could not serve any state or state organization, on pain of being labeled a *suka* (literally, *bitch*, but figuratively, a turncoat or traitor), whom any *vor* would have the right, indeed duty, to kill. The thieves' law forbade service even in so patriotic an undertaking as World War II. It was only because so many thousands of *vory* were conscripted into that war and forced to fight that the thieves themselves rebelled against their own laws, making service in that war permissible, but still not laudable.

A few of the post-Soviet *detektivy* also share the conviction of their prerevolutionary and Soviet-period ancestors that crime may be exculpated by service to the state. As we have seen, the hero of Viktor Dotsenko's *Beshenyy's Revenge* swindles a large sum out of the then-president of Chechnya, but makes this a moral act by passing the money on to Russia's prime minister of the time, Viktor Chernomyrdin. Similarly, Ivan Shitov's criminal-as-hero in *Cathedral without Crosses* wills the bulk of his ill-gotten wealth to the church. However, the increased freedom that the disappearance of censorship has permitted the *detektiv* genre suggests strongly that the path of redemption through service has become impossible for a deeper and more disturbing reason—that the essential identity of "the state" and "the people" on which that path to redemption was based has badly eroded, if not disappeared entirely.

To be sure, skepticism about individual representatives of the state is a persistent feature of Russian society, as Tim McDaniel explains. Historically, he writes, Russians have shown the tendency to revere an abstract, idealized power authority, while simultaneously anathematizing the specific individuals who exercise that authority, seeing them to be venal, corrupt, and self-interested (53)—in part because the very fact of being individuals deprives them of virtue.

The problem that Russia's new quasi-democratic system presents is that democracy definitionally emphasizes the individual exercisers of power at the expense of a more abstract "state." Russians are no longer ruled by "the Tsar" or by "the Party," but rather are governed by specific individuals, who shape, guide, and define the nature of society at the moment. The western style of democracy Russia is imitating is by nature a system of individuals, who separate themselves from "the people" by standing for election and then, if victorious, presuming to direct them.

This personification of power has been further exaggerated by the incompetence, venality, and impotence demonstrated by so many Russian public officials since 1991. Equally important, even those functions the state might still claim to fill have largely withered because of financial problems, the erosion of central authority, and general confusion about what should, and what can be, the extent of the Russian government's function. To judge at least by the genre of the *detektiv*, one important result of the changes in Russia's government is that there is no longer any agent in Russia to credibly decide the moral valence of individual acts. This makes it impossible for the genre to describe ways in which transgressors might rejoin society, but even more important, it suggests that Russians—or at least those who read *detektivy*—may no longer see any way in which right can be distinguished from wrong.[24]

That possibility explains the directions in which the *detektiv* genre seems now to be moving. The genre is splitting into two subgenres, as the violent action thrillers called *boyeviki* increasingly establish themselves as a genre distinct from the more traditional *detektivy*. As has already been noted, the *boyeviki* are basically wish-fulfillment tales, similar in their deeper structures to the comic books of caped superheroes. The heroes of the *boyeviki* prevail because they are stronger, faster, and more fierce than their opponents, suggesting that the "morality" underlying these books is nearly that of Darwin. The implication that might equals right is furthered by a recent development in the subgenre, in which the authors of popular series have begun to collaborate to produce novels pitting one popular superhero against another. A case in point is the new Beshenyy vs. Lyutyy series being jointly produced by bestselling authors Viktor Dotsenko and Fyodor Butyrskiy.

Perhaps not surprisingly, those who write, and probably most of those who read, these *boyeviki* are almost entirely men, which only seems to highlight further the equally interesting development that the more traditional forms of the *detektiv* seem increasingly to be written by women. To be sure, this feminization of the genre is not as complete as is the male domination of the *boyevik* subgenre. A number of men also continue to publish more traditional *detektivy* (although it may be significant that Vinnichenko, for example, whose first works were thoughtful explorations of the more traditional genre, has now turned to writing superhero *boyeviki*). The increased numbers of female *detektiv* writers are undoubtedly also due in part to the alacrity with which Russia's publishers have mastered the tricks of capitalism. The phenomenal popularity, and hence commercial success, of writer Aleksandra Marinina has obviously prodded other publishers actively to recruit other female authors (and, it is rumored, to encourage men to assume female *noms de plume*). One publisher has even gone so far as to set up an entire series, "The *Detektiv* Through Female Eyes."

The real significance of this trend lies not in the gender of the authors, but rather in the changes this new crop of writers has brought to the shape of the traditional genre. Although Marinina's central character is a law enforcement official, as is the heroine of the much less prolific Irina Zarubina, most of the heroines of these female writers have no relation to the state or its apparatus. Indeed, one of the most common features of these characters' lives is that the state is failing them in fundamental and significant ways. For example, the two main figures of Yelena Yakovleva's *All Joking Aside* are single women, one a journalist and the other a chemist—neither is paid on time, neither receives either help or respect from the authorities to whom the disappearance of a child forces her to turn, and neither has the slightest bit of confidence that her interests are being served by the society in which she lives. One of the pair collapses in self-recriminating hysteria, but the other woman (the journalist) manages, by novel's end, to solve the crimes and find her vanished niece by relying solely upon her own intelligence, bravery, and initiative. Zarubina's heroine is a *sledovatel*, and thus a state official, but she too seems to suffer more than she gains from the state. Made the sole support of her family because Russia's new economy has thrown her engineer husband out of work, the *sledovatel* lives the hand-to-mouth existence of a poorly paid official, performs the traditional domestic miracles of a Russian housewife and mother, and still manages—in spite of the fumbling stupidities of the men who remain in authority above her—to solve the crimes Zarubina sets before her.

Perhaps the most eloquent explorations of the collapse of the Russian state, however, come in the novels of Polina Dashkova. All of Dashkova's heroines are private persons who are thrust into danger either because of the state's incompetence, or because of its venality. In *No One Will Weep*, the heroine is a single mother and translator who must defend herself against the mafiosi who think she is shielding swindlers, merely because she has the bad luck to be assigned the swindlers' telephone number after they have absconded with someone else's cash. In *Golden Sand*, the heroine is doubly trapped because she has had the bad judgment to marry a rising politician—elected governor of their *oblast* during the course of the novel—who is also a vicious and manipulative criminal. In *Flesh for Sale*, the heroine is a student and aspiring actress who has the bad luck to become embroiled in the messy and venal politics surrounding Chechen separatism. Perhaps the most extravagant, but thoroughly representative illustration of Dashkova's conviction that Russia's citizens may rely only upon themselves is *Image of the Enemy*. In that novel, a young woman vacationing in Israel chances to glimpse a former lover, who after their long-ago affair had become a Carlos-like international terrorist. Since law enforcement officials had decided this former lover was dead, the woman understands she is in great danger, particularly since the terrorist is also the father of her son. For most of the course of this novel, the heroine is pursued by the terrorist, by the terrorist's jealous, crazed girlfriend (a terrorist in her own right), by the criminal elements who had hired the terrorist in the first place, by a shadowy former KGB colonel who now works in the twilight regions between private enterprise and the state's security apparatus, and even by an agent of the CIA. Although the criminals, the FSB (the KGB's successor), and the CIA all offer to help and protect her, the heroine rejects all of them, both because their offers are at least as self-interested as they are genuine (curiously enough, it is the CIA agent whose offer appears the least self-interested, in that his desire to help her is motivated only by the fact that he has fallen in love with her) and because she understands that none of these agencies is capable in fact of delivering the protection it promises. In the end, the heroine prefers to rely only upon herself, not for purposes of catching the terrorist, or of assisting the state, but simply because she has no other way of keeping herself and her son alive.

Such plot descriptions may suggest that the Russian *detektiv* is finally beginning to move in the direction of its western—and especially its American—cousins, to glorify the capacity of the individual to right wrong, or to seek justice, above that of the state. The suggestion, however, is misleading, for it overlooks, as discussed above, that this increased reliance upon non-state heroes is also accompanied by a pronounced blurring of the boundaries between right and wrong, or good and bad. The combined effect of these two impulses means that in *Image of the Enemy*, for example, Dashkova's heroine is fully justified in lying to the state authorities and in putting other people at physical risk, because of the overriding necessity to protect her child. The book also deals sympathetically with the desire of the terrorist to see his son (who is his only child), with a Russian-born scientist involved in Israeli germ-warfare research who betrays (Israeli) state interests to protect himself and his family once he is captured by terrorists, and even with the efforts of one of the senior *mafiosi* who is bankrolling the kidnapping of the scientist to make certain that he receives the payment, and the respect, he is due.

To western eyes, the universe the *detektiv* describes may seem a lawless and violent place, where crime is not punished and virtue is not rewarded. This may also seem an accurate-enough description of life itself in modern Russia, if one is to judge by newspaper headlines and media stories. It should be recalled, however, as this study has repeatedly argued, that such views of good and bad, or right and wrong, are, to a far greater extent than is usually acknowledged, based upon a conception of the universe that most Russians do not share. It is westerners who try to draw sharp distinctions between good and bad, right and wrong, for a variety of historically and culturally determined reasons.

As we have noted, the legal tradition used in most western countries derives from "natural" law, as shaped by the traditions and practices of Roman law. This is primarily a commerce-based form of law that imposes specific sanctions for specific acts, and so permits all other actions, which thus, by definition, may be viewed as "good." By contrast, the legal tradition in Russia has, for most of its history, been "positive," meaning that laws grant the license to perform specific acts, and so make all other acts forbidden, and thus "bad."

The same distinction may be seen in the differing religious traditions that lie beneath Russian and western societies. The enforced secularization of Russia during the Soviet period, and the separation of church and state that is a hallmark of American democracy, as well as the trend of western democracies more broadly, might lead one to presume that little remains of the religious underpinnings of the two societies. In fact, though, the legacy of Orthodoxy seems as apparent in Russian views of crime and guilt as does the legacy of Catholicism, and its Protestant offspring, in the west. Perhaps the most striking difference, in the present context, is the far greater weight the western church places upon sin, or transgression. As Timothy Ware explains in his book on Orthodoxy,

> Orthodoxy, holding as it does a less exalted idea of man's state before he fell [than does Catholicism], is also less severe than the west in its view of the consequences of the fall. Adam fell, not from a great height of knowledge and perfection, but from a state of undeveloped simplicity; hence he is not to be judged too harshly for his error. Certainly, as a result of the fall man's mind became so darkened, and his will-power was so impaired, that he could no longer hope to attain the likeness of God. Orthodox, however, do not hold that the fall deprived man entirely of God's grace. . . . Orthodox do not say, as Calvin said, that man after the fall was utterly depraved and incapable of good desires. They cannot agree with Augustine, when he writes that man is under a "harsh necessity" of committing sin. (228)

The west's insistence upon a greater distinction between the state of grace and the fallen state is also reflected in its preoccupation with criminal investigation, prosecution, and punishment. The necessity of identifying who precisely has committed a certain act arises from and is conditioned by the severity with which punishment is prescribed. The consequences of transgression in the western systems of justice are highly stigmatized, therefore requiring that the legal system take enormous pains to be as certain as possible that the real perpetrator has been identified. The western system, in other words, requires that great care be taken to be sure that the proper Adam is expelled from Paradise.

By contrast, the Russian system reflects the value system of Orthodoxy. In Ware's words, "However sinful a man may be, [in the Orthodox understanding] he never loses the image [of his likeness to God]" (224). One consequence of this view is that criminality is less stigmatized; the lawbreaker remains as human, as Godlike, as a law-abiding citizen. As legal philosopher Lon Fuller points out, an inevitable corollary of such a view is that details of prosecution, and of punishment, become correspondingly less important. In his words, "How much time and energy must be expended to be certain that no innocent person is ever convicted of a crime?" (179), particularly if one's fellow citizens are going to be inclined—as Russians have repeatedly been described to be—to sympathize with those who have fallen beyond the nation's laws. No doubt that sympathy also arises from the obvious corollary of Ware's observation: If every person, no matter how sinful, may still bear some modicum of virtue, it must also be true that even the most virtuous of humans is also going to carry a portion of evil.

Paradoxical as the argument may seem, the genre of the *detektiv* could thus be said to be elaborating a view of good and evil that in fact makes crime fiction impossible, or at least unnecessary. If there is no substantial barrier between good and bad, if law by definition contravenes justice, and if crime and law enforcement are going to battle one another to a draw for all eternity, then the conventions of crime fiction—at least as defined by the western countries that gave birth to them—have no place in Russia. The genre refuses to show that crime may be stopped, that good may triumph, or that humans may grow less evil.

The fact, however, that crime fiction is just about the *only* form of literature that continues to enjoy mass popularity in the new Russia obviously argues that this conclusion is incorrect. So what then is the social purpose of the *detektiv*? Upon close inspection, it seems very likely that it is much the same as the social purpose that Dostoyevsky found in *Anna Karenina*, the publication of which served as the springboard for a larger meditation on Russian views of crime and guilt. In his review, Dostoyevsky first described two opinions on the question that he called characteristic of the west. The first is a Pashukanis-style bill of crimes for which transgressors paid in accordance with the letter of the law. The other is the conviction of social engineers, that crimes were no more than the results of social injustice, which would disappear when the present society was destroyed and a scientifically constructed new society was set up in its stead. In his review, Dostoyevsky then contrasted these western views with the Russian understanding of crime and guilt, as exemplified by the novel of his great rival, Tolstoy:

> However, in the Russian author's [i.e., Tolstoy's] approach to culpability and human delinquency it is clearly revealed that no anthill, no triumph of the

"fourth estate," no elimination of poverty, no organization of labor will save mankind from abnormality, and therefore—from guilt and criminality.... It is clear and intelligible to the point of obviousness that evil in mankind is concealed deeper than the physician-socialists suppose; that in no organization of society can evil be eliminated; that the human soul will remain identical; that abnormality and sin emanate from the soul itself; and finally, that the laws of the human spirit are so unknown to science, so obscure, so indeterminate and mysterious, that, as yet, there can neither be physicians nor *final* judges, but that there is only He who saith: "Vengeance belongeth unto me; I will recompense."[25]

While it is striking in this regard that Vinnichenko constructs at least three of his novels around the conceit that the hero is drawn increasingly into Orthodoxy, and that Dashkova ends *Golden Sand* with a quotation from the Bible to the effect that "All rivers flow to the sea, but the sea grows not full" (509), it is not necessary to argue that the *detektiv* is beginning to proselytize Orthodoxy, or religion more broadly, as the solution to Russia's ills. What does seem clear, however, is that the moral assumptions upon which the *detektiv* is based were always derived from a universe in which good and evil are hopelessly, irremediably, and even indistinguishably mixed. What seems to be new in the genre, however, is that these writers, and presumably their readers, no longer seem willing to accept the authority of abstract, but human, arbiters who will tell them what is good and what is bad. In line with Dostoyevsky, the *detektiv* seems increasingly to argue that justice, if it is to be found at all, will be found only in heaven.

Notes

1. *Kommentarii k ugolovno-ispolnitel'nomu kodeksu Rossiyskoy federatsii i minimalnym standartnym pravilam obrashcheniya s zaklyuchënnymi* (Moscow: Ekspertnoye byuro, 1997), 43.

2. Maria Los, *Communist Ideology, Law, and Crime* (New York: St. Martin's Press, 1988), 113.

3. It is perhaps worth pointing out that Russia, for all its reputation for brutality, also has been among the nations most reluctant to use the death penalty. As Peter Juviler recounts in his *Revolutionary Law and Order* (New York: Free Press, 1976), "De jure capital punishment was abolished from Russian codes during the thirteenth and most of the twelfth and fourteenth centuries, under Elizabeth from 1742 to 1754, and up until the 1770s when Catherine II used it against the Pugachev rebels. From then until the execution of the five Decembrist putschists in 1825 no-

body was executed for political offenses either. Since 1812 the death penalty applied for some military crimes, but not for common crimes like murder or rape. . . . Ten days in power, the Provisional Government abolished all capital punishment, later restoring it July 25, 1917, at the front . . . [the death penalty has been listed] as a "temporary" measure in every major piece of criminal legislation [in the Soviet period]. . . . Stalin briefly suspended it in 1947–50. . . . Intensity of use of the death penalty appeared to abated during NEP. . . . By the end of 1927 capital punishment applied only to military crimes, state crimes under Article 58, and 'banditry.' The maximum sentence other than death ran to ten years confinement" (24–25).

4. *Kommersant,* 7 December 1996, 16.

5. *Itogi,* 1 October 1996, 56.

6. Andrei Sinyavsky, *Soviet Civilization: A Cultural History* (New York: Arcade, 1988), 183–84.

7. "Potomstvo 'chërnoy koshki' v eru miloserdiya" *Sovetskaya militsiya,* No. 10, 1990, 7.

8. B. Polubinskiy, *Blatyaki i fenya* (Moscow: ob. Red. MVD Rossii, 1997), 22.

9. See for example the first chapters of *Moskovskiy ugolovnyy rozysk: Istoriya v litsakh* (Moscow: Ob"ed. red. MVD Rossii), 1998.

10. Yuri Glazov, "Thieves in the USSR—A Social Phenomenon," *Survey,* 22/1 (Winter 1976), 141.

11. V. Polubinskiy, 5-6.

12. Valery Chalidze, *Criminal Russia: Crime in the Soviet Union* (New York: Random House, 1977), 57.

13. Vladimir Yanitskiy, "Mugface Kingdom," in *Poyedinok No. 16* (Moscow: Moskovskiy rabochiy, 1989). 289.

14. *Sovetskaya militsiya,* No. 10, 1990, 8.

15. *Sovetskaya militsiya,* No. 11, 1990, 10.

16. Chalidze informs us in *Criminal Russia* that it was a frequent practice among professional criminals escaping from labor colonies to take along at least one non-*vor,* who might be used as food if other sources of nourishment failed (113). Udintsev's story suggests that he is depicting a tamer version of this same thing.

17. See Chalidze, especially 36-43.

18. Oleg Kharkhordin, *The Collective and the Individual in Russia* (Berkeley: University of California Press, 1999), 322.

19. *Sovetskaya militsiya,* No. 11, 1990, 10.

20. *Itogi,* 9 February 1999.

21. *Sovetskaya militsiya,* No. 11, 1990, 13.

22. *Moscow Times,* 28 November 1997, 2.

23. Anatoly Gagarin, "Detektiv—literatura plyus igra," in *Russkiy syshchik* (Moscow: Otechestvo, 1994), 360.

24. This was written before the election of Vladimir Putin. Although it is too early to see whether Putin is going to be successful in reestablishing the moral primacy of a disembodied Russian State, the fact that the thrust of his policies since

taking office is precisely to "recreate the power vertical" suggests that Putin and his advisers are aware of this trait of Russian thought. Some Russian political observers have begun to explain Putin's phenomenal popularity as a conscious decision to be the "un-Yeltsin"—a gray, selfless servant of a great state. It is instructive that after a visit with Putin in September 2000, Russian nationalist and one-time dissident Aleksandr Solzhenitsyn praised Russia's new president as having "no personal ambition." Solzhenitsyn's enthusiasm is particularly striking since Putin was an officer in the KGB at the very time that the KGB was harassing Solzhenitsyn, eventually throwing him out of Russia.

   25. Fyodor Dostoyevsky, *Diary of a Writer*, vol. 2 (New York: Scribners, 1949), 788.

CHAPTER FIVE

Confirmation from Afar

M OST RUSSIANS WOULD FIND IT PERVERSE to seek confirmation of the profound differences between their own views of good and evil and that
of westerners in the many mysteries and thrillers that western writers have
set in Russia, for it is their deep conviction that foreigners simply do not
understand their homeland. This opinion is spelled out in *Stolen Dream*,
when Marinina says of the heroine, Nastya Kamenskaya, that "Even
[Russian-born] writers who have lived many years in Russia [before emi-
grating] can't avoid errors in their depiction of contemporary Russian reality, and as for writers like Martin Cruz Smith . . . Nastya . . . couldn't even
finish [his books], because she could not overcome her irritation at the obvious stupidities and clumsiness of his description of Moscow life" (142).

It is not difficult to prove that western writers have committed an enormous number of errors in their depiction of Russia, as the first part of this
chapter will demonstrate. What may be harder to understand, at first glance,
is the irritation and impatience that Marinina's heroine (and most Russians)
exhibit in regard to what they call *klyukvy*, or *klyukvenitsa* ("cranberries" or
"cranberry tree").[1] After all, the hundreds of western thrillers and mysteries
claiming to portray Russia are only entertainments, not serious political or
cultural analyses. As David Ignatius reminds us sternly in the afterword to
his novel *Siro*, which insinuates that the breakup of the USSR in 1991 was
the fruition of plots first laid down by the CIA twenty years before, "This
book is a novel, drawn from the author's imagination. Readers will search in

vain for real counterparts to the events and people described. They do not exist. This is not a *roman à clef* or a veiled description of real events. It is a work of fiction, as will be evident to those who know the true details of the period I have described" (467).

While accurate in fact, Ignatius's disclaimer is disingenuous in spirit, as the innuendo of the last part of his warning implies. The fact that Ignatius is a senior Washington journalist who enjoys access to highly placed sources in the U.S. government and the intelligence community and someone whom readers may presume does "know the true details of the period" suggests the ambiguity on which most of these Russian-based entertainments depend for their success. Novels and thrillers set in Russia—a huge percentage of which were written either by journalists like Ignatius or by former intelligence officers like John le Carré—enjoyed their greatest popularity during the Cold War precisely because they *seemed* to give information about Russia, and about East-West competition, just at the time when the Soviet government was making it as difficult as possible for outsiders to get reliable information by any other means. Unlike novels written by foreigners, but set in England, France, or other more congenial countries, the claim for attention made by thrillers set in Russia was that they were providing factual information. It is for reasons of authenticity that, for example, Tom Clancy's *The Cardinal of the Kremlin* includes among its characters a Marshal Yazov, who was an actual Soviet military commander, and provides in the text what appear to be real satellite reconnaissance photos of Tajikistan. Characteristically for the genre, however, Clancy, in that same book, simultaneously steps away from authenticity, by making the general secretary of the Communist Party in his novel not Mikhail Gorbachev, who in fact was in charge at the time depicted in Clancy's novel, but rather "Secretary Narmonov."

The Irritation of Being Misunderstood

There is a certain condescension inherent in pointing out the errors other writers have made in their depictions of Russia, particularly when the works of such authors as Ian Fleming, Martin Cruz Smith, and Tom Clancy have engaged and satisfied readers by the tens of millions. Since it was their unfamiliarity with Russia that made the errors invisible to most readers in the first place, to point them out only makes the corrector seem pedantic.

How is the average reader to judge whether such a "correction" is accurate, or to decide how necessary it is to the verisimilitude of the work in which the errors occurred?

Fortunately, the freedom from censorship that post-Soviet Russia enjoys has permitted authors there to imagine America in their writings just as American writers imagine Russia. In fact, one author, Viktor Chernyak, has suggested that to set a plot in America was one way to get around the fact that in the 1970s, "It was impossible to tell the truth about ourselves, but I had no desire to lie."[2] Although there are not nearly as many Russian books set in America as there are American books set in Russia, there are enough of them to give American readers a chance to feel the same combination of amusement and irritation Russians feel at *klyukvy*, by seeing some of the "cranberries" that Russian have committed about America. Igor Bunich's *Absolute License*, for example, is a sprawling thriller, most of which purports to be narrated by one Gerald Michael Macintyre, who is supposed to have headed up the CIA's covert operations in Moscow for more than a decade, and who is thus the real architect of the USSR's collapse. While Russians might find the plot compelling, and Bunich's explanation of the "real" reasons for the collapse of the USSR convincing, an American reader can not help but notice the slow accumulation of false details—of "cranberries"—that combine to make the novel seem merely silly. Thus, for example, Macintyre and his American colleague are described as following "the American custom" of having dinner, *after* which they have cocktails (19). Because Macintyre describes himself as having been drafted into the Navy (30), at another dinner he and the same colleague later speak "Navy slang" (396) in order to foil eavesdropping microphones. In another place, Macintyre admits that he paid off a gaggle of corrupt Soviet officials with a "suitcase filled with $1000 bills" (191). (Although they exist, bills in that denomination were withdrawn from circulation in the 1930s, which makes them so rare that, among other things, the few that are available now trade for more than their face value. This would seem to undercut their usefulness as the stuff of bribery.) American geography in particular gives Bunich a lot of trouble. Bunich's novel offers excerpts from a book said to be published by Cornell University Davidson-Macintyre Book Corporation, which for some reason is based in Boston (106), while Macintyre's superior in Washington cuts short a transatlantic telephone conversation by explaining that he is in a hurry "to get away to Silver Springs for the weekend" (103). Bunich plainly has little idea about the location of this suburb contiguous to Washington—which in any event is called Silver Spring—because, in another place, he marvels that Macintyre's American boss has arrived from an overnight flight to St. Petersburg, Russia, looking as carefree and relaxed "as if he had just flown in from Washington for a simple weekend in Silver Springs" (385).

American geography also trips up Vladimir Shitov, in *Cathedral without Crosses*. In the book, Shitov's main characters dine at a fancy New York nightclub called The Tired Cowboy, said to be at the intersection "of Twelfth Avenue and Eighth Street" (351). Some of Shitov's other "American" atmospheric details are equally startling. For example, his Russian hero's American doctor drives a Packard, and the car his hero prefers to lease when he flies to America (invariably through Washington) is a Citroen, which he uses to reach his "villa on the outskirts of New York."

Seeing the clumsiness of such errors about the country with which they are familiar may make it easier for Americans to understand how Russians react to similar infelicities that foreign authors make about them. Moscow and St. Petersburg, the two most common settings for Russian thrillers and mysteries, each have unique architecture and distinctive weather, which are relatively easy for foreigners unfamiliar with them to evoke in a believable way. Nevertheless, even here some foreign writers are prone to gaffes, especially if they do not understand the ways in which Russian place names are formed, or copy them incorrectly from whatever source they have chosen to supply their background color. Thus, for example, Craig Thomas in *A Wild Justice* slips in a "Moskba Prospekt" ("Moscow" in Cyrillic letters looks like the Latin letters "MOCKBA," but only when capitalized) and a "Cheremetievo Airport" (239), suggesting he may have used a French-language guidebook as his source, while Stuart Kaminsky has a "Tvetnoi Boulevard" (for "Tsvetnoi") in his *A Fine Red Rain* (39).

The farther from Russia's "two capitals" a foreign author moves, the greater the errors he is likely to commit. Thus, Philip Kerr introduces a region called "Dazakhstan" (inhabited by "Tazaks") into *Dead Meat*, while Greg Dinallo in *Red Ink* lists "Sverdlovsk" among the cities that, like Tbilisi and Minsk, he supposes became the capitals of new states when the USSR collapsed (114).

Russian names present much greater problems for foreign authors. Again, the best way to get some sense of how western gaffes will grate on Russian ears is to show the monstrosities Russian authors have concocted in trying to set their plots in the United States. Vladimir Shitov, for example, offers the wife of his hero's first American partner, one *Badzhen Foster*, a doctor *Buno Pochivano*, the crucial witness to a break-in named *Lorentsia Zulfit*, and, best of all, that witness's cook, *Sarda Baislaks*. Even Polina Dashkova, who to judge by the way in which she portrays it in several of her novels seems reasonably familiar with America, makes a bit of a clunker in *Golden Sand* when she dubs a minor American character Richard Mc-Dandley (27).

Probably the most common mistake American writers make in naming their Russian characters is to assume that in order to be "Russian," a character's name need only be long and unpronounceable. Kaminsky's several novels about Moscow detective Porfiry Rostnikov provide scores of examples of this "Scrabble-tile" approach to characters' names. The novel *A Fine Red Rain* offers, in addition to Rostnikov himself, such names as Timis Korostyava, Valerian Duznetzov, Oleg Pesknoko, Dimitri Mazaraki, the brothers Felix and Osip Gorgasali, and police inspectors Snitkonoy and Khabolov, all of which bear approximately the same relation to plausible Russian names as Shitov's "Sarda Baislaks" does to plausible American ones.

Even when Kaminsky creates the perfectly plausible Vadim Dunin, he undermines verisimilitude by giving the same character the extravagant patronymic of "Malkoliovich." In general, patronymics are a problem for Kaminsky. Formed from the father's given name, patronymics are used with a person's given name in formal address, and so serve as the functional equivalent of "Mr." or "Mrs." in Russian conversation. Not realizing this, Kaminsky in *The Man Who Walked Like a Bear* describes Rostnikov's father as having named his son Porfiry Petrovich (6) out of admiration for the character of the same name in Dostoyevsky's *Crime and Punishment*, while, in *A Fine Red Rain*, one of Kaminsky's characters boasts, "My father was an assistant to Lunacharsky. He, my father, called him Anatoly Vasilyvich. That's how close they were" (50).

Although Kaminsky may be the most egregious in his creation of Russian-sounding but impossible names, tamer versions of Scrabble-tile naming are very common, especially among authors who don't have much experience in Russia. In addition to reprising his Estonian submarine commander Ramius, introduced in *The Hunt for Red October*, Clancy introduces such names as Filitov, Vatutin, Altunin, and Narmonov into *The Cardinal of the Kremlin*, while Joseph Hone in *The Sixth Directorate* envisions a Soviet KGB composed of such names as Flitlianov, Chechulian, and Sakharovsky (in addition to the real Yuri Andropov). James Burch, in

Lubyanka, introduces such characters as Davilov, Saunin, and General Drachinsky, all names which are as Russian (or un-Russian) as are the characters Grechukha and Zapotkin created by John Kruse in *Red Omega.* The rich ethnic mix of the USSR was such that even knowledgeable authors could slip into "cranberries" when they took their plots outside the Slavic regions with which westerners were most familiar. This happened, for example, with Ralph Peters, who gave his Uzbek mafia chieftain in *Flames of Heaven* the family name of Talala.[3] Something similar happens to Martin Cruz Smith when he includes among the crew of the Polar Star in his eponymous novel both a character named Izrail Izrailovich and a young Uzbek girl named Dynama. While both names are entirely possible, it is extremely unlikely that so obvious a Jew or, even more so, an unmarried Uzbek female might have been among the crew of an Arctic fishing boat.[4]

Another way in which authors may "Russify" their characters' names is to choose authentic names, culled from some other source. Some authors take the route of caution, giving their characters unremarkable common Slavic names such as Slanski and Panov, as Ted Allbeury did in *The Man with the President's Mind,* or Krasin and Soloviev, as he did in *Moscow Quadrille.* The choice of such generic names is also common in the novels of journalists who have once been posted to Moscow: Michael Killian's main villain in *Blood of the Czars* is Marshal Kuznetsov; James O. Jackson also made use of the name Kuznetsov in *Dzerzhinsky Square,* which further includes the names Chudov, Volkova, and the unusual but possible name Malmudov; and Anthony Hyde creates such wholly possible names as Glubin, Shastov, Osipov, and Subotin in *The Red Fox.*

A number of western writers, however, have taken a much more clever, but oddly unsettling, approach to this problem, by giving their characters the names of real public figures. This approach has the advantage of authenticity, particularly in the case of non-Russian names, but it creates problems of another order, by appearing to introduce into a story real people who are not, in fact, being depicted. At least, Dinallo acknowledges this confusion, when his main character says of another in *Red Ink* that, "I once teased [the character Valery Shevchenko] that he shares his surname with a famous poet who advocated Ukrainian independence from Russia and a high-ranking UN diplomat who defected to the United States" (8). By contrast, Martin Cruz Smith makes no such acknowledgment that his characters Patiashvili (also the name of a Brezhnev-era head of Georgia) and Chukovskaia (also a famous writer and dissident) in *Polar Star,* or Minin (also one of the two saviors of the Russian state in 1613, who has a statue in his memory in Red Square), Fedorov (also a prominent Moscow eye surgeon) and Gubenko (also an actor, who at the time of Smith's novel was Minister of Culture) in *Red Square*, all bear the names of real people prominent in Russian history or society, but who have nothing to do with his plots. Craig Thomas's choices for names in *A Wild Justice* run to literature and politics. Among his characters are a Turgenev, a Bakunin, and a Kropotkin. (To be fair, he also has an American character called John Lock.)

Philip Kerr appropriates the names of prominent Russians or Soviets for his characters in *Dead Meat*, including Sobchak (in real life the perestroika-era mayor of St. Petersburg), Kornilov (also a general who tried to seize power from the Provisional Government in 1917), Ordzhonikidze (also a Red Army commander who conquered the Caucasus for Soviet power), and Voznesensky (also a famous poet). What is more confusing, however, is that Kerr also gives his characters names taken from Russian fiction, a particularly eerie practice, since his novel is set in St. Petersburg; *Dead Meat* appropriates for its characters such Dostoyevskian and Gogolian names as Lebezyatnikov, Stavrogin, Svridigailov [*sic*], and even Chichikov.

Another of Kerr's characters, a certain "Skorobogatych," illustrates a possibility of which very few western authors have taken advantage, that of using the meaning of the constituent parts of a name to "color" a particular character. In this case, Kerr would seem to have created the perfect name for a villain in a post-Soviet novel, since it may be translated "of the rapidly rich." However, the fact that Kerr never makes much use of this character, or the possibilities of his name, suggests that he is unaware of the rich associations his character's name might conjure up.

Ian Fleming seems to have been more cognizant of the ways in which Russian names can work to characterize those who bear them. Among the chief villains of *From Russia, With Love* is General Grubozaboyshchikov, whose name, most appropriately, might be translated as "Gross-slaughter."

Fleming's familiarity with the Russian meaning of his characters' names is related to a third technique western writers have adopted in order to give their novels the air of expertise necessary to sustain the plausibility of their plots—that of sprinkling Russian words and phrases through their texts. Although the fact that most readers do not know Russian creates the awkward necessity to translate such phrases as soon as they are used, if employed sparingly this technique can create the impression that the author knows what he is talking about—unless it happens that a reader knows Russian better than does the author. Ian Fleming, for example, is generally correct in the phrases he sprinkles throughout *From Russia, With Love* although it sometimes seems far from clear why he chooses the Russian words he has. It is difficult to see, for example, what authenticity Fleming gains in this description: "On the left-hand wall . . . stands a large *Televizor*, or TV set" (29). Some of Fleming's Russian expletives go a bit awry, such as his beautiful female spy's exclamation of "Bogou moiou" ("bozhe moi" would be correct), but most are authentic, such as "*Sookin Syn*" (son of a bitch) (italics and capitalization by Fleming) and "*Y*b**na mat!*" (m*th*rf*ck). Fleming's use of asterisks in this instance is a nice touch, implying that his western readers share not only Fleming's mastery of Russian curses, but also his delicacy about spelling them out.

Although the texts of many writers suggest that they have at least consulted Russian-speakers before sprinkling Russian words and phrases throughout their books, Fleming's relative accuracy in the use of Russian is the exception, not the rule. Far more often, the Russian phrases an author plants in his text to increase authenticity have the opposite effect instead, for any reader who knows Russian. Sometimes the false note is nothing more than an omitted, mistaken, or additional letter, as in Nelson DeMille's slip ("khula" for "khuyom") in the impeccably Russian-sounding expression "whacking pears with my dick" (*The Charm School*, 115). In a similar, if less colorful, way Clancy uses "Samogan" for "samogon" (home-brew)—like Fleming, Clancy sometimes capitalizes Russian words without clear reason—and "pokazhuka" for "pokazukha." (This is a very Russian concept that is difficult to translate succinctly. It means, essentially, to *pretend* to do something—a job, a project, a building—rather than do it properly [*The Cardinal of the Kremlin*, 114]). Sometimes the error is in usage, as in Clancy's "translation" of the American vulgarism "shit-eater" into "Govnoed!" (186). The word is correctly constructed, but is not one that Russians much used, at least until it gained currency after being brought into Russian by the frequency with which it appeared in translations of American films and books.[5] Indeed, as Craig Thomas's insertion of the English phrase "it's brass monkey weather out here" into the mouth of a Russian character demonstrates, it is not always necessary even to provide the original to make a mistake in Russian language usage: The "testicle of a brass monkey" is an entirely Anglo-American unit of thermal measurement.

Also common are attempts at what might be called "near-Russian," along the lines of the "near-names" detailed above. Thus, Dinallo seems to be attempting the well-known Russian toast of "na zdorovye" (for health), but what he writes is "Zadrovnye," which means approximately "for the logging sleds." Similarly, Dinallo's main character later describes being caught "by the *karotkii volaskiis*, as we say in Russia." (201). This translation of the un-Russian expression "by the short and curlies" (approximately) is made more mysterious by Dinallo's use of an English plural on the Russian noun.[6]

The greatest Russian-language problems occur with writers who rely on dictionaries or phrase books for their touches of authenticity, without having any knowledge of the structure of Russian itself. Among other problems, the use of phrase books can introduce puzzling spelling and punctuation into familiar Russian phrases, as in Kaminsky's rendering of the common phrases "Sko'l'ka sto'eet" ("how much"), "Tavah/reeshch ("comrade") or "Spasee'bo" ("thanks"). Any reader with even a little Russian is likely to be mystified by Kaminsky's rendering of these everyday phrases, until he or she realizes that Kaminsky has lifted not only the phonetic transcription from his phrasebook source, but also the marks meant to indicate which syllables are stressed. Kaminsky's phrase "Krasee'v/iy doch" looks hopelessly bizarre, until a Russian speaker realizes that Kaminsky has paired the adjective "beautiful" with the noun "daughter" without understanding that the letters to the right of the slash are meant to vary by the gender of the noun (in this case requiring "aya," not "iy"). Sometimes the phrasebook approach to authenticity leads to straight-out errors, as in Kaminsky's phrase, "the smell of *rassolnik rybny*, noodle soup, had reminded Rostnikov of his hunger" ("rybny" means "fish," not "noodle").

A fourth strategy western thriller writers have used to authenticate their Russian plots is a general demonstration of close familiarity with daily life in Russia. As with the other strategies, however, such details can as easily prove to be "cranberries." Sometimes the mistakes come with physical objects, such as Kaminsky's assigning to a character a Chaika automobile that is painted white (151); government-issue, the Chaikas came only in ministerial black. Similarly, Greg Dinallo describes in *Red Ink* two security officers who are "about the size of [a] refrigerator" (47), by which he appears to mean they are large; even the biggest of Russian refrigerators, however, would be not much larger than a good-sized footlocker stood on end, a fact that drains Dinallo's comparison of most of its threat.

Similar problems arise with depictions of Russian institutions, customs, and practices. Craig Thomas, for example, imagines a town, Noviy Urengoy, laid out on an American-style grid, resulting in addresses that would seem better suited to Washington, D.C. ("Junction of K Street and Fourteenth") than to Siberia. In a similar vein, Kaminsky introduced private ownership of small businesses into Russia long before it existed in fact. For example, in *A Fine Red Rain*, one police investigator is described as "assigned [to] a new case, something to do with a gang of youths who were involved with some kind of extortion against shopkeepers beyond the Outer Ring Road" (123). Robin White, in his otherwise generally accurate *Siberian Light*, has his Russian hero remark that he was forced as a schoolboy to memorize Pasternak's *Zhivago* poems (278), when, in fact, even to read them would have been forbidden.

Finally, some of the problems this strategy for authenticity can create arise from the simple mechanics of the novel. It is extremely common in foreign-produced "Russian" mysteries that characters be called upon to assist their authors in providing details of local color or history, resulting in conversations that seem highly unlikely actually ever to have taken place, as in this example from Kaminsky:

> "History repeats itself," the man said, shaking his head wisely.
> "As Marx said," Rostnikov continued. "Where I now stand and you sit once stood the walls of the White City. This is where the Arbat Gate stood and where in 1812 Napoleon's army entered the city, set up their cannons, and destroyed the Troitskaya Gate of the Kremlin. (7)

The need for scene-setting can induce this kind of lumpy conversation even among American characters, as in DeMille's *The Charm School*:

> The Prague Restaurant was to their left. . . . On the north side of the square was Dom Svyasi. . . . [U.S. Embassy worker] Lisa said, "That's where the church of Saint Boris used to stand, and over there was the seventeenth-century church of Saint Tikhon. The communists demolished both of them. (99)

Cranberry or Ideology?

The fact that it is only unlikely, not impossible, that such conversations might take place in real life touches on a larger problem of the genre of Russia-set thrillers, which is that the stuff of so many of them, while not demonstrably inaccurate in any particular detail, seems as a whole to be false. It is very likely that it is this broader, less specific sense of incorrectness that particularly irritates Russian readers of these books, just as Americans might find themselves exasperated by such assertions as that of Igor Bunich, who has his "CIA Director" remark off-handedly,

> Unfortunately we [i.e., the CIA] didn't have time to enjoy the sense of victory [after the United States brought down the USSR]. . . . We had to provide security for the new democratic leaders of Russia, maintain surveillance on the underground political and commercial structures, point the militia toward the most odious of the mafia groups and clans, and work in full and open contact with the KGB. (5)

Although the mad exploit of German teenager Matthias Rust, who managed to cross Soviet air space and land his single-engine airplane in Red Square in May 1987, made the invulnerability of Soviet borders much less plausible than it had seemed before, it still seems most unlikely that, for example, in the mid-1960s Andrew Garve's journalist-hero would have been able to penetrate the Baltic defenses of the Soviet Union in a small sailboat *twice*, first to find the Russian ballerina whom he has married, and the second time to spirit her out of the USSR (in *Two if by Sea*). Even after Rust's exploits, Lionel Davidson seems implausible in *Kolymsky Heights* when he sneaks his polyglot hero into Russia as a Korean sailor on a Japanese cargo boat, and then spirits him out disguised as a native Chukchi, who skis to Alaska across the frozen Bering Strait. Still more implausible are plots such as that of James Burch's *Lubyanka,* which posits that the CIA could first spirit an operative into the most famous of the KGB's prisons, find a particular Soviet scientist who is being held there, and then get both the scientist and himself out again. The plot of Kruse's *Red Omega* seems impossible, not implausible: The book purports to detail a western plot to assassinate Joseph Stalin inside the Kremlin.

Whatever their degree of implausibility, all of these plots share the common feature that the western hero triumphs over his Soviet adversaries. This should not be surprising, since the Russian thriller emerged as a genre during the Cold War, when it was important, in little and in large, to reaffirm the superiority of west over east. A more complex question, which various of the thrillers seem to answer in different ways, is what precisely constitutes that superiority.

For many novelists, of course, the superiority of the west over Soviet Russia was so much a given that they saw no need even to explain it. Their supposedly Russian characters had only to catch a glimpse of the west, or even a westerner, in order to be ready to change sides immediately. In Ted Allbeury's *Moscow Quadrille,* French bed-manners convince Viktor Krasin, a Moscow actor, to defect in order to remain in France with Adele de Massu, the ex-wife of a British diplomat whom he had originally been assigned to seduce and suborn. Tatiana Romanova, the heroine of *From Russia, With Love,* doesn't even need France; one night sharing a pillow with James Bond is enough to convince her that life is better in the west, because "There was a wonderful sense of freedom being alone with a man like this and knowing that she would not be punished for it" (172). Stepan, a Soviet fisherman who is kidnapped by the escaping British journalist in *Two if by Sea,* needs neither sex nor a peek at the west to convince him to run away from his homeland. After a few days as a captive in the Englishman's small sailboat, he asks plaintively, "Can I not, perhaps, come to England with you?" (225).

Other thrillers are more explicit about the ways in which they see Soviet Russia to be inferior to the west. In some novels, the Soviets are portrayed as conniving, power-mad fiends, who seek victory for its own sake. Thus Joseph Hone in *The Sixth Directorate* depicts Yuri Andropov, who at the time really was in charge of the KGB, musing after a Politburo meeting that "There had been a hundred interpretations of the true faith [of Marxism] over the years . . . and none of them had really mattered; they could be identified, isolated, and crushed, as had happened so many times before: with Trotsky, with Hungary in 1956, and in Czechoslovakia twelve years later" (17). In the same vein, Ian Fleming's more fictional General Grubozaboyshchikov gloats in *From Russia, With Love* that "The reactions of our enemies are clumsy, their strategy disorganized. . . . At the same time . . . we continue to forge everywhere stealthily ahead—revolution in Morocco, arms to Egypt, friendship with Yugoslavia, trouble in Cyprus, riots in Turkey, strikes in England, great political gains in France—there is no front in the world on which we are not quietly advancing" (34). Other thrillers portray the Soviet threat as less surreptitious and more straightforward. Ralph Peter's *Red Army,* for example, describes in great detail how a Soviet *blitzkrieg* through the Fulda Gap might manage to swallow up West Germany.

Perhaps the writer who was most consistently paranoid about a Soviet threat was Ted Allbeury, most of whose books revolve in one way or another about the fear that the USSR might take over the west. *The Man with the President's Mind* details "Operation 471 [in which] a man was to be re-cruited who would be the analog of the US President" (21) in order to avoid future fiascoes like the Cuban missile crisis, while *All Our Tomorrows* goes even further, to imagine an England so torn by Moscow-inspired strikes and political bickering that England's prime minister finally appeals directly to Moscow to impose order on the United Kingdom.

Another way in which western writers implied the evils of Soviet Russia was to view the country through the eyes of a western hero, thus allowing readers to suffer Russian life vicariously. The result in a great many thrillers was to stress the ways in which Soviet Russia was not a consumer culture. Alan Williams in *Gentleman Traitor*, a "what-if" about Kim Philby rede-fecting to the west, describes Russia as a place where "several hundred yards of balding carpet" lead to a hotel room, where one might go "into the tiny bathroom to get a glass, but there wasn't one; nor was there any soap or plug for the bathtub. The only consolation was a brand-new roll of toilet paper" (49), while Dick Francis makes his hero in *Trial Run* muse in the "cathedral-like stations of the Moscow metro" that on the "achingly long and boring escalators I found myself quite missing London's vulgar adver-tisements for bras. Ritzy, jazzy, noisy, dirty, uninhibited old London, greedy and gutsy and grabbing at life" (113). DeMille is even more pointed about the material deprivations of Russia in *The Charm School*, where he imag-ines a mock American town erected deep in the secret heart of Russia as a place in which the KGB may acclimatize spies before infiltrating them into the United States. This pretend town has a 7-Eleven, a laundromat, a Bank of North America complete with logo, a place called Sweeney's Liquors, a barbershop called Mane Event, and a beauty parlor named Tresses, but the goods within them are only props. One of the American POWs from Viet-nam, who is forced to live in the center as an involuntary "instructor," ex-plains to DeMille's hero that "Everything is only for loan. . . . For fresh meat and produce, we go to a warehouse near the main gate and get whatever is available on a rationed basis. *That* is the same as everywhere else in this country" (466–68).

Many western thriller writers were also horrified by Soviet censorship. Le Carré's *Russia House* conveys the struggles of a Sakharov-like Russian sci-entist to get his musings published in an uncensored arena, while Richard Lourie, in *First Loyalty*, characterizes the depths of Soviet perfidy by sug-gesting that the Joseph Brodsky-like dissident poet of his thriller is a KGB agent. David Lippincott's *Salt Mine* revolves about the attempts of a group of desperate dissidents to seize western hostages, as a means of publicizing Russia's censorship policies. As the main dissident explains,

> [Our demands] are designed to force the world to see the Soviet government as it really is, not as the Soviet tells the world it is. For it is true that we have a constitution. To you Americans it would read very much like your own. But your constitution is observed as a matter of law; the Soviet constitution is just words on a piece of paper. For instance, our constitution, like yours, guarantees freedom of speech. Yet if one says one wrong thing—even to a friend—one may well end up in prison. (254)

In fairness, it must be said that at least one western writer saw that censorship had a positive side as well: To be persecuted for what you have written is at least to be read, while not to be read at all is, for a writer, the darkest nightmare imaginable. Lourie explored this faint sense of western envy in his ironic mock-thriller *Zero Gravity*, which has the United States and the USSR locked in a furious competition to be the first nation to send a poet to the moon. Once on the moon, the American poet laments to his Soviet counterpart, as the two split a celebratory bottle of vodka, "I envy you because in your country poets are taken seriously enough that three KGB men had to accompany you to the moon. That could never happen in America. Poetry is of no consequence in America" (213).

Other thrillers used their western central characters to convey a less specific but far broader sense of paranoia and alienation, suggesting that only a Russian might ever feel at home in Russia. Michael Frayn's *The Russian Interpreter* was a particularly vivid example, using as its central character a British exchange student in Moscow to embody the bewilderment and fear an outsider might feel in a place where he is "small and vulnerable among large forces that were indifferent to him" (159). As seen through the eyes of this puzzled student, Russia is a place where "Everything was . . . unnecessarily complicated, never more than half-explained. The simplest of life's arrangements had to be heaved into place against the gravitational pull of indifference and muddle. There were always two left shoes, and one finger too many to go in the holes of the glove." Frayn makes particularly vivid his fears about Soviet Russia when this graduate student seems to be making good progress toward picking up a Russian girl at a picnic:

> Now she was laughing. He caught up with her and kissed her again. They fell into the wet grass together. Laughing and laughing, Raya sat up and stuffed handfuls of dead leaves into his mouth.

He was sitting up and spitting out leaves when an unhappy thought occurred to him. It was too good to be true. That was what was wrong with it. She had joined the expedition uninvited—sat opposite him on the train—followed him into the forest—kissed him. The whole thing was being organised not by him but by her. Wasn't it all somewhat reminiscent of those cases one heard about, where foreigners in Russia were compromised, and then blackmailed into working for Soviet intelligence? . . . It was a horribly anaphrodisiac thought. (59)

This fear of Frayn's hero, that the Soviet system might turn even the impulses of human love against him, was widely shared by other western thrillers. Garve's *Two if by Sea* excoriates the Soviet Union for the determination of Soviet officials to prevent the marriage of a British journalist to a Russian ballerina: "The attitude of the authorities to foreign marriages seemed to be hardening. It was never quite clear what their motives were, but they had a morbid fear and suspicion of the outside world, and just didn't want any mixing" (8). Conversely, in *Moscow Quadrille* Allbeury shows the Soviet authorities doing all they can to encourage a liaison between British Ambassador James Hoult and one Lydia Ouspenskaya, because they wish to use Hoult's attraction to the woman as a lever by which to control a senior, influential politician; as Allbeury's Soviet spymaster explains, "The Presidium subcommittee wants this man to be either well-disposed toward us or under an obligation" because he "will not be our only weapon, but he could be the decisive one. When weak men, ambitious men [like the Prime Minister] are under pressure, then seemingly neutral advice can tip the scales. We want them to tip our way" (17, 19).

Ian Fleming also shows Soviets using sex as a lure in *From Russia, With Love*, although the Russians' goal there is to kill Bond rather than to recruit him. To homophobic Fleming, the picture of spymistress Rosa Krebs getting her own lesbian kicks from a tryst with Tatiana Romanova, the KGB's "Bond-bait," is a vivid indicator of the depths of Soviet depravity.

Family affections were another arena in which the thrillers accused Soviet authorities of cynical unprincipled abuse. Lourie's *First Loyalty* shows the Soviet authorities attempting to force an émigré living in New York to do their bidding by threatening to harm her brother who remains in Russia. In the same book, Lourie also builds suspense about what might become of one of his heroes, a dissident Russian physicist, by showing how great is his affection for his tiny daughter, thus magnifying the horror of what the KGB might do to the little girl in order to hurt the father. Kruse plays on those same fears and vulnerabilities in *Red Omega*, giving his hero's former lover Liudmilla two young children, who inevitably are taken away by the KGB, to be used as levers through which to try to pressure the hero into giving himself up.

Len Deighton shows the perfidy of the Soviet system coming from another quarter. In *Berlin Game,* the Communist spymaster, whom hero Bernard Sampson is trying to unmask, turns out to be his own beloved wife (who, to be fair, is an agent of East German, not Soviet, intelligence). A similar fear, that a man's nearest and dearest might actually be working against him, also haunts le Carré's *Our Game.* In that book, the hero pursues his former friend and protégé not so much because the protégé has apparently gone over to the Soviets, but out of jealous rage because the protégé has been successful in outwitting the hero by seducing away the hero's girlfriend, enlisting her intimate knowledge of the hero to help defeat him.

Indeed, westerners were so certain that the Soviet authorities would scruple at nothing in order to get the information they needed, or to hurt people whom they wished to punish, that in *Russia House*, le Carré made the *failure* of the Soviets to hurt someone in their power a major basis for the suspicion of authorities in British intelligence that the Russians might be playing them for fools. As the hero of *Russia House* ruminates while trying to decide whether or not their Russian contact person is genuine, "[The KGB] have not stolen her children, ransacked her flat, thrown Matvey [another Russian helping her] in the madhouse or displayed any of the delicacy traditionally reserved for Russian ladies playing courier to Soviet defence physicists who have decided to entrust their nation's secrets to a derelict Western publisher. Why?" (317).

The Individual as Hero, the Collective as Villain

Probably the fullest exploration of the supposed evils of the Soviet system came in those novels that claimed to make Russians, rather than foreigners, their heroes. The use of western heroes highlighted the ways in which westerners might react to specific features of the Soviet system as outsiders, but it did not lend itself to any consideration of what that system might do to universal human values—or at least to what the thriller writers assumed were such values. It probably was in part to widen the criticism of Soviet Russia that western thriller writers began in the early 1980s increasingly to make Russian characters their heroes.

As the angry reaction of Marinina to the novels of Martin Cruz Smith may suggest, Russians tend to find such characters utterly false, not only because of errors of language, detail, or geography committed by the western writers, but also because the psychology of these supposed Russians seems—to Russian readers—utterly and unrecognizably alien. It is difficult to respond to such criticisms though, in large part because they rely upon generalizations about the existence of a Russian national character, which, like pornography, is as difficult to define as it is easy to recognize when you see it. By fortunate coincidence, however, there exist two western thrillers, one written by an Englishman and the other by a Russian émigré, which allow the sensation of a comparative "Russianness" to be illustrated, rather than simply asserted.

Although the plots of the two thrillers are quite different, both Lionel Davidson's *Kolymsky Heights* and Edward Topol's *Red Snow* are set in Russia's Far North, which allows both books in passing to discuss the despoliation of the taiga and the degradation of the native northern peoples who are being destroyed by alcohol, disease, and Russian exploitation of their natural resources. In his book, Lionel Davidson creates a Russian doctor, Tatiana Komarova, who was born in the Far North and has spent her life working among the aboriginal Evenk people. Davidson describes the woman's thinking:

> She loved the work and she loved the country—the native people better than the Europeans. So she kept her distance, and was considered aloof; yes, she knew it. But better that than join a white elite and patronize the natives . . . [the natives] were not treated equally. . . . Plenty of extras for Europeans in these northern parts, but natives excluded, even in such matters as drink. (190)

Topol also imagines a heroine who has been born and raised in the Russian Far North. Unlike Davidson's sensitive Dr. Komarova, however, Topol's militia investigator, Anna Kovina, is contemptuous towards the natives, including particularly a "simple Nenets reindeer herder" (35) who had courted her years before while they were both in university. Although, as Kovina remarks with unsympathetic sarcasm, "he wasn't actually brought [to Moscow] by reindeer" (35), she had expected the fellow would kill himself while at the university, since "In the four years I'd been at the university, there'd been nine cases of suicide among students from the arctic territories—Chukchi, Evenki, Nentsi, and Khanti. Eskimo boys and girls just can't handle the stress of a big city" (35). Despite her prediction, however, the Nenets has not only survived, but has become a senior militia official. In the novel's present, this "reindeer herder" has now become a committed nationalist, who gets his fellow Nenets so stirred up that they delay the construction of a natural gas pipeline, thus requiring that Moscow send in Russian troops to restore order. When she sees the soldiers arriving, Kovina exults,

> Hell, it feels good to be a citizen of a country that's got military strength like ours! Never mind the rationing, or that there's no meat or butter in the shops. At least we can sleep securely knowing that we need have no fear of any Chinese, American, West German, or Israeli aggressor. My heart warmed to see the huge potbellied Antons [airplanes] disgorging tanks, armored cars, and tracked amphibians straight onto the frozen Ob [river]. With revving engines they formed into columns ready to storm through tundra, taiga, or desert, wherever the Homeland might require. (298)

The fact that both Davidson and Topol intend their respective heroines to be positive characters only serves to reinforce the differences between the two depictions. Without in any way wishing to assert that it is "un-Russian" to show sensitivity towards the aborigines, it must nevertheless be admitted that, when compared to Topol's Inspector Kovina, Davidson's Dr. Komarova feels and sounds like an Englishwoman.

Unfortunately, no such ready comparison exists to illustrate the "un-Russianness" of Martin Cruz Smith's hero, militia detective Arkady Renko, whom Marinina dismisses with such contempt. Renko was one of the first, and most popular, of the western-produced Russian heroes who purport to show westerners how ordinary Russians think and feel. Although, as the son of a war-hero general who himself was a senior law enforcement official, Renko was not so ordinary; the struggles of this appealing character, as he tries to do what he considers to be right in a corrupt society bent on stopping him, constituted in their whole a powerful denunciation of Soviet society. Smith began the series with *Gorky Park,* which portrays Renko's struggle to solve a vicious murder crime that, he soon learned, far more powerful people wished to cover up. Much of the tension and the pathos of Smith's enormously successful thriller derived from the way in which Renko was hounded and nearly destroyed by the agents of the state for which he himself worked, as he plunged stubbornly towards his solution. Smith enlarged upon this conceit in his subsequent Russian novels, showing how the fact that Renko has a little bit of honesty and a certain measure of pride are enough, in the Soviet system, to turn him into an outlaw. In

Polar Star, the second of Smith's Russian novels, Renko is disgraced and banished to a trawler in the Bering Sea. Another murder occurs, but no one in authority wants it solved. Driven by his sense of justice, Renko finds the murderer but cannot rely upon Soviet law to punish the man, and so hounds the culprit into ending his own life. Reinstated to the police force in *Red Square*, the third book in the series, Renko once again finds himself having to pursue a murderer who is better connected politically than are the people searching for him, so that, in the end, the culprit escapes justice.

At the end of *Red Square*, Renko stumbles upon the spontaneous demonstration that sprang up during the attempted coup of August 1991, when a few thousand Muscovites surrounded the Russian parliament building, the so-called White House, in a gallant and quixotic attempt to "defend democracy." Although Smith has pointedly drawn Renko to become ever more cynical and disaffected over the three novels, the sight of these brave but pathetic volunteers suddenly prompts him to join them, because, as Smith explains,

> All his life Arkady had avoided marches and demonstrations. This was the first one he had ever willingly come to. The same could be said, he suspected, of the other Muscovites around him. . . . The mystery [he thought] is not the way we die, it's the way we live. The courage we have at birth becomes hoarded, shriveled, blown away. Year after year, we become more alone. Yet, holding Irina's hand, for this moment, for this night, Arkady felt that he could swing the world. (381–82)

Since the demonstrations that Smith has Renko join did in fact occur, and thousands of ordinary Russians volunteered themselves as a feeble human shield against an "attack on democracy," which in the end never materialized, it seems difficult to argue that Renko's reaction is "un-Russian"—even if those thousands of defenders were more than outnumbered by the many millions of Muscovites who did *not* rush to defend "democracy." Nevertheless, for all the indisputable reality of the demonstrators whom Renko is supposed to have joined, Smith's suggestion about what motivates them seems to derive from a western value system, not a Russian one.

Smith depicts this spur-of-the-moment decision to join the demonstration as Arkady Renko's assertion of his individualism. This reflects two assumptions Smith shares with virtually all of his fellow writers of Russian thrillers, as well as, presumably, most of his millions of readers—that the drive to assert one's individualism is innate in every human being, and that the chief evil of the Soviet system was that it tried in every possible way to destroy that impulse of the self by burying it beneath communalism.

The western thrillers about Russia illustrate their criticisms of communalism in a number of ways. In many novels, the western heroes defeat their Soviet enemies precisely because the individual has greater flexibility, greater inventiveness, and greater drive to succeed than do his rule-bound, paper-shuffling, herd-following opponents. Davidson's hero in *Kolymsky Heights* outfoxes the KGB because he "thinks outside the box," heading deeper into Siberia rather than making for the closest border, as his collective-minded pursuers assume he would. In *Red Snow*, Topol's hero may have been born in Russia, but he grew up in America, and so has the wit and inventiveness to escape from his KGB pursuers by masquerading as a Georgian fruit seller from the Caucasus. In Kruse's *Red Omega*, Russian reverence for documents, uniforms, and following orders is such that the novel's hero is able to bluff his way into the heart of the Kremlin, and even to lie well enough to allay the suspicions of Joseph Stalin himself.

Other novels suggest that the efforts of the Soviet system to suppress individuality are sufficiently heinous as to justify the illegal responses of the heroes who struggle against the state. Thus, for example, Garve's *Two if by Sea* asserts that the right of its British hero to marry whomever he pleases so fully outweighs Soviet laws about passports, citizenship, and the manner in which one may enter and leave the country that the book makes a hero of the central character for illegally entering the Soviet Union, illegally spiriting a Soviet citizen out of the country, destroying state property, and kidnapping another Soviet citizen as he does so. Lourie's *First Loyalty* finds the Soviet system so villainous that the book has no moral qualms about its heroes' efforts to assist a Soviet citizen in smuggling military secrets out of Russia. The hero of Davidson's *Kolymsky Heights* lies repeatedly, falsifies documents, destroys both public and private property in his efforts to spy on a Russian military installation, and then fires on the Russian troops who are doing their duty by trying to stop him from illegally crossing the border. In *The Cardinal of the Kremlin*, Clancy not only lionizes his central character, Jack Ryan, for kidnapping a senior Soviet official, but also makes heroes of a squad of mujaheddin guerrillas who penetrate deep into Soviet Tajikistan to blow up a military installation, causing scores of deaths and millions of dollars in property damage. Finally, in *Red Omega*, Kruse takes it as a fictional given that the assassination of the head of state, Joseph Stalin, would be an act of highest heroism.

Other authors attacked the Soviet system on broader grounds, suggesting that the suppression of individualism was self-destructive and would inevitably bring down the state itself. Curiously, many such authors understood nationalist aspirations and individual aspirations to be essentially the same thing. Thus in *Salt Mine,* David Lippincott makes the mastermind of his hostage-taking terrorists be what he calls an Azerbaidzhani, because, as Lippincott explains, "The Azerbaidzhanis are a clannish lot; even had they known who he was and what he had done, they would never tell anyone from the Party. To them the Party represented a hated Moscow" (330). Kaminsky, in *The Man Who Walked Like a Bear,* imagines a "Turkistani" freedom fighter (with the improbable name of Peotor Kotsis) who plots to blow up Lenin's Tomb in Red Square as a means to air his grievances against the state, while the better-informed David Ignatius in *Siro* has the head of his CIA covert operation say, "Moscow's biggest fear is that someday these ethnic groups will all get together and start shooting Russians. That's why the KGB works so hard to keep them suspicious of each other" (283). Later in that same book, another character concludes that this same CIA overseer had been correct to surmise that "for all their bullying, [the Soviets are] terribly weak under the surface, and he's right to think that we should give them a good hard shove, rather than accommodate them forever" (463).

The degree to which western writers saw the Soviet system as a distinct entity was underscored by a small group of works which pitted that system against Russia itself. One representative was Anthony Hyde, who in *The Red Fox* has his hero wonder whether the Soviet Union's "vast, rebellious empire . . . desperately backward economy, and . . . cruelly repressive government" is not going to create "a *Russian* dissent within the 'Soviet Union'— a dissent that might truly matter?" (244).

Dealing with the Unthinkable: Russia without the Soviet Union

A decade after the collapse of the USSR, it is difficult to recall how unimaginable it once seemed that that vast state might ever even modify itself, to say nothing of vanishing overnight. Even in 1988, when David Madsen published *USSA,* the only mechanism by which he could imagine the USSR might come to an end, and western-style economic and political structures be erected in its stead, was through a nuclear war, which in his thriller the

United States has won. After this, the United States occupies the country in order to reform it, much as America occupied Japan and Germany after World War II. Madsen's conception of a post-Soviet Russia at least had the advantage of a certain moral clarity, allowing his novel, for the most part, to make members of the former administration into bad guys and the dissidents and democratic activists of the past now be good guys. The actual collapse of the Soviet system proved to be far more confusing, as can be seen in the plots of the relatively small number of Russian thrillers that westerners have published since 1991.

As many thriller writers have lamented, the end of the Cold War has brought very hard times to what once was among the most popular of western genres. Reader interest in Russia has waned dramatically, which explains a great deal about why so few post-Soviet thrillers exist. Even many of those that are technically post-Soviet contain details or conceits that make it seem certain they were partially or entirely composed while the Soviet Union still existed. Davidson, for example, attempts in *Kolymsky Heights* to imagine a new Siberia populated with private companies, such as the Tchersky Transport Company, but most of the tension in his novel, as well as the central conceit of a highly expensive underground military research facility, depends upon the kind of centralized authority—and financing—that had largely vanished by 1994 when the book actually appeared. Similarly Philip Kerr sets *Dead Meat* in what purports to be the St. Petersburg of independence, but such details as the "deficit of lavatory paper in all the state shops" (25) make the background seem more like the very end of the Gorbachev period, rather than the beginning of the new era.

A much more difficult problem was that the change in Russia's political system left western writers uncertain about who the villains were. The most obvious quarter from which to find a threat was in a Communist resurgence. Dinallo's *Red Ink,* for example, explores the moral dilemmas presented by a man who is counterfeiting currency in an effort to support under-financed democrats in the struggle against the pro-Communist masses, whom the book's finale picture as "A sea of Soviet regalia, flags, banners and posters surges through [Red] Square. The Hammer and Sickle. The glowering images of Lenin and Stalin. A mass of humanity eagerly protesting the fall of tyranny and the advent of freedom" (336). Dinallo's hero, a Russian named Nikolai Katkov, decides at novel's end simply to ignore the counterfeiting democrat they have been searching for because, as he explains to his American opposite from the Treasury Department, "At the moment, there are more important things in Russia than the letter of the law." The American asks, "More important than the truth?" to which Dinallo's hero, and presumably Dinallo himself, replies, "I'm not sure" (336).

As even Dinallo acknowledges in that novel, however, the problem with seeing the Communists as a continued peril was that they had so bungled the last few years of their rule in Russia, including the sad farce of their badly botched coup attempt, that when independence finally came to Russia, communism seemed more a pathetic joke than a threat, the silly dream of feeble pensioners and beefy, steel-toothed hausfraus. Some writers thus divorced the ideological aims of the Communist Party from a more basic drive for power and so imagined that the threat behind their plots would derive from a neofascist, nationalist reincarnation of the Bolsheviks' will to power, resulting in a kind of National Bolshevism, which married the conventions of anti-Nazi and anti-Soviet thrillers, as in Frederick Forsyth's novel of 1998, *Icon*.

Other writers chose to marry the conventions of another genre to that of the Soviet thriller, by portraying the mafia, as Russians and westerners alike began to refer to Russia's new class of criminal. While Brian Freemantle remained undecided in *Bomb Grade* whether the mafia were a greater threat than the outmoded habits of confrontation between Russians and Englishmen, other writers seemed distinctly uneasy about taking as their villains people who were generally engaged in what in the west would pass as business, even if their methods were sometimes a bit crude. This view was articulated in Philip Kerr's *Dead Meat*, albeit in the form of an abusive letter sent to a now-murdered journalist:

> There is no such thing as "the Russian mafia." There are just businessmen providing people with what they want and, just as often, what they need—the things they can't buy in the state shops. Our business methods have to be ruthless sometimes if only because in this stupid, backward country of ours there exists no understanding of supply and demand and free enterprise. If someone lets you down in business there is no real legal mechanism to enforce a contract or to have him pay compensation. So we break his legs, or threaten his children. (52)

Other writers were less inclined to see the mafia as businessmen and more apt to view them as Bolsheviks in a new guise. As early as 1992, Martin Cruz Smith had depicted Max, one of the villains in *Red Square*, as someone who is "like liquid. He changes shape. He fills the container, whatever the container is. In a fluid situation, he's king . . . [Max] used to say a fortune could be made out of the collapse of the Soviet Union. He said it was like any huge bankruptcy; there were still assets and property. . . . Max said that all [the Communist Party] had to do was change its name, call itself a company, and restructure" (234).

Thomas takes much the same tack in *A Wild Justice*, published four years after the appearance of independent Russia. Although it is a Russian policeman, Alexei Vorontsyev, who eventually manages to break up an international band of criminals who are shipping nuclear scientists to Iran in exchange for the heroin they sell in Europe, this victory is tempered by Vorontsyev's weary recognition that "'We did it. We got one of the bastards. One of the very biggest. . . .' He gestured toward the Kremlin. 'They're out there—hundreds, thousands of them. The politicos, the old *apparatchiks*' the *mafiosi*, and the *biznizmen*. This country is endemically corrupt'" (357).

Dinallo comes to very much the same conclusion in *Red Ink*, although the man who ought to have been a villain proves at novel's end to be a hero, of an inverted sort, because he has lied, cheated, and stolen in order to "buy equipment and raw materials, to create jobs and fill empty stomachs, to put meat on the table and bread on the shelves! . . . to insure that the average Russian doesn't give up on democracy before this wretched economy gets turned around" (325). The reason that such desperate measures are required is that, as the same man says, "Whether we have a Communist, fascist, or democratic government, it's still going to be a *Russian* government—a bottomless pit of bureaucratic quicksand that'll suck up everything in its path" (325).

Instinctive Russophobia

The handful of western books set in Russia that the postcommunist environment has produced makes a somewhat slender base on which to draw conclusions, but it is nevertheless curious that the few such thrillers that have been published seem to bear out the gloomy predictions of Sam, the cynical CIA agent who is one of the heroes of DeMille's *The Charm School*. Lisa, an American girl of Russian extraction, tends to wax rhapsodic about what Russia could be, if only the Communists could be removed. As much as he would like to get her into bed, however, Sam is unable to agree:

[Sam said] "You make a distinction between the people and the government here. But I think people get the kind of government they deserve. In this case, probably better."

[Replied Lisa] "That's not true, Sam. The Russians may not understand democracy, but in some curious way they are passionately devoted to *svoboda*—freedom . . . I always thought that communism is an historical fluke here. It won't make it to its hundredth birthday."

[Sam] replied dryly, "I'd hate to think what these people will come up with next." (103)

What Sam is arguing, in essence, is that communism is a creation of Russia and Russianness, and so the west's victory over the first in no way reduces the threat posed by the second. A similar assumption underlies Frederick Forsyth's novel *Icon*, which sees the only solution to Russia's problems to be the restoration of the monarchy—under a tsar who also happens to be a member of the House of Windsor.

As this chapter has demonstrated, the western thriller writers do not, as a group, have a particularly strong grasp of the details of the Russian language, Russian culture, or Russian life. That collective unfamiliarity does not make their hostility toward Russia especially puzzling. As any number of thinkers have observed, ignorance is one of the mediums in which dislike flourishes best. What is more striking, however, is the degree to which the western thriller writers have fastened upon what the earlier chapters of this book have argued are essential features of the Russian worldview. As noted, even the most poorly informed thrillers seem to sense the Russians' comparatively greater disdain of material things, their greater deference to and respect for the state, and their instinctual communalism. For all the western insistence on rule of law and the supposed lawlessness of the communist state, or its successor, the thrillers have no qualms about allowing their heroes to commit acts that break not only Soviet laws, but that would be illegal even in the west, as long as those acts assert the primacy of the individual over the state. Russian heroes as depicted by westerners are mavericks, individuals who rebel against the society that surrounds them, while those who submit or conform to the expectations of group behavior are portrayed, at best, as humans turned to sheep by communism, and, at worst, as a faceless force bent on overrunning the west.

To be sure, for most of this century, this western animus was directed more toward communism than toward Russia. As noted above, some writers did tend to see communism as the essence of Russia, but many more saw it as an ideology enchaining ordinary Russians, who would be only too happy to embrace western values and practices once those chains were slipped off. The west has only a decade of modern experience with a noncommunist Russia, most of which has been consumed in a turbulent swirl of economic reforms, constitutional battles, financial crises, and civil wars. All of these the west has been inclined to interpret as impediments slowing Russia's natural and inevitable transformation into a western-style state. As noted in the introduction, however, Russia's stubborn insistence upon remaining distinct from the west seems increasingly to provoke a kind of surprised exasperation among westerners, who find it incomprehensible that Russia should persist in viewing itself as a great power, that Russia should resent assuming its "proper" place in the world economy as a supplier of raw materials and a consumer of imported products, that Russia should greet western political and economic advice with truculence and resentment rather than with gratitude.

In the arena of popular culture, that exasperation is increasingly being reflected by the frequency with which the so-called Russian mafia or Russian neonationalists appear as villains, suggesting that a great deal of what western thrillers used to make the hairs on the backs of their readers' necks stand up was not communism, but rather was Russia itself.

At least one scholar has suggested that this instinctive Russophobia is nothing new to the west. In examining the causes leading up to England's decision to invade Crimea, John Howes Gleason remarked that "Within the United Kingdom there developed early in the nineteenth century an antipathy toward Russia which soon became the most pronounced and enduring element in the national outlook on the world abroad."[7] In Gleason's description, this antipathy grew from the fear and disdain that England's Romantics felt for the absolutism of Russia's monarchy. The antipathies of that earlier Russophobia, according to Gleason's description, were precisely the same as those exhibited by the popular writers of the later, anti-Soviet thrillers. Those who celebrated individualism, the primacy of individual sentiment, and the tragedy of individual fate recoiled instinctively from a country which exalted the state above the individual, seeing Russia to be not just alien, but actually evil.

Gleason suggests that this earlier form of Russophobia required a certain informed ignorance to sustain itself; that is, the pro-invasion factions of English society, and of Parliament, were driven by a conviction that they understood what Russia's real nature and true aims were. For this reason they felt not just a geopolitical, but a moral duty to fight Russia. Significantly, Gleason identifies popular literature as the most influential agent in the dissemination and maintenance of English Russophobia. Gleason cites in particular the role played by a novel called *Thaddeus of Warsaw*. Terming this "the first historical novel in the English language,"[8] Gleason shows how author Jane Porter's emotionally charged descriptions of the miseries suffered by the Catholic, westernized Poles during Catherine the Great's partition of their state galvanized English public opinion, leading to what—as Gleason points out—was the only invasion of Russia that England ever mounted. Gleason's conclusions about the intent and effect of Jane Porter's novel seem applicable to the entire genre of Soviet and Russian thrillers:

> Of great importance [in understanding the genesis of Russophobia] are the stereotypes of things Russian which developed in Great Britain, the well-worn molds into which . . . ideas with regard to remote and unfamiliar objects tend to fall at all times and in all societies. (7)

This is not to suggest that it is only westerners who have misunderstood the Russians. As we have noted, there are fewer Russian depictions of the west in popular literature than there are western ones of Russia. There are probably many reasons for this, but one certainly is that Russian intellectual history has generally been more successful in defining what Russia is not than in declaring what it is. This uncertainty of definition has been reflected in a number of famous images, such as the silence of the Russian troika at the end of Nikolai Gogol's *Dead Souls*, the notion that Russia's page in world history is still blank, waiting to be written, and even the persistent attempts of Gorbachev and his supporters to find a "third way" for Russia's economy that was neither communist nor western. As Tim McDaniel has put it, "Russianness was always defined *in opposition* to something else" (28).

The inability to define and articulate a positive statement of Russianness, however, does not diminish the sharpness with which Russians sense the alien nature of much that the west understands to be natural. One of the problems in demonstrating that point is that statements by Russians directly disputing western values—especially those from the Communist era—are easily dismissed as being ideological and polemical, rather than sincere. Thus, for example, it is difficult for westerners to accept as genuine the heroine's protest in Lev Ovalov's Russian "counter-thriller" of the 1960s, *Comrade Spy*, already quoted in chapter 2, to the effect that

"Whether [luxurious goods and exclusive privileges] belong to me personally isn't all that important" (123).

It is no easier for westerners to accept similar claims for Russian unique-
ness made after the collapse of the USSR, because they seem as hopelessly
romantic as they are totally unprovable. A good example of this pro-
Russian sentiment is the following, taken from what purports to be the
KGB's secret history of Russia in Igor Bunich's sprawling *Absolute License*.
Describing the first Russian state, which the Russians themselves had
formed before the appearance of the Vikings (whom this "secret manuscript" terms "an armed commercial mafia-like group"), Bunich fantasizes
that this prehistorical Slavic Eden

> had a sociopolitical structure which was completely incomprehensible to its
> contemporaries. The people had no kings, no khans, no emirs, no princes,
> and no leaders. Everyone was equal and they governed themselves collectively.
> It is already difficult for us to believe this, but they had some form of un-
> known but exceptionally effective form of popular government [*naro-
> dovlastiye*]. This was neither ambitious nor aggressive, but rather was directed
> solely toward flourishing. In fact, there were many villages and small cities,
> and to judge by the findings of archeologists, they had existed for at least a
> thousand years before the events being described. But there is no sign any-
> where in these parts of so much as a single cataclysm! In those years when
> everybody slashed and killed everybody else, when invasions followed inva-
> sions, when the clang of sword and whistle of arrows didn't fade for so much
> as a second, in this region it was all quiet and calm. (272)

Westerners inclined to ascribe such sentiments to extreme nationalism, or
to see Bunich as a figure from the fringes of Russian thought, would do well
to realize that the sentiments expressed or implied in the passage above are
in fact held, in one form or another, by a large swath of the Russian population. This may be demonstrated by a passage from a completely different
sort of book—this a history of Russian agriculture—which begins with the
premise that

> No other country of the world has suffered so many tests of its strength and
> given so much civilization to Earth as has our country, Russia! It is Russia
> which
>   —considered the highest values to be the family, the Motherland, and na-
> ture, striving to achieve the optimal social exploitation of these riches;
>   —saved Europe from the Tatar-Mongol invasion and the aggression of
> Napoleon;

—gave the world the example of the world's largest state, in terms of territory, in terms of the numbers of people who made it up, and in terms of its military and industrial might. It is important that Russia achieved this not with the aid of arms and the forcible introduction of religion, but by defending smaller peoples, preserving their indigenous ways, leading them through Russia culture to world culture, bringing the best minds of the world into the country by creating good working and living conditions for them;

—led the world out of the dead end of the first world war, which had come about from the sins and selfish interests of capitalism, and in many ways realized the thousand-year-old dreams of all peoples of the world for the creation of a just state for people of labor, who wished to live according to the principle "from each according to his abilities, to each according to his labor," and guaranteed a high level of social support;

—saved the world from fascism, thermonuclear war, helped colonialism to collapse, created a commonwealth of socialist countries, the might and successes of which forced capitalism, in order to survive, to transform itself into a more humane and civilized form of market economy. The practices of socialism were the primary basis of this, as were the experience of the Russian Empire and of pre-Christian Rus. Obviously, this experience was not so bad. . . . In saving earth's civilization from the worst and most unpredictable consequences, Russia three times emerged as the world's leader, but each time was the victim of a conspiracy by foreign governments (pre-Christian Rus by Byzantium; and the Russian Empire and the USSR by the developed capitalist countries of the world) and the treachery of its own leaders.[9]

Perhaps the best demonstration, though, of the instinctive anti-westernism that lies just beneath the skin of most Russians, just as an instinctive Russophobia does in most westerners, is the figure of Michael Baron, an American professor of Russian history who plays a supporting role in Polina Dashkova's *The Light Steps of Madness*. Dashkova appears from her books to be familiar with the west and to have no particular love or nostalgia for the Communist past. The characters in her many books enjoy the comforts of western consumer culture, and are perfectly content to travel abroad, as money and time permit. Her portrait of this prominent American professor of Russian history is well observed, with no obvious "cranberries" to suggest that Dashkova's judgments are ignorant or based on misunderstandings.

Baron figures in Dashkova's plot in part as a device of protective coloration, a character who allows the novel's heroine to travel to Siberia as the professor's translator, to search out the reasons why someone from her youth has suddenly begun stalking her. A middle-aged professor of Russian history who cannot speak Russian, Michael is cast as a good-hearted but garrulous and light-minded eccentric. A vegetarian who is said to be a founding member of the "Brooklyn Anti-Smokers Club," Michael stumbles blithely through a landscape of mafiosi and killers, lecturing Russians on their health habits, until he is suddenly mistaken for a more serious participant in Dashkova's unfolding plot. Fired upon, he permits himself to be whisked immediately away by the militia who have been surreptitiously following the heroine (who is the wife of one of their colleagues). Despite insisting that he will not depart Siberia until he knows that the heroine is well, Baron, in fact, lets himself be shipped back to Moscow immediately, where he is secured in a hotel for the duration, because what the militia officer fears most is that "All that was missing here was a dead American! After all, if anything were to happen to a U.S. citizen, God forbid, on his territory, there would blow up such an international scandal that it was terrible even to imagine" (393–94). Unlike the heroine, who forges ahead to the solution of the novel's crimes despite enormous danger to herself and her family, Baron sulks furtively in his hotel room, because "I don't want to risk my life" (385). Self-righteous, self-absorbed, preachy about subjects about which he knows less than those to whom he is lecturing, judgmental and condescending to the Russians whom he studies, and so concerned for his own well-being that he is content to hide in his hotel room and leave it to the FSB to "do something" to save his imperiled Russian female friend, the figure of Michael Baron speaks all the more eloquently about the general Russian perception of Americans because Dashkova obviously intends him in her book to be a positive character.

Conclusion

Early western euphoria, when the USSR broke up, over the prospect that Russia would now become an "ordinary country" has, over the past decade, been transformed into a growing exasperation, as Russia continues to frustrate western hopes and expectations. Western businessmen have been frightened by the bloody directness with which ownership battles have been fought, mystified by the intricacies of shareholder laws, license granting, and insider trading, and scared away by the insouciance with which the government repudiated its own short-term debts, in the economic meltdown of August 1998. Policy makers and politicians have been affronted by Russia's determination still to be considered a party to be consulted in the conduct of world affairs and have professed incomprehension that Russia would find the expansion of NATO right up to the country's borders a threat. Democracy builders have thrown their hands up in dismay at the conduct of national voting, first in 1993, when free elections brought the mad-mouthed nationalist Vladimir Zhirinovskiy to prominence, then in 1996 when only vividly unfair media treatment permitted a deeply unpopular Boris Yeltsin to snatch the presidency back from a choice between a Communist and a general, and finally in 2000, when Yeltsin's surprise New Year's resignation paved the way for a first-round victory by a presidential candidate who was entirely unknown to the world just a few short months before.

To sympathetic western eyes, the course of Russian politics, economic reform, and the general tenor of Russian life all seem incompetent, chaotic, and naive, while unsympathetic westerners prefer to view the actions of the state and its leaders as proof that Russia remains a cruel and Byzantine place, where the only currency of value is raw power, and no price—financial, political, or human—is too high to pay in its pursuit. Both camps tend to see Russia as unpredictable and illogical, lurching drunkenly from one lunacy to the next, giving vivid geopolitical embodiment to the famous Russian joke of the leader who announces somberly to the nation that "Comrades! Until last week we stood on the edge of the abyss, but now we have taken great strides forward!"

What the west may fail to appreciate in this self-deprecating Russian joke is that Russia has trembled above this abyss for more than six centuries, and indeed can make a plausible claim to have existed as a continuous geopolitical ethnic and linguistic unity for at least a millennium. Even during the period they term the Tartar-Mongol Yoke (usually dated 1240–1480), the Russians remained in nominal control of their principalities, albeit at the price of a heavy tribute paid to their Mongol conquerors. The northwestern part of their state—Novgorod and Pskov—remained wholly independent of the Mongols (although also paying a heavy tribute), before being conquered by other Russians. The Russian religious heritage, attenuated though the practice of it may be in modern Russia, is also a millennium old. What is more important, from the Russian point of view, is that Orthodoxy can trace its lineage back to the very earliest days of the Christian era, while the Catholicism of the west is a deviation and apostasy. The Protestant faiths that have so profoundly shaped the most active of the modern western states, including England, Germany, and America, are, from the Russian Orthodox point of view, little more than quibbles within quibbles among apostates from "the right faith"—Orthodoxy. As the Russians themselves will occasionally point out, they were building massive churches before any of the present states of Europe existed, while the walls that surround the Kremlin were built (yes, following the design of an Italian architect, but using bricks cast and laid by Russian hands) at about the same time as Christopher Columbus set sail to discover what took several more centuries to become America.

Although the tenets and assumptions of social Darwinism lurk just beneath the surface of most public discourse in the west, public and government opinion has generally accepted the premise that the wealth and power of certain individuals are not the direct result of greater virtue or better qualities. In judging the comparative virtues of states, or of belief systems, however, the world remains relentlessly Darwinian—the west is "better" because of the greater material advantage it has accumulated in relationship to the rest of the world. The process of the collapse of communism appeared to reinforce that perception, as the vast Soviet Russian state proved incapable of keeping even bread on the shelves of its stores, and so had to turn in humiliating appeal to the west to stave off a widely threatened—but never materialized—famine. Present-day western images of Russia focus on the country's crime rate, but rarely add that it is the United States that has the greatest percentage of its adult population behind bars and leads the developed world in executions. Much is written about Russia's swelling underclass of the poor and disenfranchised, but rarely do such articles point out that the percentage of Russians who live beneath their country's official poverty line is virtually identical to the number of Americans who live beneath the U.S. poverty line (about 26 percent in each case). Russia's protracted war in the north Caucasus has been taken as proof of Russian brutality, militarism, and latent dreams of empire, yet no serious western effort has been mounted to reply to the question that the Russians themselves have raised to such criticism: What is the difference between their destruction of Grozniy and the U.S.-led bombing of Serbia (to be sure, under the banner of the United Nations) that makes the latter "good" and the former "bad"?

It is not the intention of this book to argue that the Russians are right and the west wrong. The Russians themselves acknowledge that their country faces great problems, and there is little consensus about how these might be addressed, to say nothing of solved. Indeed, the argument about whether Russia can find the resources to solve these problems somewhere within itself, or whether it must, in essence, surrender to the west by adopting western solutions, has run through Russian society for at least the past three hundred years. What this book has tried to demonstrate, however, is that the differences between Russia and the west are far more profound than westerners—and probably Russians too—like to acknowledge. Perhaps the fault for this lies in Russia's apparent similarity to the west. No westerner expects the Chinese or the Ethiopians to think, behave, or react as westerners do. Forgetting that Russians do not share most of the cultural, economic, and philosophical history that has shaped the western world—they had no Renaissance, no Reformation, no Enlightenment, but what is even more important, neither did they need them, since their attachment to their faith remained constant—westerners expect Russians to think and act as we do, and then grow first puzzled, then condescending, then hostile when they do not.

Crime fiction depends upon a consensus about what is normal. English and American readers expect that humans will not die violent and unexpected deaths, that they will not have their property forcibly taken from them, that governmental authorities will protect them, and thus crime fiction readers are able to enjoy the vicarious pleasures of seeing what might happen when those normal situations are violated by abnormal events called crimes.

What a close reading of the *detektivy* shows is that the "natural" world of the Russians is very different from that of the west. Much of what the west calls "crime," the Russian genre finds to be simply human weakness, or an inescapable part of an imperfect world. Conversely though, many of the relations between people that the west accepts as a matter of course seem so barbaric to Russians as to become a kind of crime. The unit of measurement that the western genre finds supreme—the individual—is to the Russian genre, at best, a solipsism and, at worst, a criminal, actively working to destroy the Russian basic unit, an amorphously defined but acutely felt larger community (the *mir* or *obshchestvo* or *narod* or *Rodina*). To the Russian, the much-vaunted laws of the west are hubris, the attempt to abrogate to man what rightly belongs only to God. It is the duty of society, in the person of its duly empowered representatives, to battle those elements that would put their interests and pleasures above those of the group as a whole, but the only expected result of that battle is that the defenders and the attackers will battle in dynamic stasis forever. In both the defenders and the attackers, however, the spark of God's likeness glows, ready at the appropriate moment to be fanned up by the cognition of justice.

Crime fiction tries to convince its readers that justice will eventually be served. What people tend to forget is that the perception of what constitutes justice varies widely, and that no one people's notion of it is more correct or natural than that of another. Rather, the notion of justice grows from the culture, the religion, the history, and the tradition of a people. Commercialized, individualistic, and convinced at some level or another that heaven (or fate) "repays" people as they have earned by their deeds, western readers want crime fiction that punishes malefactors, returns property, and exacts revenge. More accustomed to the ebb and flow of material fortune, inclined to find their true identity in some kind of communal group larger than themselves, and willing to recognize that sinner and saint alike share the qualities of being human, the Russian readers of the *detektiv* have created a variant of the crime genre that maps out the specifically Russian understandings of crime, punishment, absolution, and retribution.

Notes

1. The origin of this term used to describe the errors of fact that foreigners commit in their descriptions of Russia is obscure. The usual explanation is that a French journalist interviewing Tolstoy—or, in some versions, Turgenev—failed to understand the source of the unfamiliar juice with which they were refreshing themselves, and so began his article with the words, "As we sat in the shade of a spreading cranberry tree...."

2. Viktor Chernyak, "A Thin Layer of Falsehood" in *Detektiv No. 1* (Moscow: Prometey, 1989), 81.

3. It is possible that Peters intends Talala to be a Lakai, rather than an Uzbek, particularly since he describes his villain as having been "born in a yurt" (73), something highly unusual for the sedentary Uzbeks, but not at all unusual for the various hill and mountain peoples of the part of the former Emirate of Bukhara which Peters describes as Talala's home region (122).

4. It also seems unlikely that a girl born in the late 1960s or early 1970s might have been "named Dynama in honor of the electrification of Uzbekistan" (35); such "industrial" names were common in the 1920s and 1930s, but were replaced by traditional Uzbek and Islamic names later on.

5. A more likely equivalent would seem to be "dermoyed" or "darmoyed," although I have only heard this used descriptively of third parties, and never as the equivalent is used in Clancy's book, as a face-to-face insult.

6. Fellow pedants will also note that Dinallo properly indicates vowel reduction (o for a), but keeps the adjective singular.

7. John Howes Gleason, *The Genesis of Russophobia in Great Britain* (Cambridge, Mass.: Harvard University Press, 1950), 1.

8. Gleason, 14.

9. V. P. Zvolinskiy, *Pravda vsegda odna: Rossiyskaia derevnya na istoricheskom razlome* (Moscow: Mezhdunarodnyy tsentr nauchnoy i tekhnicheskoy informatsii, 1996), 6–7.

Bibliography of Works Consulted

Detektivy

Adamov, Arkadiy, et al. *Moya militsiya (My Militia)*. Moscow: MVD, 1997.

Adamov, Arkadiy. *Bolotnaya trava (Swamp Grass)*. Moscow: Sovetskiy Pisatel, 1990.

——. *Idyot Rozysk (Search Underway)*. Moscow: Yuridicheskaya Literatura, 1986.

——. *Inspektor Losev*. Moscow: Moskovskiy Rabochiy, 1989. Also contains the novels *Na svobodnoye mesto (Into an Empty Place)* and *Zlym vetrom (Evil Wind)*.

——. *Inspektor Losev*. Kishinyov: Lumina Publishing, 1985. Also contains the novels *Zlym vetrom (Evil Wind)* and *Petlya (Noose)*.

——. *Petlya (Noose)*. Moscow: Eksmo Press, 1997.

Afanasyev, Aleksandr, and Danil Koretskiy. *Gat (Log Road)* and *Zaderzhaniye (Arrest)*. Moscow: Molodaya Gvardiya, 1991.

Afanasyev, Anatoliy. *Moskovskiy dushegub (Moscow Mankiller)*. Moscow: Martin Press, 1996.

Aitmatov, Chingiz. *The Place of the Skull*. New York: Grove Press, 1989.

Akunin, Boris. *Azazel*. Moscow: Zakharov, 2000.

——. *Koronatsiya (Coronation)*. Moscow: Zakharov, 2000.

Aleksandrov, Nikolai. *Two Leaps Across a Chasm*. New York: Scribners, 1992.

Ardamatskiy, Vasiliy. *Sud (The Trial)*. In *Roman-Gazeta*, no. 17, 1987.

Arestova, Lyubov. *Poslednyaya ulika (Last Clue)*. Moscow: Yuridicheskaya Literatura, 1988. Also contains the short stories "Last Clue," "Supplementary Investigation," "Regarding the Disappearance of . . . ," and "Search in the Taiga."

——. *Tayna dvoynogo ubiystva (Secret of a Double Murder)*. Moscow: Kvadrat Press, 1995.

Aryasov, Igor. *Tri chasa na vyyasneniye istiny (Three Hours to Clarify the Truth)*. Moscow: Molodaya Gvardiya, 1989.

Astafyev, Viktor. *Pechalnyy detektiv (Sad Detective)*. In *Roman-Gazeta*, no. 5, 1987.

Astakhova, Inna. *Myortvaya voda (Dead Water)*. Rostov-na-Donu: Prof-Press, 1995.

———. *O proshlym prikazano zabyt (Ordered to Forget the Past)*. Rostov-na-Donu, Elista: Prof-Press and Dzhangor Press, 1995.

Ateyev, Aleksey. *Chyornoye delo (Black Deed)*. Moscow: Eksmo Press, 1998.

Aytmatov, Chingiz. *Plakha (The Executioner's Block)*. Moscow: Molodaya Gvardiya, 1987.

Babkin, Boris. *Ozherelye smerti (The Jewelry of Death)*. Moscow: Lokid Press, 1995.

Barabashov, Valeriy. *Krestnaya mat (Godmother)*. Moscow: Eksmo Press, 1996.

———. *Vyshak (The Big Jump)*. Moscow: Eksmo Press, 1997.

Barkovskiy, Vyacheslav, and Andrey Izmaylov. *Russkiy tranzit (Russian Transit)*. St. Petersburg: Folio Press, 1995.

Belousova, Yana. *Rasplata manyaka (Maniac's Payback)*. Moscow: Vagrius Press, 1988.

Bezuglov, Anatoliy. *Chyornaya vdova (Black Widow)*. Moscow: Moskovskiy Rabochiy, 1989.

———. "Cupid's Arrows." In *Slovo Prokurora*. Moscow: Sovetskaya Rossiya, 1987.

———. *Prestupniki (Criminals)*. Moscow: Molodaya Gvardiya, 1987.

———. *Slovo prokurora (The Procurator Speaks)*. Moscow: Sovetskaya Rossiya, 1987. Contains "Cupid's Arrows."

Bunich, Igor. *Bespredel (Absolute License)*. St. Petersburg: Shans, 1994.

Bushkov, Aleksandr. *Kapkan dlya Beshenoy (Trap for Beshenaya)*. Moscow: Olma-Press, 1997.

Cherginets, Nikolay. *Sledstviye prodolzhayetsya (The Investigation Continues)*. Minsk: Mastatskaya Literatura, 1986.

Chernyak, Viktor. *The Hour Is Come*. Moscow: Raduga Publishers, 1989.

———. *Tonkiy sloy lzhi (A Thin Layer of Falsehood)*. Moscow: Prometey, 1989.

Chernyonok, Mikhail. *Losing Bet*. Garden City, N.Y.: Dial Press, 1984.

Danilova, Anna. *Vykhozhu tebya iskat (I'm Coming to Find You)*. Moscow: Eksmo Press, 1998.

Dashkova, Polina. *Krov nerozhdyonnykh (Blood of the Unborn)*. Moscow: Eksmo Press, 1999.

———. *Lyogkiye shagi bezumiya (The Light Steps of Madness)*. Moscow: Eksmo Press, 1998.

———. *Mesto pod solntsem (Place under the Sun)*. Moscow: Eksmo Press, 1998.

———. *Nikto ne zaplachet (No One Will Weep)*. Moscow: Eksmo Press, 1999.

———. *Obraz vraga (Image of the Enemy)*. Moscow: Eksmo Press, 1999.

———. *Pitomnik (Nursery)*. Moscow: Astrel Publishing, 2000.

———. *Prodazhnyye tvari (Flesh for Sale)*. Moscow: Eksmo Press, 1998.

———. *Zolotoy pesok (Golden Sand)*. Moscow: Eksmo Press, 1999.

Davydenko, Vladimir. *U krutogo ovraga (By a Steep Ravine)*. Donetsk: Donbas, 1984.

Dementyev, Nikolay. *Lyudi, prostite menya (People, Forgive Me)*. Leningrad: Lenizdat, 1987.

Derevyanko, Ilya. *Otmorozki (Thugs).* Moscow: Eksmo Press, 1995.

Dontsova, Darya. *Obed u lyudoyeda (Lunch with a Cannibal).* Moscow: Eksmo, 2001.

Dorenko, Viktor. *Stavka na banditov (Bet on Bandits).* Moscow: Eksmo Press, 1996.

Dotsenko, Viktor. *Lyubov Beshenogo (Beshenyy's Love).* Moscow: Vagrius Press, 1997.

———. *Mest Beshenogo (Beshenyy's Revenge).* Moscow: Vagrius Press, 1996.

———. *Tridtsatogo unichtozhit! (Destroy Number Thirty!).* Moscow: Vagrius Press, 1996.

Dotsenko, Viktor, and Fyodor Butyrskiy. *Chyornyy tribunal (Black Tribunal).* Moscow: Vagrius Press, 1999.

Dvoretskiy, Lev. *Bezoruzhna i ochen opasna (Unarmed and Very Dangerous Woman).* Moscow: Vagrius Press, 1996.

Filatov, Nikita. *Myshelovka (Mousetrap).* St. Petersburg: Folio Press, 1996.

———. *Provereno elektronikoy (Electronically Tested).* Moscow: Olma Press, 1995. Includes the short stories "Static," "4:15 Moscow Time," and "Electronically Tested."

———. *Safari Mayora Vinogradova (Major Vinogradov's Safari).* St. Petersburg: Azbuka, 1997.

Gagarin, Stanislav. *Russkiy syshchik (Russian Investigator).* Moscow: Otechestvo, 1994. Also contains Pronin "Snezhnaya Versiya (Version in Snow)."

German, Yuryy. *Odin god (One Year).* Moscow: Moskovskiy Rabochiy, 1989.

Gonik, Vladimir. *Preispodnyaya (Out from Under).* Moscow: Pilgrim, 1993.

———. "Edge of the World," in *Poyedinok No.17.* Moscow: Moskovskiy Rabochiy, 1991.

Imanov, Mikhail. *Chistaya sila (Pure Force).* Moscow: Sovremennik, 1988.

Ivanov, Nikolay. *Department nalogovoy politsii (Tax Police).* Moscow: Eksmo Press, 1995.

———. *Vzyat na mushku (Take Aim).* Moscow: Eksmo Press, 1997.

Ivanov, Nikolay, and Sergey Ivanov. *Pridyotsya vas ubit (You Must Be Killed).* Moscow: Eksmo Press, 1996.

Izmaylov, Andrey. *Belyi ferz (White Queen).* Moscow: Lokid Press, 1996.

———. *Idiot (Male Idiot).* Moscow: Lokid Press, 1996.

———. *Idiotka (Female Idiot).* Moscow: Lokid Press, 1996.

———. *Tryukach (Stuntman).* St. Petersburg: Teks, 1995.

Kayyak, V. *Chudo Brigity (Brigita's Miracle).* In *Latyshskiy detektiv (The Latvian Detektiv).* Riga: Liesma Publishing, 1985. Also contains Tsirulis, *Milyi, ne speshi . . . (Don't Rush, Darling),* and Kolbergs, *Nochyu, v dozhd (At Night, In the Rain).*

Khristoforov, Igor. *Russkiye rabyni (Russian Slave Girls).* Moscow: Eksmo Press, 1996.

Kivinov, Andrey. *Masliny dlya pakhana (Olives for a Crime Boss).* Moscow: Olma-Press, 2000.

———. *Ment obrechennyy (Doomed Cop).* Moscow: Olma-Press, 1998. Also contains the short stories "Made of Waste Products" and "Doomed Cop."

————. *Okhota na krys (Rat Hunting)*. St. Petersburg: MiM-Delta Press, 1996. Also contains the short story "Rat Hunting."

————. *Sled bumeranga (Track of the Boomerang)*. Moscow: Tsentrpoligraf, 1997. Also contains the short stories "Baby Doll" and "Track of the Boomerang."

————. *Strakhovochnyy variant (Backup Plan)*. St. Petersburg: Valeri SPb, MiM-Delta Press, 1995. Also contains the short stories "Nightmare on Stachek Street," "Backup Plan," "Gone with the Wind," "Chance Companions," "Petersburg Present," "Seductive Dreams," "Absence of Proof," and "Kisses, Larin."

————. *Umirat podano (Death Is Served)*. St. Petersburg: Neva, 1999.

Klarov, Yuriy. *Pyat eksponatov iz muzeya ugolovnogo rozyska (Five Exhibits from the Museum of Criminal Investigation)*. Moscow: Molodaya Gvardiya Press, 1985.

Klyuyeva, Varvara. *Unikum (Unicum)*. Moscow: Olma-Press, 2000.

Kolbergs, Andris, and Viktors Lagzdins. *Ten (Shadow)*. Moscow: Sovetskiy Pisatel Press, 1986. Also contains the novel *Nochyu, v dozhd (At Night, In the Rain)*.

————. *Nochyu, v dozhd (At Night, In the Rain)*. In *Latyshskiy detektiv (The Latvian Detektiv)*. Riga: Liesma Publishing, 1985.

————. *The Shadow*. Moscow: Progress Publishers, 1991. Contains Kolbergs, *The Shadow* and Lagzdins, *A Night at Elk Farm*.

Koretskiy, Danil. *Peshka v bolshoy igre (Pawn in a Big Game)*. Moscow: Eksmo Press, 1996.

————. *Printsip karate (The Karate Principle)*. Moscow: Molodaya Gvardiya, 1988.

————. *Privesti v ispolneniye (To Bring to Execution)*. Moscow: Eksmo Press, 1996.

Kozlovskiy, Yevgeniy. "Four Sheets of Plywood." In *Poyedinok*, no. 18. Moscow, Moskovskiy Rabochiy, 1992.

Kruglov, German, and Anatoliy Matsakov. *Vedyotsya sledstviye (Investigation Underway)*. Minsk: Mastatskaya Literatura, 1985. Contains Kruglov's short story of the same name.

Krutin, Vasiliy. *Terror-95 Krasnaya Ploshchad (Terror-95, Red Square)*. Moscow: Vagrius Press, 1995.

Lagzdins, Viktors, *A Night at Elk Farm*, in Kolbergs and Lazdins, *The Shadow*. Moscow: Progress Publishers, 1991.

Latynina, Yuliya. *Okhota na izyubrya (Hunting Mongolian Deer)*. Moscow: Olma-Press, 1999.

Latyshskiy detektiv (The Latvian Detektiv). Riga: Liesma Publishing, 1985. Also contains Kayyak, *Chudo Brigity (Brigita's Miracle)*, Tsirulis, *Milyy, ne speshi . . . (Don't Rush, Darling)*, and Kolbergs, *Nochyu, v dozhd (At Night, In the Rain)*.

Lazutin, Ivan. *Serzhant militsii (Militia Sergeant)*. Moscow: Pravda, 1988.

Leonov, Nikolay. *Brosok kobry (The Cobra's Strike)*. Moscow: Eksmo Press, 1996.

————. *My s toboy odnoy krovi (You and I Are One Blood)*. Moscow: Eksmo Press, 1995.

————. *Narkomafiya (Narcomafia)*. Moscow: Eksmo Press, 1995.

————. *Obrechyon na pobedu (Condemned to Victory)*. Moscow: Eksmo Press, 1996.

————. *Shakaly (Jackals)*. Moscow: Eksmo Press, 1997.

———. *Zashchita Gurova (Gurov's Defense)*. Moscow: Eksmo Press, 1997.

Lipatov, Vil. *A Village Detective*. Moscow: Progress Publishers, 1970.

Makarov, Artur. "Five Summer Days." In *Poyedinok No. 17*. Moscow: Moskovskiy Rabochiy, 1991.

Maltseva, Valentina. *KGB v smokinge (KGB in a Tuxedo)*. 2 vols. Moscow: Terra, 1995.

Marinina, Aleksandra. *Chuzhaya maska (Alien Mask)*. Moscow: Eksmo Press, 1997.

———. *Kogda bogi smeyutsya (When Gods Laugh)*. Moscow: Eksmo Press, 2000.

———. *Prizrak muzyki (The Ghost of Music)*. Moscow: Eksmo Press, 2000.

———. *Rekviyem (Requiem)*. Moscow: Eksmo Press, 1999.

———. *Shestyorki umirayut pervymi (Small Fry Die First)*. Moscow: Eksmo Press, 1998.

———. *Stilist (Stylist)*. Moscow: Eksmo Press, 1997.

———. *Svetlyy lik smerti (The Bright Face of Death)*. Moscow: Eksmo Press, 1997.

———. *Ukradyennyy son (Stolen Dream)*. Moscow: Eksmo Press, 1996.

———. *Ubiytsa po nevole (Unwilling Murderer)*. Moscow: Eksmo Press, 1996.

———. *Za vsyo nado platit (Everything Must Be Paid For)*. Moscow: Eksmo Press, 1996.

Maslov, Valeriy. *Mafiya po-russkiy (Mafia Russian-Style)*. Moscow: Eksmo Press, 1996.

———. *Mafiya v zakone (Made Mafia)*. Moscow: Eksmo Press, 1996.

———. *Moskva vremyon Chikago (Moscow in Chicago Times)*. Moscow: Eksmo Press, 1997.

———. *Odin protiv mafii (One Against the Mafia)*. Moscow: Eksmo Press, 1996.

Matsakov, Anatoliy. *Vedyotsya sledstviye (Investigation Underway)*. Minsk : Mastatskaya Literatura, 1985. A collection of short stories, including "Nasty Weather."

Medvedovskiy, Leonid. *Prervannyy reys (Interrupted Journey)*. Riga: Liesma Press, 1987.

Milevskaya, Lyudmila. *Kikimora bolotnaya (Swamp Goblin)*. Moscow: Eksmo Press, 2001.

Mir-Khaydarov, Raul. *Peshiye progulki (Walkabouts)*. Moscow: Molodaya Gvardiya, 1988.

———. *Sudit budu ya (I Will Do the Judging)*. Kharkov: Grampus Ekht, 1995.

Monakh, Yevgeniy. *Kitayskaya zabava (Chinese Amusement)*. Moscow: Lokid Press, 1996.

Monchinskiy, Leonid. *Osobo opasnoye zhivotnoye (Especially Dangerous Animal)*. Moscow: Lokid Press, 1996.

Mozhayev, Boris. "Propazha svidetelya (The Witness Vanishes)." In *Podvig*. Moscow: Molodaya Gvardiya, 1986.

Myasnikov, Viktor. *Igra po-krupnomu (Big Game)*. Moscow: Eksmo Press, 1996.

———. *Lyudoyedy (Cannibals)*. Moscow: Eksmo Press, 1996.

Nezrimyye poyedinki (Invisible Duels). Voronezh: Tsentralno-chernozemnoye knizhnoye izdatelstvo, 1985.

Nilin, Pavel. *Zhestokost (Savagery)*. Moscow: Moskovskiy Rabochiy, 1987.

Obukhov, Platon. *Nesostoyavshchiysya shantazh (Blundered Blackmail)*. Moscow: Lokid Press, 1995.

Oganesov, Nikolay. *Igrayem v Sprint (We Are Playing Sprint)*. Moscow: Molodaya Gvardiya, 1985.

Ovalov, Lev. *Comrade Spy*. New York: Award Books, 1965.

——. *Sekretnoye Oruzhiye (Secret Weapon)*. Moscow: Molodaya Gvardiya, 1963.

Paniyev, Nikolay. *Rassvet posle nochi (Dawn after Night)*. Moscow: Molodaya Gvardiya, 1985.

Petrov, Dmitriy. *Podstava dlya lokha (Setup for a Sucker)*. Moscow: Eksmo Press, 1996.

Polyakova, Tatyana. *Chego khochet zhenshchina (What a Woman Wants)*. Moscow: Eksmo Press, 1988.

——. *Moy drug Tarantino (My Friend Tarantino)*. Moscow: Eksmo Press, 2001.

Pomchenko, Yuriy. *Gotovnost (Readiness)*. Moscow: Sovetskiy Pisatel, 1988.

Poyedinok No. 16, containing the stories Yanitskiy, "Mugface Kingdom," Anatoliy Stepanov, "Soccer Star," and Udintsev, "Search." Moscow: Moskovskiy Rabochiy, 1989.

Poyedinok No. 17, containing the stories Gonik, "Edge of the World," Romov, "Man in an Empty Room" and Makarov, "Five Summer Days." Moscow: Moskovskiy Rabochiy, 1991.

Poyedinok No. 18, Moscow: Moskovskiy Rabochiy, 1992. Also contains Yevgeniy Kozlovskiy, *"Chetyre lista fanery (Four Sheets of Plywood)."*

Primost, Valeriy. *Shtabnaya Suka (Barracks Bitch)*. Moscow: Tramvay Press, 1994.

Printsev, Yuzef. "Wedding Postponed." In *Skhvatka (Hand-to-Hand Combat)*. Leningrad: Lenizdat, 1987.

Pronin, Viktor. *Bolshaya okhota (Big Hunt)*. Moscow: Eksmo Press, 1997.

——. "Version in Snow." In Gagarin, *Russkiy syshchik (Russian Investigator)*. Moscow: Otechestvo, 1994.

Psurtsev, Nikolai. *Bez zlogo umysla (Without Evil Intent)*. Moscow: Molodaya Gvardiya, 1985.

Puchkov, Lev. *Krovnik (Blood Matter)*. Moscow: Eksmo Press, 1997.

——. *Professiya—Killer (Profession—Killer)*. Moscow: Eksmo Press, 1996.

Rasputin, Valentin. *Siberia on Fire*. DeKalb: Northern Illinois University Press, 1989. Also contains the novella "The Fire."

Rayevskaya, Veronika. *Pomiris s sudboy (Make Peace with Fate)*. Moscow: Makhaon Press, 2000.

Radyshevskiy, Dmitriy. *Russkiye strakhi (Russian Fears)*. Moscow: Eksmo Press, 1995.

Romov, Anatoliy. "Man in an Empty Room." In *Poyedinok*, no. 17. Moscow: Moskovskiy Rabochiy, 1991.

Ropskiy, Grigoriy. *Delo ugolovnogo rozyska (Matter for Criminal Investigation)*. Tashkent: Matbuot Press, 1987.

Samovarov, Aleksandr. *Terroristka (Lady Terrorist)*. Moscow: Assotsiyatsiya Press, 1994.

Savelyev, Kirill. *Stavka na predatelstvo (Bet on Treachery)*. Moscow: Bukmen Press, 1995.

Semyonov, Yulian. *Auktsion (Auction)*. Moscow: Sovremennik, 1986.

———. *Petrovka No. 38,* Moscow: Sovremennik, 1984.

———. *Semnadtsat mgnoveniy vesny (Seventeen Moments of Spring)*. Leningrad: Lenizdat, 1982.

Serova, Marina. *Glavnyy printsip gadaniya (The Main Principle of Fortune-telling)*. Moscow: Eksmo Press, 1997.

———. *Okhotnik na znamenitostey (Celebrity Hunter)*. Moscow: Eksmo Press, 1999.

———. *Vperyod i s pesney (Forward! And with Singing!)*. Moscow: Eksmo Press, 1999.

———. *Za chto borolis (What They Fought For)*. Moscow: Eksmo Press, 1999.

Shchyogolev, Aleksandr. *Lyubov zverya (A Beast's Love)*. Moscow: Lokid Press, 1996.

Shevtsov, Ivan. *Grabezh (Burglary)*. Moscow: Molodaya Gvardiya, 1988.

Shitov, Vladimir. *Angely v belykh vorotnichkakh (Angels in White Collars)*. Rostov-na-Donu: Tandem Press, 1996.

———. *Ekho byloy vrazhdy (Echo of Former Emnity)*. Rostov-na-Donu: Tandem Press, 1996.

———. *Igrok, ili Lastochkino gnezdo (Player, or Swallow's Nest)*. Rostov-na-Donu: Tandem Press, 1996.

———. *Sobor bez krestov (Cathedral without Crosses)*. Kharkov: Revansh Press; Rostov-na-Donu: Don-Ars Press, 1995.

———. *S otkrytym zabralom (With Open Visor)*. Rostov-na-Donu: Tandem Press, 1996.

Shkatulo, Igor, *Tanets myortvetsa (Dance of the Dead Man)*. St. Petersburg: Diamant Press, 1995.

Skhvatka (Hand-to-Hand Combat). Leningrad: Lenizdat, 1987. Contains a collection of stories, including Printsev, "Wedding Postponed."

Slovin, Leonid. *Bronirovannyye zhilety (Bulletproof Vests)*. Moscow: Nedra, 1991.

———. *Dopolnitelnyy pribyvaet na vtoroy put (Extra Train Coming on Track Two)*. Moscow: Moskovskiy Rabochiy, 1987. Also contains "Five Days and the Morning of the Fifth."

Sovetskiy detektiv (The Soviet Detektiv) (Moscow, 1990). Thirty volumes, of which I was able to find volumes 5, 21, 29.

Stepanov, Anatoliy. "Soccer Star." In *Poyedinok No. 16*. Moscow: Moskovskiy Rabochiy, 1989.

Svetoteni (Lightdark). Moscow: Politicheskaya Literatura, 1991.

Svetov, Vladimir. *Rokovaya oshibka (Fatal Error)*. Moscow: Eksmo Press, 1997.

Timakov, Viktor. *Krovavyye dengi, ili zharkoye leto v Magadane (Bloody Money, or Hot Summer in Magadan)*. Magadan: Maobti, 1993.

Tsirulis, G. "Milyy, ne speshi . . ." *(Don't Rush, Darling)*. In *Latyshskiy detektiv (The Latvian Detektiv)*. Riga: Liesma Publishing, 1985.

Udintsev, Anatoliy, "Search." In *Poyedinok No. 16.* Moscow: Moskovskiy Rabochiy, 1989.

Ushakov, Aleksandr. *Kriminalnyy ekspress (Criminal Express).* Moscow: Tsentrpoligraf, 1998.

Ustinov, Sergey. *Kto ne spryatalsya (Who Didn't Hide).* Moscow: Eksmo Press, 1996.

———. *Mashina smerti (Car of Death).* Moscow: Eksmo Press, 1996.

———. *Mozhete na menya polozhitsya (You Can Count on Me).* Moscow: Eksmo Press, 1996.

Valovoy, Dmitriy. *Poisk (Search).* Moscow: Sovremennik, 1987.

Vayner, Georgiy. *Umnozhayushchiy pechal (Multiplying Sadness).* Moscow: AST, 2000.

Vayner, Georgiy, and Arkadiy Vayner. *Era miloserdiya (Era of Charity).* Moscow: Moskovskiy Rabochiy, 1988.

———. *Lekarstvo protiv strakha (Medicine against Fear).* Moscow: Sovetskiy Pisatel, 1986.

———. *Telegramma s togo sveta (Telegram from the Next World).* Moscow: Sovetskaya Rossiya, 1985.

Vedeneyev, Vasiliy. *Kazino Bon Shans (Bon Chance Casino).* Moscow: Martin Press, 1996.

Vinnichenko, Igor. *Igra v detektiv (Playing at Detektiv).* Moscow: Lokid Press, 1995. Contains the novel *Honeymoon.*

———. *Krasotka iz GRU (The Beauty from the GRU).* Moscow: Eksmo Press, 1998.

———. *Rosomakha (Wolverine).* Moscow: Eksmo Press, 1998.

Volchiye yagody (Wolf Berries). Moscow: Molodaya Gvardiya, 1986. Also contains Leonid Zalata, "Wolf Berries."

Voronin, Andrey. *Slepoy protiv manyaka (Slepoy vs. Maniac).* Moscow: Martin Press, 1996.

———. *Slepoy v zone (Slepoy behind Bars).* Moscow: Martin Press, 1996.

Vysotskiy, Sergey. *Belaya dur (White Dope).* Moscow: Eksmo Press, 1996.

Vysotskiy, Vladimir, and Leonid Monchinskiy. *Chyornaya svecha (Black Candle).* 2 vols. Moscow: Lokid Press, 1997.

Yakovleva,Yelena. *Shutki v storonu (All Joking Aside).* Moscow: Eksmo Press, 1998.

Yanitskiy, Vladimir. "Mugface Kingdom." In *Poeydinok No. 16.* Moscow: Moskovskiy Rabochiy, 1989.

Zalata, Leonid. "Wolf Berries." In *Volchiye yagody (Wolf Berries).* Moscow: Molodaya Gvardiya, 1986.

Zarubina, Irina. *Gospozha sledovatel (Mrs. Inspector).* Moscow: Olimp Press, 1998.

———. *Kompromat.* Moscow: Olimp Press, 1998.

Zlobin, Anatoliy. *Goryacho-Kholodno (Hot-Cold).* Moscow: Sovetskiy Pisatel, 1988.

Zvyagintsev, Aleksandr. *Russkiy Rembo (Russian Rambo).* Moscow: Eksmo Press, 1996.

Reference Books

Allensworth, Wayne. *The Russian Question.* Lanham, Md.: Rowman & Littlefield, 1998.

Barker, Adele, ed. *Consuming Russia: Popular Culture, Sex, and Society Since Gorbachev.* Durham, N.C.: Duke University Press, 1999.

Belousov, Vladimir. *Kto ubil Vlada Listyeva? (Who Killed Vlad Listyev?).* Minsk: Sovremennaya Literatura, 1995.

Binyon, T. J. *Murder Will Out.* Oxford: Oxford University Press, 1989.

Boym, Svetlana. *Common Places: Mythologies of Everday Life in Russia.* Cambridge, Mass.: Harvard University Press, 1994.

Brooks, Jeffrey, *When Russia Learned to Read.* Princeton, N.J.: Princeton University Press, 1985.

Chalidze, Valery. *Criminal Russia: Crime in the Soviet Union.* New York: Random House, 1977.

Chamberlain, Lesley. "Communism and the Politics of John LeCarré." *Détente* (Fall 1986).

Connor, James E., ed., *Lenin on Politics and Revolution: Selected Writings.* Indianapolis: Bobbs Merrill, 1968.

Cullen, Robert. *The Killer Department.* New York: Pantheon, 1993.

Eco, Umberto. "Narrative Structures in Fleming." In *The Poetics of Murder,* edited by Glenn Most and William Stowe. New York: Harcourt Brace Jovanovich, 1983.

Freeling, Nicolas. *Criminal Convictions.* Boston: Godine, 1994.

Fuller, Lon L. *The Morality of Law.* New Haven, Conn.: Yale University Press, 1969.

Generalnaya prokuratora Rossiyskoy Federatsii, *Kommentariy k ugolovnomu kodeksu Rossiyskoy Federatsii.* Moscow: Norma-Infra-M, 1996.

———. *Kommentariy k ugolovnomu kodeksu Rossiyskoy Federatsii. (Commentary on the Criminal Code of the Russian Federation),* 2nd ed. Moscow: Norma-Infra-M, 1997.

Gleason, John Howes. *The Genesis of Russophobia in Great Britain.* Cambridge, Mass.: Harvard University Press, 1950.

Grazhdanskoye i sluzhebnoye oruzhiye (The Civilian and the Service Weapon). Moscow: Prior, 1997.

Graffy, Julian, and Geoffrey Hosking, eds. *Culture and the Media in the USSR Today.* London: Macmillan, 1989.

Gurov, A. *Krasnaya mafiya (Red Mafia).* Moscow: Samotset, 1995.

Holquist, Michael, "Whodunit and Other Questions." In *The Poetics of Murder,* edited by Glenn Most and William Stowe. New York: Harcourt Brace Jovanovich, 1983.

Ivanov, O. L., ed., *Moskovskiy ugolovnyy rozysk (Moscow Criminal Investigation).* Moscow: MVD, 1998.

Juviler, Peter H. *Revolutionary Law and Order.* New York: Free Press, 1976.

Kelina, S. G., ed. *Ugolovniy kodeks Rossiyskoy Federatsii (The Criminal Code of the Russian Federation).* Moscow: Bek, 1996.

Kharkhordin, Oleg. *The Collective and the Individual in Russia.* Berkeley: University of California Press, 1999.

Korolev, Yuriy. *Kremlyovskiy sovetnik (Kremlin Advisor).* Moscow: Olimp Press, 1995.

Kuznetsova, N. F. *Kriminologiya: posobiye (Criminology—Study Guide).* Moscow: Zertsalo, 1998.

——. *Kriminologiya: uchebnik (Criminology—Text Book).* Moscow: BEK, 1998.

Lambert, Gavin. *The Dangerous Edge.* New York: Grossman, 1976.

Larin, A. M., E. B. Melnikova, and V. M. Savitskiy. *Ugolovnyy protses Rossii (The Criminal Trial in Russia).* Moscow: Bek, 1997.

Los, Maria. *Communist Ideology, Law, and Crime.* New York: St. Martin's Press, 1988.

McDaniel, Tim. *The Agony of the Russian Idea.* Princeton, N.J.: Princeton University Press, 1996.

Ministerstvo yustitsii Rossiyskoy Federatsii. *Ugolovniy kodeks Rossiyskoy Federatsii, Ugolovno-protsessualnyy kodeks RSFSR, Ugolovno-ispolnitelnyy kodeks Rossiyskoy Federatsii (Criminal Code of the Russian Federation, Criminal Trial Code of the RSFSR, Criminal Executive Code of the Russian Federation).* Moscow: Norma-Infra-M, 1997.

Mishchenkov, P. G., ed. *Kommentarii k ugolovnomu–ispolnitelnomu kodeksu Rossiyskoy Federatsii i minimalnym standartnym pravilam obrashcheniya s zaklyuchonnymi (Commentaries on the Criminal–Executive Code of the Russian Federation and on Minimum Standard Rules for Treatment of Prisoners).* Moscow: Ekspertnoye Byuro, 1997.

——. *Kommentariy k ugolovnomu kodeksu Rossiyskoy Federatsii i minimalnym standartnym pravilam obrashcheniya s zaklyuchennymi (Commentaries on the Criminal Code of the Russian Federation and on Minimum Standard Rules for Treatment of Prisoners).* Moscow: Ekspertnoye Byuro, 1997.

Morris, Brian. *Western Conceptions of the Individual.* Oxford: Berg Publishing, 1996.

Modestov, Nikolay. *Mosvka banditskaya (Bandit Moscow).* Moscow: Tsentrpoligraf, 1996.

Moskovskiy ugolovnyy rozysk: Istoriya v litsakh (Moscow Criminal Investigation: A History in Personalities). Moscow: MVD Rossii, 1998.

Nersesyants, V. S. *Yurisprudentsiya (Jurisprudence).* Moscow: Norma-Infra-M, 1998.

O'Dell, Felicity. *Socialisation Through Children's Literature: The Soviet Example.* Cambridge: Cambridge University Press, 1978.

Polubinskiy, V. *Blatyaki i fenya (Criminal Words and Slang).* Moscow: MVD, 1997.

Praviteli prestupnogo mira (Rulers of the Crime World). Moscow: Zelyennyy parus, 1991.

Rancour-Laferreire, Daniel. *The Slave Soul of Russia: Moral Masochism and the Cult of Suffering.* New York: New York University Press, 1995.

Razzakov, Fyodor. *Bandity vremyon sotsializma (Bandits in the Time of Socialism).* Moscow: Eksmo Press, 1997.

Savage, William, Jr. *The Cowboy Hero.* Norman: University of Oklahoma Press, 1979.

Shumilov, Yu. A. *Spetssluzhby Rossii: Zakony i kommentariy (Russia's Special Forces: Laws and Commentary).* Moscow: Yurist, 1997.

Sinyavsky, Andrey, *Soviet Civilization: A Cultural History.* New York: Arcade, 1998.

Slovar tyuremno-lagerno-blatnogo zhargona (Dictionary of Jail-Prison Camp-Criminal Jargon). Moscow: Kraya Moskvy, 1992.

Sommerville, John. *Soviet Philosophy.* New York: Philosophical Library, 1946.

Stites, Richard. *Soviet Popular Culture.* Cambridge: Cambridge University Press, 1992.

Timofeyev, Lev. *Russia's Secret Rulers.* New York: Knopf, 1992.

Usmanov, U. A. *Spravochnik sledovatelya (Sleodvatel's Handbook).* Moscow: Prior, 1998.

Vasilyev, I. *Yuridicheskaya psikhologiya (Juridical Psychology).* St. Petersburg: Piter, 1998.

Ware, Timothy. *The Orthodox Church.* Hammondsworth, England: Penguin Books, 1975.

Yani, Pavel. *Pod sledstviyem: Besedy o prave (Under Investigation: Conversations about the Law).* Moscow: Raduga, 1997.

Yarochkin, V. I. *Informatsionnaya bezopasnost (Information Security).* Moscow: Letopisets, 2000.

Zvolinskiy, V. P. *Pravda vsegda odna: Rossiyskaya derevnya na istoricheskom razlome (The Truth Is Always Singular: The Russian Village at a Historical Breaking Point).* Moscow: Mezhdunarodnyy tsentr nauchnoy i tekhnicheskoy informatsii, 1996.

Western Thrillers Cited in Text

Allbeury, Ted. *All Our Tomorrows.* New York: Warner, 1990.

———. *Moscow Quadrille.* London: Ulverscroft, 1985.

———. *The Man with the President's Mind.* London: Ulverscroft, 1988.

Burch, James. *Lubyanka.* New York: Atheneum, 1983.

Clancy, Tom. *The Cardinal of the Kremlin.* New York: Berkley, 1989.

———. *The Hunt for Red October.* New York: Berkley, 1985.

Davidson, Lionel. *Kolymsky Heights.* New York: St. Martin's Press, 1994.

Deighton, Len. *Berlin Game.* New York: Ballantine, 1997.

DeMille, Nelson. *The Charm School.* New York: Warner, 1988.

Dinallo, Greg. *Red Ink.* New York: Pocket Books, 1994.

Fleming, Ian. *From Russia, With Love.* New York: Macmillan, 1957.

Forsyth, Frederick. *Icon.* New York: Bantam Books, 1997.

Francis, Dick. *Trial Run.* New York: Fawcett, 1987.

Frayn, Michael. *The Russian Interpreter.* London: Collins, 1966.

Freemantle, Brian. *Bomb Grade.* New York: St. Martin's Press, 1997.

Garve, Andrew. *Two if by Sea.* New York: HarperPerennial, 1986.

Hone, Joseph. *The Sixth Directorate.* London: Collier, 1990.

Hyde, Anthony. *The Red Fox.* New York: Knopf, 1985.

Ignatius, David. *Siro.* New York: Farrar, Straus and Giroux, 1991.

Jackson, James O. *Dzerzhinsky Square.* New York: St. Martin's Press, 1986.

Kaminsky, Stuart. *A Fine Red Rain.* London: Mandarin, 1991.

————. *Cold Red Sunrise.* New York: Ivy Books, 1989.

————. *The Man Who Walked Like a Bear.* New York: Macmillan, 1990.

Kerr, Philip. *Dead Meat.* New York: Mysterious Press, 1995.

Killian, Michael. *Blood of the Czars.* New York: St. Martin's Press, 1984.

Kruse, John. *Red Omega.* New York: Random House, 1981.

LeCarré, John. *Our Game.* New York: Ballantine, 1996.

————. *Russia House.* New York: Knopf, 1989.

Lippincott, David. *Salt Mine.* New York: New American Library, 1980.

Litvinov, Ivy. *His Master's Voice.* London: Virago Press, 1989.

Lourie, Richard. *First Loyalty.* New York: Harcourt Brace Jovanovich, 1985.

————. *Zero Gravity.* New York: Harcourt Brace Jovanovich, 1987.

Madsen, David. *U.S.S.A.* New York: Morrow, 1989.

Peters, Ralph. *Flames of Heaven.* New York: Pocket Books, 1994.

————. *Red Army.* New York: Pocket Books, 1990.

Smith, Martin Cruz. *Gorky Park.* New York: Ballantine Books, 1984.

————. *Polar Star.* New York: Ballantine Books, 1990.

————. *Red Square.* New York: Ballantine Books, 1993.

Thomas, Craig. *A Wild Justice.* New York: HarperPaperbacks, 1996.

Topol, Edward. *Red Snow.* New York: Signet, 1988.

White, Robin. *Siberian Light.* New York: Doubleday, 1997.

Williams, Alan. *Gentleman Traitor.* New York: Harcourt Brace Jovanovich, 1974.

Index

"Absence of Proof," 78
Absolute License. See Bunich, Igor
Across the Chasm in Two Leaps. See
   Aleksandrov, Nikolai
Adamov, Arkadiy, 5, 28, 130. *See also*
   Evil Wind; Into an Empty Space;
   Search Underway; Swamp Grass
Aleksandrov, Nikolai, 30, 31
All Joking Aside, 35, 42, 93, 130, 131,
   145–46
All Our Tomorrows, 165
Allbeury, Ted. *See All Our Tomorrows;*
   The Man with the President's Mind;
   Moscow Quadrille
Ardamatskiy, Vasiliy, 140. *See also The*
   Trial
Arestova, Lyubov, 28, 57, 58. *See also*
   Last Clue; "Last Clue"; "Regarding
   the Disappearance of . . ."; "Search
   in the Taiga"; "Supplementary
   Investigation"
Aryasov, Igor, 25, 62, 66–67, 88, 91,
   108–9, 114
Astafyev, Viktor, 6, 7, 55, 71, 77–78,
   116, 126, 131

Astakhova, Inna, 58. *See also Ordered to*
   Forget the Past

"Baby Doll," 95, 101
"Backup Plan," 73
Berlin Game. See Deighton, Len
Beshenyy's Love, 38
Beshenyy's Revenge, 143
Bezuglov, Anatoliy, 140. *See also Black*
   Widow; Criminals; "Cupid's Arrows"
Black Widow, 60, 69, 70
blatnoy mir, 132
Bloody Money, or Hot Summer in
   Magadan. See Timakov, Viktor
boyevik, 3, 36, 144–45
Bomb Grade. See Freemantle, Brian
The Bright Face of Death, 131
Bulletproof Vests, 28, 91
Bunich, Igor, 51, 81, 155, 180
Butyrskiy, Fyodor, 32–33, 145

The Cardinal of the Kremlin, 154, 157,
   160, 172
Cathedral without Crosses, 38, 42, 51,
   74, 107–8, 120, 143, 156

"Chance Companions," 78, 80, 82, 95, 96
The Charm School. See DeMille, Nelson
Cherginets, Nikolay, 54, 87, 91, 110
Chernyonok, Mikhail, 55
Circle of Friends, 60
Clancy, Tom, 3–4, 160, 187n5. See also The Cardinal of the Kremlin; The Hunt for Red October
Comrade Spy (Secret Weapon English title), 178–79. See also Secret Weapon
Cops (Menty), 73
Criminals, 64, 66, 69, 98, 109, 141
"Cupid's Arrows," 56

Danilova, Anna, 58. See also I'm Coming to Find You
Dashkova, Polina, 58, 141, 146–47. See also Flesh for Sale; Golden Sand; Image of the Enemy; The Light Steps of Madness; No One Will Weep; Nursery; Place under the Sun
Davidson, Lionel, 170. See also Kolymsky Heights
Dead Meat. See Kerr, Philip
Deighton, Len, 168
DeMille, Nelson, 160, 162, 165, 176–77
Derevyanko, Ilya, 50, 60–61
detektiv, 3, 43–46
Dinallo, Greg, 161, 187n6. See also Red Ink
"Doomed Cop," 26
Doretskiy, Lev, 32–33
Dostoyevsky, Fyodor, 4, 10, 21, 102, 135, 149–50, 157
Dotsenko, Viktor, 32–33, 145. See also Beshenyy's Love; Beshenyy's Revenge

Electronically Tested, 93
"Electronically Tested," 94, 96
"Elk Bone." See Lipatov, Vil
Especially Dangerous Animal. See Monchinskiy, Leonid
Evil Wind, 16, 40, 42, 76, 77, 86, 109, 117–18, 120

Filatov, Nikita, 34–35, 92–93. See also Electronically Tested; "Electronically Tested"; "4:15 Moscow Time"; "Static"
A Fine Red Rain, 156, 157, 162
First Loyalty, 165, 167, 172
"Five Days and the Morning of the Sixth," 54, 87
Flames of Heaven. See Peters, Ralph
Fleming, Ian, 3–4, 154, 160. See also From Russia, With Love
Flesh for Sale, 43, 59, 92, 113, 146
"4:15 Moscow Time," 93, 96, 97–98, 134–35
"Four Sheets of Plywood." See Kozlovskiy, Yevgeniy
Francis, Dick, 165
Frayn, Michael, 166–67
Freeling, Nicolas, 11
Freemantle, Brian, 175
From Russia, With Love, 159, 160, 164, 167

Gagarin, Stanislav, 4, 9, 11, 16, 45
Garve, Andrew, 163, 164, 167, 172
Gentleman Traitor. See Williams, Allan
The Ghost of Music, 1, 22
Golden Sand, 141, 146, 150, 157
"Gone with the Wind," 40, 52, 73–74, 101, 121
Gorky Park, 170

Hayek, Friederich von, 104–5
Hertsen, Aleksandr, 61
His Master's Voice. See Litvinov, Ivy
Holquist, Michael, 11
Hone, Joseph, 157, 164
Honeymoon, 20, 34, 113, 115, 140
The Hunt for Red October, 157
Hyde, Anthony, 158, 173

Ignatius, David, 153–54, 173
I'm Coming to Find You, 35–36, 131
Image of the Enemy, 146, 147
Interrupted Journey. See Medvedovskiy, Leonid

Into an Empty Space, 66, 128
The Investigation Continues. See
Cherginets, Nikolay
"Investigation Underway." *See* Kruglov,
German
Ivanov, Nikolay, 51, 56–57, 79, 92, 112,
130
Izmaylov, Andrey, 30, 31, 100. *See also*
Russian Transit

Kaminsky, Stuart, 161. *See also A Fine*
Red Rain; *The Man Who Walked*
Like a Bear
The Karate Principle, 68
Kerr, Philip, 156, 159, 174, 175
Khusaynov, Gafa, 99–100
"Kisses, Larin," 97, 114
Kivinov, Andrey, 3, 28–29, 44, 79–80, 97,
141–42. *See also* "Absence of Proof";
"Baby Doll"; "Backup Plan"; "Chance
Companions"; *Cops* (*Menty*);
"Doomed Cop"; "Gone with the
Wind"; "Kisses, Larin"; "Made from
Waste Products"; "Nightmare on
Stachki Street"; "Rat Hunting";
"Petersburg Present"; "Seductive
Dreams"; "Track of the Boomerang"
klyukvy, klyukvenitsa, 153
Klyuyeva, Varvara, 36
Kolymsky Heights, 163, 169, 172, 174
Koretskiy, Danil, 31, 32–33.
See also Circle of Friends; *The Karate*
Principle
Kozlovskiy, Yevgeniy, 135
Kruglov, German, 62, 65–66
Kruse, John, 158, 163, 167–68, 172

Lagzdins, Viktors, 24, 76
Last Clue, 58
"Last Clue," 72, 97, 134
Lazutin, Ivan, 5. *See also Militia*
Sergeant
le Carré, John, 3–4, 154. *See also Our*
Game; *Russia House*
Lenin, Vladimir, 43, 101–2

The Light Steps of Madness, 181–82
Lipatov, Vil, 27, 111–12
Lippincott, David, 165–66, 173
Litvinov, Ivy, 18, 109
Losing Bet. See Chernyonok, Mikhail
Lourie, Richard. *See First Loyalty*; *Zero*
Gravity

"Made from Waste Products," 60,
78–79, 131
Made Mafia. See Maslov, Valeriy
Man in an Empty Apartment. See
Romov, Anatoliy
The Man Who Walked Like a Bear, 157,
173
The Man with the President's Mind,
158, 164–65
Marinina, Aleksandra, 3, 29, 41, 58–60,
125–26, 141–42, 145, 169–70. *See*
also The Bright Face of Death; *The*
Ghost of Music; *Small Fry Die First*;
Stolen Dream; *Stylist*
Marx, Karl, 114–15, 131
Maslov, Valeriy, 42, 91, 141
McDaniel, Tim, 9–10, 72, 105, 113–14,
125–27, 139, 144, 178
Medvedovskiy, Leonid, 41, 87–88
Militia Sergeant, 39, 69–70, 97, 107
Mir-Khaydarov, Raul, 64–65, 140. *See*
also Walkabouts
Monchinskiy, Leonid, 141
Morris, Brian, 104
Moscow Quadrille, 158, 164, 167
Mrs. Inspector, 19, 20, 42, 59

A Night at Elk Farm. See Lagzdins,
Viktors
"Nightmare on Stachki Street," 73, 94,
95
No One Will Weep, 59, 146
Notes of a Criminal Investigator, 143
Nursery, 75

obshchak, 136, 137
Ordered to Forget the Past, 113

Our Game, 168
Ovalov, Lev, 5. See also Comrade Spy
(Secret Weapon English title); Secret
Weapon

Pashukanis, Yevgenii, 104–5
Peters, Ralph, 158, 164, 186n3
Petrov, Dmitriy, 19, 42, 92, 108, 141
Petrovka, 38, 28
Place under the Sun, 59, 78, 79
Polar Star, 158, 171
Printsev, Yuzef, 111. See also "Wedding
Postponed"
Pronin, Viktor, 55, 58, 107
Psurtsev, Nikolay, 56, 64, 70, 71–72, 77

"Rat Hunting," 85–86, 94
The Red Fox. See Hyde, Anthony
Red Ink, 156, 158, 161, 174–75, 176
Red Omega. See Kruse, John
Red Snow. See Topol, Edward
Red Square, 159, 171–72, 175–76
"Regarding the Disappearance of . . . ,"
67, 76, 87
Romov, Anatoliy, 58
Russia House, 165, 168
The Russian Interpreter. See Frayn,
Michael
Russian Transit, 32

Sad Detective. See Astafyev, Viktor
"St. Petersburg Present," 97
Salt Mine. See Lippincott, David
"Search." See Udintsev, Anatoliy
"Search in the Taiga," 75–76, 109–10
Search Underway, 67
Secret Weapon, 68. See also Comrade
Spy (Secret Weapon English title)
"Seductive Dreams," 78, 93–94, 109
Semyonov, Yulian, 5. See also Petrovka,
38; Seventeen Moments of Spring
Setup for a Sucker. See Petrov, Dmitriy
Seventeen Moments of Spring, 5, 25

Shevtsov, Ivan, 41, 111, 140. See also
Theft
Sheynin, Lev, 5. See also Notes of a
Criminal Investigator
Shitov, Vladimir, 156–57. See also
Cathedral without Crosses
Shmelyo, Aleksey, 100
Sinyavsky, Andrey, 126
Siro. See Ignatius, David
The Sixth Directorate. See Hone, Joseph
sledovatel (investigator), 25, 30–31
Slovin, Leonid, 5, 50, 51, 55. See also
Bulletproof Vests; "Five Days and the
Morning of the Sixth"
Small Fry Die First, 20, 59, 78–79, 92,
108, 131
Smith, Martin Cruz, 3–4, 153, 154, 169,
170–72. See also Gorky Park; Polar
Star; Red Square
Smolentsev, E. A., 99, 118
"Soccer Star." See Stepanov, Anatoliy
spravedlivost (justice), 96, 100, 115
State and Revolution. See Lenin,
Vladimir
"Static," 20, 101, 113
Stepanov, Anatoliy, 30, 32, 55–56
Stolen Dream, 26, 43, 92, 93, 112,
115–16, 130, 153
Stylist, 19, 41–42, 60, 78, 126, 130
"Supplementary Investigation," 57
Swamp Grass, 85, 91
syshchik (detective), 25, 27–31
Szamuely, Tibor, 61–62

Tax Police. See Ivanov, Nikolay
Telegram from the Other World, 16
Theft, 54, 70–71, 76, 80–81, 110, 111,
127
Thomas, Craig, 160, 162. See also A
Wild Justice
Three Hours to Clarify the Truth. See
Aryasov, Igor
Thugs. See Derevyanko, Ilya

Timakov, Viktor, 54
tolkachi, 108
Tolstoy, Leo, 149-50, 186n1 Topol,
  Edward, 169–70, 172
"Track of the Boomerang," 20, 80, 130
The Trial, 63, 65, 99, 106, 108, 109,
  141
Trial Run. See Francis, Dick
Two if by Sea. See Garve, Andrew

ubiystvo, 22
uchastkovyy (simple policeman), 25–27
Udintsev, Anatoliy, 67, 110, 134
Unicum. See Klyuyeva, Varvara

Vayner, Arkadiy and Georgiy, 5. *See
  also Telegram from the Other World
Version in Snow. See* Pronin, Viktor
veshchizm ("thingism"), 68

Vinnichenko, Igor, 46, 145, 150. *See
  also Honeymoon*
vory, 132

Walkabouts, 62–63, 74–75, 89–91, 107,
  111, 114, 119–21
"Wedding Postponed," 25, 88, 110–11
A Wild Justice, 156, 159, 176 Williams,
  Allan, 165
Without Evil Intent. See Psurtsev,
  Nikolay

Yakovleva, Yelena, 58. *See also All
  Joking Aside*

zakon (law), 96, 100, 115
Zarubina, Irina, 58, 145, 146. *See also
  Mrs. Inspector*
Zero Gravity, 166

About the Author

Anthony Olcott is associate professor of Russian at Colgate University. He is the author of several mystery novels, including the Edgar-nominated *Murder at the Red October*. He was also a Silver Dagger nominee for the Crime Writers Association in the United Kingdom, for *Mayday in Magadan*.